THE TRUE
AND
THE EVIDENT

International Library of Philosophy
and Scientific Method

FOUNDER: A. J. AYER
ADVISORY EDITOR: BERNARD WILLIAMS
EDITOR: TED HONDERICH

INDUCTIVE PROBABILITY by John Patrick Day.
SENSATION AND PERCEPTION: A History of the Philosophy of Perception by D. W. Hamlyn.
TRACTATUS LOGICO-PHILOSOPHICUS: Ludwig Wittgenstein's *Logisch-philosophische Abhandlung* with a new Translation by D. F. Pears and B. F. McGuinness and with the Introduction by Bertrand Russell.
PERCEPTION AND THE PHYSICAL WORLD by D. M. Armstrong.
HUME'S PHILOSOPHY OF BELIEF: A Study of His First *Inquiry* by Antony Flew.
KANT'S THEORY OF KNOWLEDGE: An Outline of One Central Argument in the *Critique of Pure Reason* by Graham Bird.
CONDITIONS FOR DESCRIPTION by Peter Zinkernagel, translated from the Danish by Olaf Lindum.
AN EXAMINATION OF PLATO'S DOCTRINES by I. M. Crombie. Two volumes. I: Plato on Man and Society. II: Plato on Knowledge and Reality.
PHENOMENOLOGY OF PERCEPTION by M. Merleau-Ponty, translated from the French by Colin Smith.
THE IDEA OF JUSTICE AND THE PROBLEM OF ARGUMENT by Ch. Perelman, translated from the French by John Petrie.
LECTURES ON PSYCHICAL RESEARCH by C. D. Broad. Incorporating the Perrott Lectures given in Cambridge University in 1959 and 1960.
THE VARIETIES OF GOODNESS by Georg Henrik von Wright.
METHOD IN ETHICAL THEORY by Abraham Edel.
METHOD IN THE PHYSICAL SCIENCES by G. Schlesinger.
SCIENCE, PERCEPTION AND REALITY by Wilfrid Sellars.
NORM AND ACTION: A Logical Enquiry by Georg Henrik von Wright.
PHILOSOPHY AND SCIENTIFIC REALISM by J. J. C. Smart.
STUDIES IN METAPHILOSOPHY by Morris Lazerowitz.
REASON, ACTION AND MORALITY by J. Kemp.
THE HIDDEN GOD: A Study of Tragic Vision in the *Pensées* of Pascal and the Tragedies of Racine by Lucien Goldmann, trans. from the French by P. Thody.
THE EXPLANATION OF BEHAVIOUR by Charles Taylor.
THE STRATIFICATION OF BEHAVIOUR: A System of Definitions Propounded and Defended by D. S. Shwayder.
STUDIES IN PLATO'S METAPHYSICS edited by R. E. Allen.
NEW ESSAYS ON PLATO AND ARISTOTLE edited by Renford Bambrough.
POLITICAL ARGUMENT by Brian M. Barry.
BRAIN AND MIND Modern Concepts of the Nature of Mind edited by J. R. Smythies.
BRITISH ANALYTICAL PHILOSOPHY edited by Alan Montefiore and Bernard Williams.
EXPERIENCE AND THEORY: An Essay in the Philosophy of Science by Stephan Körner.

THE TRUE
AND
THE EVIDENT

BY

FRANZ BRENTANO

EDITED BY

OSKAR KRAUS

English Edition edited by
RODERICK M. CHISHOLM

Translated by
RODERICK M. CHISHOLM
ILSE POLITZER
and KURT R. FISCHER

NEW YORK
THE HUMANITIES PRESS

Translated from the German
WAHREIT UND EVIDENZ (1930)

First published
in the United States of America 1966
by Humanities Press Inc.
303 Park Avenue South
New York 10, N.Y

Published in Great Britain by
Routledge & Kegan Paul Ltd
London

English translation
© Routledge & Kegan Paul 1966
Library of Congress Catalog Card Number
66–15644

Printed in Great Britain

CONTENTS

v

PART FOUR: THE LATER VIEW AS SET FORTH IN ESSAYS

APPENDICES

PREFACE
TO THE ENGLISH TRANSLATION

Franz Brentano's *Wahrheit und Evidenz*, edited by Oskar Kraus of the University of Prague, was first published in 1930 by Felix Meiner at Leipzig. Professor Kraus compiled and edited the material and contributed an Introduction as well as extensive explanatory notes. The Introduction and notes are included in the present edition with certain minor alterations. No further introduction is needed, but certain features of the translation require brief comment.

Brentano divides mental phenomena, or states of consciousness, into three fundamental classes: *Vorstellen*, *Urteilen*, and *Gemütstätigkeiten*, identifying these classes with what Descartes had called "ideas" (*ideae*), "judgements", and "volitions or affections". The most natural translation of "Vorstellung", therefore, is "idea", but "presentation" and "thought" are sometimes also used. The verb "vorstellen" is more difficult; it is here translated variously as "to think of", "to contemplate", and "to have before the mind".

According to Brentano's later view, set forth in Parts Three and Four, our states of consciousness take only *realia* as their objects. *Realia* is to be understood in contrast with *irrealia*—the pseudo-objects (according to Brentano) which may seem to be designated by such expressions as "the existence of God", "the non-being of the round square", "Socrates being mortal", "that Socrates is mortal", "redness", "the absence of food", and "nothing". A man who is thinking about a unicorn, however, is thinking about *ein Reales*, despite the fact that unicorns do not exist or have any other kind of being or reality. Hence "realities" and "real entities" are to be avoided as translations of *realia* and of the various German words (e.g. *Realitäten*) which Brentano uses as synonyms. "Things" would seem to be the best translation; "concrete things" has been avoided because it is not adequate for the expression of certain parts of Brentano's theory of categories.

Judgements, then, have only things or *realia* as their objects, and not so-called "propositions" or "states of affairs". The theist, for example, accepts or affirms *God*, and not the *existence* of God or the proposition *that* God exists. Brentano, therefore, does not use that-clauses or other propositional objects with his two verbs "anerkennen" and "leugnen"; these verbs are here translated by means of the disjunctive expressions, "accept or affirm" and "reject or deny".

Judgements and feelings, according to Brentano, are either correct (*richtig*) or incorrect. And of those judgements and feelings that are correct, some are also *als richtig charakterisiert*. Since a literal translation of the latter expression would be entirely misleading, "seen to be correct" has been used instead. By reference to those judgements which the subject "sees to be correct", Brentano constructs his theory of the true and the evident.

The first selection in Part One and the notes that accompany it were translated in collaboration with Prof. Kurt R. Fischer of Mill's College, and the remainder in collaboration with Mrs Ilse Politzer of Providence, R.I. In preparing the final version, I have had the good fortune to be able to consult with Professor Franziska Mayer Hillebrand, of the University of Innsbruck, and with Dr George Katkov of St Antony's College, Oxford, who assisted Professor Kraus in the preparation of the original German edition. I am responsible for any errors that may appear in the present edition.

RODERICK M. CHISHOLM

Brown University

FOREWORD

Franz Brentano authorized me to edit his unpublished writings. The notebooks for his lectures often contain brief notes and phrases in place of carefully worked out sentences; his manuscripts and dictations are frequently only sketches and they make use of as few words as possible. But in preparing the present book, I have decided that it is preferable to present the material as it stands. I have provided an introduction and detailed explanatory comments in order that the book might be a unified whole.

Hence the book itself—the publication of which has been supported by T. G. Masaryk—is my own responsibility. I decided what selection should be made from the great wealth of unpublished material; I have tried to arrange the material in such a way that the development of certain lines of thought will be made clear; I have provided an introduction and notes, which are essential, I believe, to the general understanding of what Brentano is saying; and I have replied to certain objections.

While the effect of Brentano's own publications has been relatively small, the effect of his lectures, his letters, and his conversations has been enormous, as is evidenced in the writings of those who studied with him. Yet his own books are less well known than are those of his students. Hence I have undertaken the following: to make clear that Brentano himself is the source of certain highly significant discoveries and advances, and to present in their original form views which were subsequently corrupted or distorted beyond recognition; to indicate the way in which Brentano revised his views after unceasing investigation and self-criticism; to emphasize his critique of ancient and modern errors; and to note those points of his later views which seem to be contributions of extraordinary significance.

Brentano died in 1917; he is the philosopher, not of yesterday, but of tomorrow.

OSKAR KRAUS

Prague, October 1930.

ix

INTRODUCTION

by OSKAR KRAUS

I. ON THE ARRANGEMENT OF THE BOOK AND ITS SUBDIVISIONS

1.   The essays collected in this book do not constitute a systematic statement of one and the same doctrine; they present Brentano's thinking in its living development.

Brentano's epistemology had been based upon the Aristotelian theory; but the lecture on truth, which is the first selection published here, shows that even in 1889 he was not entirely satisfied with Aristotle. Brentano had revised the Aristotelian theory of judgement and in consequence found it necessary to criticize the view that truth consists in an *adaequatio rei et intellectus*. In addition to synthetic, categorical judgements of the form "S is P", there are also, according to Brentano, simple, *thetic* judgements of the form "S is". Contrary to the Aristotelian theory, these thetic judgements, even when they are true, cannot be said to *combine* what is combined in reality, or to *separate* what is separated in reality. One can say of such judgements only that they accept something or that they reject something. Hence according to the conclusion of this early lecture, a judgement is *true* provided either that it says, of something that is, *that* it is, or that it denies, of something that is not, that it is.

Since every synthetic judgement is logically equivalent to a thetic judgement ("S is P" is equivalent to "SP is"), this particular definition of truth, representing Brentano's earlier views, was sufficiently comprehensive. Nevertheless it was untenable, and Brentano could not permanently conceal this fact from himself. It had always been characteristic of his theory of knowledge to proceed on the basis of the *insightful judgement*, or the *judgement that is seen to be correct*. For a considerable period of time, however, he felt that one could remain within the Aristotelian tradition by interpreting *truth* or *correctness* in terms of correspondence,

xi

adequacy, or appropriateness—this in contradiction with his own view. Even the break with tradition which is heralded by the work of Descartes (whom Brentano held in high esteem) and which is even more clearly set forth by Spinoza, was not enough to emancipate him from this ambiguous interpretation.

It was Brentano's conception of the existential proposition which required him to modify the correspondence theory of Aristotle; this modification may be seen in the first two selections here and also, to some extent, in the fifth. According to the modified theory, true judgements are no longer said to correspond with *things* and their properties; they correspond instead with the *being* or the *non-being* of things—with their *existence* or *non-existence*.

In Section 57 of the lecture on truth, the first of these selections, Brentano explicitly states that he would explicate the truth of an affirmative judgement by means of the correlative concept of the *existence* of the object, and that he would explicate the truth of a negative judgement by means of the correlative concept of the *non-existence* of the object.

The introduction of this doctrine of *irrealia* and of so-called "states of affairs" (existences, non-existences, possibilities, impossibilities, etc.) was necessary in order to preserve the correspondence theory. Brentano was later to give up this doctrine; yet it was destined to play a significant role in the philosophical movements that were to grow out of Brentano's thought.

The second selection—the fragmentary "Being in the Sense of the True"—shows the earlier doctrine in its classic form. One can see that at the time the selection was written, Brentano took the *linguistically* equivalent expressions, "There is someone contemplating an A" and "There is an A which is being contemplated" to indicate correlative entities.

2. The selections presented here are so arranged as to indicate the gradual emancipation from both theories—the theory of the *adaequatio rei et intellectus* and the theory of *irrealia*. Strictly speaking, the lecture on truth contains the key to the refutation of the correspondence, or *adaequatio,* theory. In Section 58b we find one consideration which would reduce any such theory to absurdity. Brentano here points out—and again in Part Two of the book— that every such theory implies that where there is a judgement constituting knowledge there must also be a comparative judge-

ment, constituting knowledge, which compares the knowing judgement with the thing that is known.[1]

3. In the first essay Brentano enters into a controversy with Windelband. He agrees with Windelband that the Aristotelian theory is not sufficient, but he contends that Windelband, in his attempt to free himself from the concept of truth as "being adequate, suitable, or appropriate", goes too far in trying to conceive it in terms of being in "an agreement with a rule of thinking". Windelband thinks that, with this concept of a rule or norm, he catches the essence of Kant's "Copernican revolution" and that Kant himself had abandoned the correspondence theory. Brentano easily shows, with abundant documentary evidence, that Windelband has really transformed the views of his master. But Brentano goes too far in his critique of Windelband's "Kantian" theory, for in one important point Windelband is close to the later teaching of Brentano: the insightful judgement, i.e., the judgement as it ought to be, the judgement which is justified, is taken to be the standard of truth and falsehood, of correctness and incorrectness.

In saying that truth consists in a way of thinking which accords with a rule that ought to be followed, Windelband is far from being entirely clear. But in saying that the mind brings its own norm to consciousness, he is speaking in terms which could also be used to express the doctrine on which Brentano had been lecturing for years. Indeed the following passage from Windelband's *Präludien* (p. 47) agrees with Brentano's views, almost to the letter: "The only thing that philosophy can do is to extract this normative consciousness from the flux of our empirical consciousness and to rely upon direct evidence; it is in this direct evidence that the normative consciousness, once it has been brought to light, has the efficacy and validity which it ought to have for every individual." But this is as far as the agreement goes, for Windelband is unable to distinguish the "ought" of judgement from the "ought" of feeling and willing; the fact that a judgement which ought to be—i.e., an insightful judgement—is at the same time a judgement which ought to be valued adds to the confusion.* Brentano touched upon

* Compare Rickert, *Der Gegenstand der Erkenntnis*, 6th edn, p. 205: "The knowing subject does not 'turn toward' reality in order to become theoretically *valuable*; but it should turn toward theoretical value if it is to know reality."

this confusion in volume 2 of his *Psychologie* (appendix VII, p. 152ff.) *and in the fourth selection of the present book (originally an appendix to the first edition of *Vom Ursprung sittlicher Erkenntnis*, 1889).[2] Windelband never freed himself from the error of treating the "realm of values" as a realm of unreal objects.

But Brentano was to expose the fictions and hypostatizations to which we are led by such substantival expressions as "truth", "eternal truth", "value", and "meaning". The renunciation of all such fictions is foreshadowed in the final four selections in Part One; it is more clearly seen in the letters and dictations which are assembled in Part Two.

4. The final four selections of Part One were originally notes appended to the first edition (1889) of *Vom Ursprung sittlicher Erkenntnis*; they are omitted or abbreviated in subsequent editions of the same work.† They are not directly relevant to the problem of the origin or source of our knowledge of value and preferability; Brentano had used the publication of the *Ursprung* merely as an occasion to set forth his critique. These selections, which were notes 21, 22, 23, and 27 respectively of the original edition of the *Ursprung*, are: "Descartes' Classification of Mental Phenomena"; "Windelband's Error with respect to the Classification of Mental Phenomena"; "Sigwart's Theory of the Existential and the Negative Judgement"; and "On the Evident".

In this context, I may call attention to the polemic against Windelband, particularly the fourth point, which is discussed in the explanatory notes at the end of the book.

The polemic against Sigwart's concept of existence is not only

---

* All references to Brentano's *Psychologie vom empirischen Standpunkt* are to the 1925 edition, edited by Oskar Kraus, and published by Felix Meiner at Leipzig. The 1925 edition, in two volumes, includes the *Psychologie vom empirischen Standpunkt* of 1874, the *Von der Klassifikation der psychischen Phänomene* of 1911, and an appendix selected from material dictated by Brentano between 1915 and 1917.—R.M.C.

† The first edition was published by Duncker and Humblot at Leipzig in 1889, the second by Felix Meiner at Leipzig in 1921, and the third by Felix Meiner in 1934; the second and third editions were edited by Oskar Kraus. The original edition was translated by Cecil Hague as *The Origin of the Knowledge of Right and Wrong* (Constable, London 1902).—R.M.C.

of historical interest; its criticism of the correspondence theory is even more penetrating than the one to be found in the lecture on truth. I have included the selection on the Evident despite the fact that it is included in the second edition of *Vom Ursprung sittlicher Erkenntnis*. The essay had been overlooked in its original context and has not yet been sufficiently noticed. In this essay we have for the first time an attack upon construing the evident in terms of any kind of feeling; in recent years this very point has been cited as one of the contributions of Husserl's attack upon psychologism.* We shall return to these questions below.

5. The basis of epistemology is the theory of the evident—the insightful judgement, the judgement which is justified in itself and which constitutes knowing. This is the topic of the final dictations in Part Four. I shall anticipate two of the more frequent objections and misunderstandings.

It has been argued that, since one can be mistaken about what is evident, an epistemology or theory of knowledge which is based upon the concept of the evident is impossible. But from the fact that we are capable of insightful judgements—judgements which are seen to be correct—it does not follow that every erroneous or incorrect judgement is seen to be erroneous or incorrect!

It has also been noted that we sometimes fail to recognize insightful judgements as such and that we sometimes mistake erroneous judgements for those that are insightful. But this very argument presupposes that there *is* a distinction between the two types of judgement and indeed that we are able to make the distinction. For if we did not know, with respect to some judgements, that they are insightful, and with respect to others, that they are erroneous, how could we know that the one type of judgement is sometimes mistaken for the other? The fact that we are able to tell that some judgements are insightful and some are not assures us that we are able to guard against such mistakes, or to correct them.

Brentano has shown, repeatedly and in detail, that it is "an absurd undertaking to try to use reasoning to guarantee the

* See, for example, "Phänomenologie und Kritizismus", by F. Klein, in *Heidelberger Abhandlungen*, edited by Hoffman and Rickert, No. 21.

evidence of what is self-evident".* He has been reproached for "never having considered the problem of the logical presuppositions of his so-called *a priori* evident judgements". If he is guilty of this charge, at least he may be said to have asked why anyone should suppose that there *is* such a problem. Presumably these mysterious "logical presuppositions" are themselves known. What is the nature of this knowledge, then? Does *this* knowledge also have "logical presuppositions", or is it ultimate—that is to say, directly evident and justified in itself? Surely one is not blind to the fact that either (i) we should give up all talk about knowledge, or (ii) we may reason in a vicious circle, or (iii) we must admit that there is ultimate knowledge—i.e., that there are judgements which are self-evident and justified in themselves. If there is anyone who doesn't see this, then, as Aristotle put it, we can only leave him behind.

But our theory of the evident is not to be held responsible for the transformation it has undergone in Husserl's *Ideen* (with its "adequate" and "inadequate" evidence and its "perceptual explosion"); nor is it compatible with Meinong's "evident surmises".

6. Kant's "Copernican revolution" contains a faint suggestion of the truth, as I have indicated elsewhere.* But Kant did not overthrow the correspondence theory. He shifted the system of co-ordinates from the object to the subject: our knowledge is not a function of the things; the things—to the extent that they are our phenomena—are a function of our knowledge. Using the terminology of practical reason, we could say that Kant transforms our knowledge from something heteronymous to something autonomous. But the correct point of view—just as in ethics and the theory of value—is neither autonomy nor heteronomy; it is *orthonomy*. The correct point of view for theoretical reason is neither Ptolemaic nor Copernican. Knowledge is not to be fitted to the things, nor are the things to be fitted to our knowledge. Certain judgements about the things, however, are judgements as they *ought* to be; they are justified in themselves, seen to be

* Franz Brentano, *Versuch über die Erkenntnis*, edited by Alfred Kastil (Felix Meiner, Leipzig 1925).

* O. Kraus, "Die 'kopernikanische Wendung' in Brentanos Erkenntnis- und Wertlehre", *Philosophische Hefte*, Vol. I, No. 3 (Berlin 1929).

correct, and therefore they are the norms for what is true and false, correct and incorrect. A judgement contradicting a judgement which constitutes knowledge cannot possibly be evident—that is to say, it cannot possibly constitute knowledge itself.

Descartes intends precisely this point with his "*Quod clare et distincte percipio verum est*"; Spinoza is even clearer in Proposition 43 of Book II of the *Ethics*, where we find that the subtle questions about "logical presuppositions" have already been exposed and repudiated. For he exclaims: "Who can know that he knows a thing unless first of all he knows the thing? That is to say, who can know that he has certainty with respect to a thing, unless first of all he does have certainty with respect to the thing? What can serve as a clearer and more certain norm of the truth than a true idea? As light reveals itself and darkness, truth is the norm both of itself and of falsehood."*

The Sophist Protagoras expressed the creed of all subjectivists and relativists with his doctrine "Man is the measure of all things, of things that are that they are, of those that are not that they are not."

Neither Plato's flight to the transcendent realm of ideas, nor the more mundane correspondence theory of Aristotle, nor even the transcendental method of Kant and the Kantians with its "Copernican revolution", could completely uproot the doctrine of Protagoras. But all these attempts were necessary in order that proper correction to the *homo-mensura* could finally be formulated: the one who judges with *insight*, that is to say, the one who *knows*, is the measure of all things, of things that are that they are and of those that are not that they are not. Here we have the Archimedean point from which both the Ptolemaic and the Copernican theories of knowledge may be uprooted. It is the logical and epistemological δός μοι ποῦ στῶ.

The demise of the correspondence theory, for Brentano, goes hand in hand with the recognition that only *things*, or *realia*, can be thought, and that such *irrealia* as being and non-being, existence and non-existence, possibility and impossibility, states of affairs and truth, are mere fictions. And we may add to this, as already noted, the fact that the correspondence theory involves a vicious circle. The essays and letters published here deal with the corres-

* Compare the review, by Oskar Kraus, of Hermann Cohen, in the *Deutsche Literaturzeitung*, 1929, No. 30.

pondence theory partly in general terms and partly in the form of a polemic against Anton Marty and the present editor. They apply, even to a greater extent, to the views of Meinong (compare Brentano's *Psychologie*, vol. II, p. 158) and Husserl.

Surely one ought to be able to see that nothing whatever is accomplished by the assumption of these ideal and unreal objects, states of affairs, eternal truths, and the highly-prized realm of "eternal values". The assumption is totally incapable of dealing with relativism and scepticism. If Protagoras says of such "truths" and "values" that they exist only for those who believe in them, and that they do not exist for those who reject them, how is one going to be able to use the "eternal truth" against him? What else can one do but appeal to the *evidence* of judgement or valuation—to the judgement or valuation which is seen to be correct? And if the judgement or valuation *is* seen to be correct, then what is accomplished by the assumption of all of these *irrealia*? If one man makes a judgement which is seen to be correct and another man makes a judgement which contradicts it, then it is not possible for the second judgement to be evident or correct. Analogously for evaluation: if a man makes an evaluation which is seen to be correct, then no other correct evaluation can contradict it. What more is needed to ensure objectivity and absolute and general validity?

Actually if we say it is an "eternal truth" that two and two are four, we mean no more than this: no judgement contradicting the apodictic denial or rejection of a two and two, which is *not* equal to four, can possibly be evident. In other words: the apodictic denial or rejection of a two and two not equal to four, cannot possibly be false. One thus denies apodictically that there can be an evident judgement denying that two and two are four.*

7. Part Two, entitled "Transition to the Later View", contains a letter and two essays. Brentano's letter, written to Marty in 1901, constitutes a turning-point in the theory of concepts. From here on, the reform moves closer and closer to the later view which is set forth in Part Three. Further progress in this direction is manifested in "The Equivocal Use of the Term 'Existent' ". This essay, from the year 1904, is of interest from the point of view of the philosophy of language. It has been superseded in some

* See Brentano's essays in Part Four.

respects, especially by Anton Marty's *Untersuchungen zur Grundlegung der allgemeinen Grammatik und Sprachphilosophie* (Halle 1908), and there are still rudiments of the correspondence theory in paragraphs 27, 28, and 29. But this essay signifies an emphatic renunciation of all *entia rationis* and *irrealia*; the concept of "being" or "existing" is now investigated from the point of view of language. In this selection—more particularly, in a comment which I have taken from a note dated 16 November, 1905—it is shown that the terms "being" and "existing" are merely synsemantic and pertain to *denominationes extrinsecae* (see the index of Volume 2 of the *Psychologie*). The selection of 1905, entitled "Language", although it is concerned with other topics, contains important material, especially in paragraphs 3 to 5 inclusive, supplementing what has previously been said.

8. Part Three is entitled "The Later View: As Set Forth in Letters". It consists of selected passages from Brentano's letters, which have already been published, in part, in the *Philosophische Hefte* (1929).

Brentano is now fully aware of the imaginary nature of so-called ideal objects, unreal entities, and states of affairs. In this context one may compare the letter of 14 September, 1909, which is published in the Introduction to Volume 1 of the *Psychologie*, as well as the essays in the Appendix of that work. The letters to Marty are easy to understand, but those that are addressed to me are more difficult. I have felt it in order, therefore, to add to my notes a general synopsis of Brentano's line of thought.*

9. The dictations on the true and the evident, which make up Part Four, present Brentano's view in its most mature form. They were written during the last years of his life and supplement what is set forth in the letters. There are certain unavoidable repetitions; but in view of the misunderstandings which Brentano's views still encounter, a certain amount of repetition can do no harm.

The Appendix includes an account of the origin of the earlier view; I owe this, along with considerable stimulation, to my

* I should like to express my thanks to Dr George Katkov for his help in connection with this synopsis, as well as for his valuable assistance in preparing the present book.

friend, A. Kastil.[3] A letter to Husserl, and a fragment which has been found of another letter to Husserl, have been also included. Brentano is here concerned with the nature of mathematical propositions, a question which he repeatedly investigated. The letters touch upon the relation between psychology and logic and protest against a certain misuse of the term "logic". And, what is more important, they throw light upon what Husserl calls "psychologism" and show that he was mistaken in his criticism of those who would set up logic in relation to psychology: there is no ground for saying that this way of conceiving logic makes "truth" dependent upon our psychophysical organization. With the exposure of Husserl's confusion, the motivating force behind the bizarre speculations of "phenomenology" is removed.

One wonders how long these efforts on the part of a thinker of Brentano's stature will continue to be neglected. Will German philosophers still refuse to consider and evaluate Brentano's critique of their phenomenological and transcendental fantasies? And will the phenomenologists and transcendentalists continue to look upon him as the representative of a psychologism long since refuted and reduced to absurdity? Let us try to see just how he is related to this psychologism.

II. PSYCHOLOGISM AND PHENOMENOLOGISM

10. Husserl is now thought of as the opponent *par excellence* of psychologism. His criticism is directed towards philosophers who fall into the following categories:

(1) those who would reduce the universal validity of truth to the particular make-up of human beings, or who would contest the universal validity of knowledge;*

(2) more particularly, those who would interpret the evident as a kind of *feeling*;†

(3) those who would affirm that the correctness of a judgement consists in something other than its appropriateness in relation to "the truth";‡

(4) those who would deny that there are "ideal objects", ideal

---

* Edmund Husserl, *Logische Untersuchungen*, 2nd edn (Halle 1913, 1921), Vol. I, pp. 191, 121.

† *Op. cit.*, Vol. I, p. 180; Vol. II, Part 2, p. 127.

‡ *Op. cit.*, Vol. I, pp. 150, 186, 191.

meanings, propositions (*Sätze*), states of affairs (*Sachverhalte*), "ideal unities", Platonic ideas which "are experienced in acts of ideation", contents of judgements, and "Affirmates" and "Negates" as ideal unities.*

These characterizations of psychologism are taken for the most part from Husserl's *Logische Untersuchungen*, which is supposed to be the basis and point of departure for all the developments and deviations of so-called "phenomenology". To call Brentano's theory of knowledge "psychologism", on the basis of these remarks of Husserl, is fantastic and contrary to all historic truth.

Let us compare certain passages from the first edition of Brentano's *Vom Ursprung sittlicher Erkenntnis* (1889) with certain characteristic statements from the second edition of Husserl's *Logische Untersuchungen*.

Brentano (pp. 80–81): "Any judgement which is seen by one person to be true is universally valid; its contradictory cannot be seen to be evident by any other person; and anyone who accepts its contradictory is *ipso facto* mistaken. What I am here saying pertains to the nature of truth: anyone who thus sees into something as true is also able to see that he is justified in regarding it as a truth for all."

Husserl (Vol. I, p. 191): "And accordingly we have the insight that if we have a genuine insight, then no one else can have a genuine insight which conflicts with it."

Brentano (p. 79): "The peculiar nature of insight—the clarity and evidence of certain judgements—which is inseparable from their truth—has little or nothing to do with a *feeling* of compulsion. . . . We can understand what distinguishes it from other judgements only if we look for it in the *inner peculiarity* of the act of insight itself."

Husserl (Vol. I, p. 189): "Evidence is not a concomitant feeling which, accidentally or otherwise, connects itself with certain judgements. It is not at all a psychical characteristic which simply happens to be attached to a given judgement of some particular class (such as the class of so-called 'true judgements')."

* *Op. cit.*, Vol. I, pp. 191, 129. Compare: "As we have said, the number three, the truth which has been named after Pythagoras, and the like, are not empirical particulars or classes of such particulars; they are ideal objects which we grasp ideationally in the correlating activities of counting, judging with evidence, and so on." (Vol. I, pp. 186–7.)

Brentano (paragraph 11): "The precepts of logic are naturally valid rules of judging; that is to say, we must adhere to them, since the judgement which accords with them is certain and that which does not is exposed to error. Thus we are concerned here with the fact that thought processes which conform to rules are *naturally superior* to those which do not."

Husserl (Vol. I, p. 157): "The general conviction that the propositions of logic are norms of thinking cannot be entirely unfounded; the self-evidence with which it enlightens cannot be pure deception. *Thought which is in accordance with rules* has a certain *inner superiority* which distinguishes these propositions from others."

It is also noteworthy that, in the polemic against psychologism in Volume 1 of the *Logische Untersuchungen*, Husserl does not attack Brentano himself. Nor does he cite Brentano as the source of his critique.

11. This comparison of passages is relevant to the first two of the psychologistic theses referred to above. Brentano's views on these points are made abundantly clear in the selections that follow. As for the third thesis, which Husserl opposes by appeal to the so-called correspondence theory, Husserl's argument is taken *directly* from the writings and lectures of Brentano, who had extended and modified the Aristotelian tradition. This is also true of the fourth point: Brentano had made the assumption of *irrealia*—of states of affairs (existences and non-existences)—in the first of the selections published here and modified the principle of *adaequatio rei et intellectus* by saying that our judgements must be adequate to these *irrealia*. At the time of the lecture, he thus taught that there are certain entities that are not things; his pupils were later to introduce new technical terms. Where others spoke of "states of affairs" or "truths", Meinong, for example, spoke of "objectives". These *irrealia*, or non-things, are what fall under Husserl's general "concept" of so-called ideal objects.

We have already noted that at one time Brentano took "existence" and "non-existence" as terms which are *correlatives* to the concept of truth. This doctrine, which Brentano long since abandoned and condemned as purely fictitious, is revived in Husserl's *Ideen*. Husserl writes (p. 265): "We recognized that the description of the essence of consciousness leads back to the description of the essence of what it is that one is conscious *of* in that consciousness; this conscious correlate of consciousness is inseparable from it and yet not really contained within it." The fact that new terms—"Negates" and "Affirmates"— have been coined for these correlates need not prevent one from recognizing the origin of the doctrine. To be sure, Brentano never deluded himself into believing that the supposed correlates of judgement are themselves the *objects* of judgement; Husserl makes this mistake, however, and in so doing is forced to abandon the distinction between affirmative and negative *judgements*, reformulating it as a distinction between the supposed *objects* of judgement.[4] One finds nothing about "perception of states of affairs" in Brentano's work.* And Brentano is far from thinking of "the number three" as an ideal object. It was rather Bolzano who was responsible for these doctrines. (Brentano recognized the value of Bolzano's work and recommended it—not, however, because of these doctrines, but because of Bolzano's critical attitude with respect to Kant and his affinity with Leibniz.)

After continued research and self-criticism, the later Brentano recognizes that the correspondence theory and the doctrine of states of affairs, states of value, meanings, ideal objects, and *irrealia* are mistaken, and he rejects them. (Compare the third and fourth points in the statement of "psychologism" in Section 10 above.) This later view was first published in 1911, in the new edition of the *Klassifikation der psychischen Phänomene*, but it had been set forth in letters to friends and students since 1905.

The 1925 edition of Volume 2 of the *Psychologie* (which includes the third edition of the *Klassifikation*) contains a series of far-reaching discussions of these questions taken from Brentano's unpublished writings. As already noted, these have gone unappreciated up to the present time. Despite the attitude of the phenomenologists and transcendentalists, I am confident that to compile and publish these works, left to us by the foremost philosophical mind of our age, will contribute to the regeneration of philosophy. I venture to say that the most significant advance in philosophy since antiquity may be found here: in the final overthrow of the correspondence theory; in the consequent liberation of the theory of the evident, and hence of epistemology, from the correspondence theory; and finally in the realization that

* See Husserl's *Logische Untersuchungen*, Vol. 2, Part 2, pp. 140, 122.

there can be awareness or consciousness only of things—that is to say, of *realia* or real entities (the *onta* of Aristotle's theory of categories).

III. WHAT IS TRUTH?

12. Our contention is this: All such expressions as "true" and "false", "correct" and "incorrect", "truth", "eternal truth", "objective validity", and "tenability", function in the language only to call up the thought of one who judges with evidence. But the idea of one who judges with evidence does not constitute the *meaning* of these words. The point is, rather, that the locutions in which these words are used cannot be understood without *thinking* of one who judges with evidence.

What do we mean when we speak of "one who is judging truly"? The concept of "justified in itself"—or, what comes to the same thing, "completely correct", "perfectly right", "judgement of insight", "insightful judgement", or "knowing judgement"—is drawn immediately from intuition. In analogy with what is generally true of the acquisition of concepts, the distinguishing mark of such judgements stands out when they are contrasted with judgements which lack this mark. No psychologistic investigation of the natural causes of judgement and no "transcendental" investigation of the logical presuppositions of judgement can reveal to us the nature of knowledge. The theory of knowledge must be based upon the concept of the evident judgement.

But it is essential to recognize this distinction: although all insightful judgements are true, not all true judgements are evident. In other words, no two judgements having the same object can contradict each other and at the same time be such that both of them are evident.[5] Here we have an ultimate insight—one that is axiomatic, *a priori*, and apodictic. No evident judgement can contradict another evident judgement; hence the general validity of our knowledge is secured, absolutely and *a priori*.

But we say that there are "true" judgements which are not evident. For there are judgements which resemble those that are evident in the following respects: they can never be brought into contradiction with an insight; we may accept what follows from them; and so they have the same practical value as do judgements which are evident. We may thus consider the fact that these judgements cannot contradict what is evident and look upon it fictitiously as though it constituted a characteristic of the judgements themselves. We may then construct a term—a *denominatio extrinseca*—which applies not only to insightful judgements but also to those blind judgements which cannot be brought into contradiction with any insightful judgement. Both types of judgement, neither of which can contradict what is evident, may be said to be *true*. And from this it follows that, although all insightful judgements are true, not all true judgements are evident.

We can now see why it is that the truth of a judgement is generally taught to be a matter of logic and not a matter of psychology. For the grammatical predicate "true" does not indicate *any* real property of the judgement; hence it does not indicate any psychological property, such as that of being evident. There is no act of judgement which refers directly to any so-called true judgement.[6]

One may see the justification of what we have said if one notes that a judgement, without itself being altered in the slightest, may change from true to false. Thus I may judge "it is raining" and continue so to judge after the rain has ceased. But if in saying, "The judgement A is true", we are not in fact predicating anything of the judgement A, what is it that we *are* saying? We are rejecting the possibility of there being an evident judgement which has the same object as the judgement called "true" but which does not have the same quality as the judgement called "true".[7] We are apodictically denying or rejecting any judging consciousness which is judging with evidence but which is not making a judgement of the same quality as the one that we are calling "true".*

13. Ehrenfels has proposed an objection, and this will throw light upon our problem. Suppose there are certain things which, for one reason or another, are entirely inaccessible to any knowledge, positive or negative; it is impossible, say, to find out whether or not there is a diamond weighing exactly 100 kilograms. Hence neither a judgement affirming such a diamond nor one denying it can be brought into contradiction with what is evident. And therefore, according to what we have said above, both judgements —the one affirming that there is such a diamond and the one denying it—would have to be called "true". And both would

* See the references under "richtig" in Vol. 2 of Brentano's *Psychologie.*

have to be called "false" as well, since neither an affirmative nor a negative judgement about this diamond could be evident.

The objection is easy to answer. Let us suppose that there is such an unknowable diamond. Then *if* it were possible for someone to know about the diamond, the knowledge could not possibly be *negative*—the knowledge could not be a judgement that denies or rejects the diamond. But it would be a mistake to say that, *if* there were such knowledge of the diamond, it could not possibly be *affirmative*. Hence, on our assumption about the unknowable thing, an evident denial is impossible for *two* reasons. First, our general assumption (that the diamond is unknowable) precludes the possibility of any knowledge about the thing. But secondly, our additional assumption (that there is such a diamond) implies that even if such knowledge *were* possible, it could *not* be knowledge which is negative. But there is only *one* reason for saying that affirmative knowledge about the thing is impossible—namely, our assumption that the thing is unknowable.*

Inaccessibility to our knowledge, then, is no reason for concluding that the negative judgement is true. For what we have been saying is this: a true judgement about a thing is one such that, whether or not knowledge about the thing is possible, knowledge contradicting the judgement is impossible. The affirmative judgement about the unknowable diamond, although it is a judgement which cannot be evident, is one which we must call true. For, whether or not it is possible to know anything about the diamond, negative knowledge contradicting the affirmative judgement is impossible.

14. It should be sufficiently clear from what has preceded that we are far from immersing logic in the psychology of evidence.†
We have noted that, in saying of a judgement that it is true, we are not predicating evidence of the judgement; indeed, we are not predicating anything of the judgement. But the assertion "Such and such a judgement is true" unavoidably contains the thought of an evident judgement—the thought, namely, that any judgement contradicting the one that is being called "true" cannot possibly be evident: one apodictically denies that any such judge-

---

* By altering our second assumption and supposing now that there is *no* such diamond, we arrive at analogous results, *mutatis mutandis*.

† See Husserl's *Logische Untersuchungen*, Vol. I, p. 184.

ment is evident. What is asserted, then, may also be expressed by saying that it is *impossible* for an evident judgement to contradict the one that is being called "true". In saying this we are not merely expressing something which is logically equivalent to the statement that the judgement is true; we are expressing its *meaning*, its *sense,* what must be thought if the statement is to be understood.

Husserl, on the other hand, would connect the "concept" of truth with the "*possibility* of evident judgement", saying that a true judgement is one such that it is *possible* for it to be evident. This "transformation of the concept of truth into that of the *possibility* of evident judgement" is a thought which played a role in Brentano's earlier lectures and writings. In one passage in the *Psychologie* (Vol. 2, p. 90), where he takes up the problem of correct evaluation, he asks "whether the object is of such a sort that one could stand in the appropriate relation to it". In the notes for his logic lectures of 1875, we read: " 'The object is' means . . . that the object is to be accepted or affirmed, i.e., that it can be correctly affirmed."*

Here we have the source of the definition of the true—or of being in the sense of the true—as that which can be correctly affirmed. This was incorporated in the writings of Husserl and also in those of Anton Marty.

But this definition is the one which is least satisfactory. Among the alternatives are: "that which is to be affirmed (*das Anzuer-kennensein*)";† Marty's "that which it is possible to affirm (*das Anerkenntliche*)"; "that which is affirmable", or "worthy of being affirmed (*das Anzuerkennende oder Anerkennenswerte*)"; and "that which ought to be affirmed (*das, was anerkannt werden soll*)". The latter expressions come closer to the correct one, viz., "that, the affirmation of which cannot possibly be false", or "that, the denial of which cannot possibly be evident".

We have seen that Brentano finally rejected all those definitions which refer to the *possibility* of evident affirmation and replaced them by those that we have been defending. But why should we reject the attempt to characterize the true by reference to a *possible* evident consciousness? First, because, as we have already shown, a possible evident consciousness is not included in the so-called

---

* " 'Der Gegenstand ist' bedeutet . . . das der Gegenstand anzuer kennen ist, d.h. dass er mit Recht anerkannt werden kann."

† *Psychologie*, Vol. II, p. 89.

concept of the true. And secondly, such a definition leads to the monstrous assumption of the *a priori* possibility of an evident consciousness, which not only is aware of everything that is, but also denies with evidence everything that is not and everything that cannot be. If we were to take this assumption seriously, we should be led to affirm the *a priori* possibility of an omniscient mind encompassing all *vérités de fait* and all *vérités de raison*. And this road, as we know, leads inescapably to the ontological argument for the existence of God.[8] Husserl, to be sure, attempts to avoid this consequence by distinguishing between "real" and "ideal" possibility.* He would have it that there are evidences which are psychologically impossible but which—"to speak in ideal terms"—constitute a *possible* psychical experience. These "ideal possibilities of evidence" are finally transformed, in Husserl's *Ideen,* into the fiction of a "pure consciousness". Whether it be "pure consciousness", "transcendental consciousness", or what, one wishes to avoid "psychologism" and is driven instead into a kind of *hyperpsychologism*, with its invention of a fairy-tale hyperconsciousness. All this only because, as we have already said, one confuses "the *impossibility* of a judgement contradicting a judgement we call 'true' " with "the *possibility* of a judgement which is qualitatively the same as one we call 'true' ".

But all these constructions have an element of truth, at least to the extent of indicating that every thought about truth *somehow* includes the thought of an insightful consciousness (*ein einsichtiges Bewusstsein*).[9] The whole question, however, turns upon this "somehow", and it is here that both phenomenology and transcendentalism go wrong.

The motivation behind such hyperpsychologistic fictions is commendable enough, for it is the old Platonic striving to secure what is called the absolute and general validity of truth.[10] Elsewhere Husserl objects to Sigwart's assertion that it is a fiction to regard a judgement as being true unless there is some mind or other that thinks that judgement.† There is a perfectly good sense in which "Two and two are four" may be said to be an eternal truth, holding whether or not anyone happens to be thinking about it. But the point is not what Husserl and the dogged defenders of "the realm of eternal truths" have had in mind. In

* *Logische Untersuchungen*, Vol. I, p. 185.
† *Logische Untersuchungen*, Vol. I, p. 127.

saying that "Two and two are four" is an eternal truth, we are expressing an apodictic judgement—namely, that it is impossible for there to be anyone judging with insight, judging as one ought to judge, and in so doing judging that two and two are *not* equal to four.

Part One

THE EARLIER VIEW

I

ON THE CONCEPT
OF TRUTH

(Lecture delivered to the Vienna Philosophical
Society on 27 March, 1889)

1. When Aristotle laid the foundations of science, in the broadest
sense of that term, he needed a scientific terminology. None existed.
He had to invent one himself, and his accomplishment showed
great perspicacity and a delicate scientific touch.

A whole set of terms was entirely his own invention; other
terms he took over from ordinary speech; where these were vague
he provided sharp delineation, and where they were ambiguous
he distinguished between their various meanings, always attempt-
ing to elucidate their content by breaking it up into its conceptual
components.

2. Unanticipated equivocations emerged in connection with the
term *cause,* the term *part,* and even in connection with *being.*

Generally speaking, certain kinds of equivocation were found
in almost every word, or at least in entire classes of words. Consider, for example, the ambiguity which stems from our using one
and the same term to designate sometimes an activity, sometimes
a power, sometimes a capacity for an activity. We may say of a
man that he sees, even if his eyes happen to be closed, thus distinguishing him from a blind man; we mean that he has the capacity
to see. We may say of someone that he doesn't hear, and in saying
this we wish to convey that he is deaf. We say that man is a thinking
being, and yet without contradiction we may speak of a man who
has just lost consciousness. We say that a man has knowledge if he
is able to supply good grounds for his opinion; but we attribute

3

knowledge even to the sleeping scholar provided that he has acquired certain dispositions. Again, we may say of a man "I know what it is that he wants" even though the man himself may not be thinking about what it is that he wants. We say of someone that he plays the flute, sometimes when we want to say that he is actually playing, but at other times when we wish merely to attribute to him the skill of flute-playing. And so on.

3. Aristotle did not eliminate equivocations of this sort; they have a kind of regularity and might be said to belong to the spirit of language. On the contrary, he imitated and multiplied them. No one who properly considers the matter will condemn him for this. The many attacks which have been levelled against Aristotle because of this ambiguity of his terms are without justification. It is true that his way of writing often gave rise to misunderstandings; the compression of his style really presupposes another Aristotle as a reader.

4. He was aware of the danger presented to logic by equivocation, and he studied this linguistic phenomenon thoroughly. He distinguished three classes: accidental equivocations, equivocations due to analogy, and equivocations based upon relations of a set of terms to a given term which bears the name in its strict or proper (*eigentlichen*) sense.

5. Accidental equivocations are, for the most part, limited to one language. Plays on words are usually lost in translation. Other equivocations, based on a kind of connection among ideas shared by various nations, are likely to be found in the languages of all of them.

6. So it is with the equivocations which Aristotle pointed out in the traditional, important term ἀληθές. What he says about this term would hold equally well had he said it about the Latin "*verum*" or the German "*wahr*". Thus Aristotle's distinctions between the different senses of "the True", as well as what he has to say about the concept of truth itself, could become authoritative far beyond the confines of Hellas, and throughout the ages during which the torch of philosophy passed into the hands of other nations.

4

7. Let us see, then, how the most powerful scientific mind ever to influence the fate of man explained the term "truth".

The expressions "true" and "false", he said, are ambiguous; and their ambiguity is of the type, already mentioned, in which a term has a variety of senses, but each standing in a certain relation to one strict or proper sense.

We call many *thoughts*, ideas, or presentations (*Vorstellungen*) true, and we call others false (hallucinations, for example, we call false); we call concepts true or false, we call *judgements* true or false; we call conjectures, hopes, and anxieties true or false; we call a heart, a mind, true or false (*un esprit faux*); we call external things true or false; we call sayings true or false; we call conduct true or false; we call expressions, letters of the alphabet, and many other signs, true or false; we call a friend, we call gold, true or false. We speak of true happiness and of false happiness, and the latter locution, in turn, we may use for very different purposes, sometimes because we only seem to be happy, and sometimes because the happiness we have had has treacherously forsaken us. Similarly, we say on occasion: a false woman, namely when she is a flirtatious girl teasing us; but in another sense a false woman would be a man posing as a woman, as in the case of a thief who was wearing women's clothes when he was arrested; and still in another sense a false woman would be a man who has no thought of pretending to be a woman but nevertheless is taken for one, a thing that actually happened to me at dawn one morning in the entrance to the Würzburg fortress. At the time I was wearing a cassock, and the horror and bafflement of the man was all the greater, and the more comic.

8. When we thus spell out the various uses of the expression "true" its ambiguity leaps to the eye. But it is equally obvious that these multifarious uses are all related to one use which is standard for all the others. A comparable case is provided by the expression "healthy", an expression we sometimes use in connection with a body, at other times in connection with a complexion, and then again in connection with food, medicine, a region, or a walk. It is the healthy body that is healthy in the strict or proper sense; other things are called healthy because they impart, enhance, or establish health.

9. What, then, is this one use to which all the others are related? Where is truth in the strictest sense to be found? Aristotle says that it is found in judgement.

It is with reference to the truth or falsity of judgement that the other things which bear these names may properly be said to be true or false: some things because they express a true or a false judgement, such as a false assertion, or a false utterance; some things because they produce a true or false judgement, as in the case of hallucination, or a slip in uttering or in writing a word, or a metal which is taken for gold because of similarity in colour; some things because they are intended to produce a true or false judgement, as for instance a true spirit or a false mannerism; and some things because one who considers them real judges truly or falsely —for example, a true god, or a true stone in contrast to one that is painted. Some concepts are called true or false with respect to that which coincides, or fails to coincide, with their content, since here a true or erroneous judgement turns upon a discovery about this content; thus we may speak of rectangular figure as not being the true notion of square, and so forth.

10. Truth and falsity in the strict or proper sense, therefore, are found in judgement. And every judgement is either true or false.

11. But when—according to Aristotle—is a judgement true, and when is a judgement false? His answer is this: a judgement is true if the one who makes the judgement is related to things in a way which corresponds to them, and a judgement is false if the one who makes the judgement is related to things in a way which is contrary to them. "He who thinks the separated to be separated and the combined to be combined has the truth, while he whose thought is in a state contrary to that of the objects is in error." *Metaphysics* IX, 10, 1051, b 3.*

12. And so it was that truth was explicated as being a kind of agreement or correspondence obtaining between things and judgement.

* Ὥστε ἀληθεύει μὲν ὁ τὸ διῃρημένον οἰόμενος διαιρεῖσθαι καὶ τὸ συγκείμενον συγκεῖσθαι, ἔψευσται δὲ ὁ ἐναντίως ἔχων ἢ τὰ πράγματα.

[Trans. W. D. Ross.]

13. A long history had prepared the way for this definition.

a) According to the ancient Ionians, we know external things and forces by means of similar things that are within us.

> For with earth do we see earth, with water water,
> with air bright air, with fire consuming fire;
> with Love do we see Love, Strife with dread Strife.
>
> Empedocles*

b) And the paradoxical theses of the Sophists also play upon difficulties bound up with these early opinions. We have Gorgias denying that anything real can be known, and then adding that, even if there were anything that could be known, it would be impossible to communicate the knowledge from one person to another. There is nothing which corresponds completely to anything other than itself. What is external to me is not in me, and what is and remains in me, does not pass over into anyone else. Thus truth, as well as the communication of truth, is impossible. If any of our thoughts can be said to be true, then, according to Gorgias, everything else can be said to be true. For every thought is identical with itself as well as different from all other thoughts. But that every thought should be called true, even when I think of a chariot race on the sea, is an absurdity.

c) Nevertheless, another Sophist comes forth to present the contrary thesis. Protagoras does not say that all our beliefs are false; he says instead that all our beliefs are true. Whatever one thinks a thing to be, it is, and whatever one thinks it not to be it is not.

It is easy to see, I think, how Protagoras arrived at this idea. If a belief is true provided only it corresponds completely with something that exists, then every belief is true, for every belief is identical with itself. Aristotle also connects this thought with the doctrines of the Ionic school upon which the contrary thesis of Gorgias depends. Protagoras, who was a true Sophist, according to the classical portrait (that is to say, the portrait that was drawn by Plato and Aristotle, and not the one by Grote, who lived somewhat later), now quite obviously turns the paradox he had come

---

* γαίη μὲν γὰρ γαῖαν ὀπώπαμεν, ὕδατι δ'ὕδωρ,
αἰθέρι δ'αἰθέρα δῖον, ἀτὰρ πυρὶ πῦρ ἀίδηλον,
στοργὴν δὲ στοργῇ, νεῖκος δέ τε νείκεϊ λυγρῷ.
Aristotle, *Metaphysics*, B 4, 1000 b 6; trans. W. D. Ross.

upon into the starting-point of an ingenious game. The Down-Throwers (καταβάλλοντες) was the name of the text in which Protagoras defended his thesis. In it, apparently, blows are being dealt, and threatening objections parried.

To the objection that, if his view were correct, a thing could be said both to be and not to be at one and the same time, Protagoras seems to have replied that such a consequence is not absurd; the point just is that the thing *is* for one, and *is not* for another.

But Protagoras did not even attempt to provide a scientific justification for his position. This is clear from the fact that neither Plato nor Aristotle—to whom the text was surely available —could trace the means by which he arrived at it. Both were guided wholly by conjectures, a procedure in which Aristotle, completely acquainted with the historical antecedents, and certainly more abundantly equipped with a historical sense, was the more successful.

I have pointed out the steps on the path towards the Protagorean thesis. Parmenides also says: "What can be thought is only the thought that it is."* What could be more obvious than the paradox that every thought is true? Every belief, obviously, is in complete agreement with itself, and therefore, given the presupposition in question, every belief is in complete agreement with its object.

14. But let us not remain any longer with the historical antecedents of the Aristotelian definition of truth. Let us see the effect it has had upon later thinkers. What we find is that, with insignificantly few exceptions, it is standard up to our own time.

15. Medieval thought agrees in saying that true and false in the strict sense is to be found in judgement, and defines truth as *"adaequatio rei et intellectus"*.

16. In the Cartesian logic which Arnauld offers us in the *Port Royal Logic* (Part 2, Ch. 3) we read: "Propositions are divided, again, according to their matter, into true and false. And it is clear that there are none which are not either true or false, since every proposition denoting the judgement which we form of things is true when that judgement is conformed to truth, and false when

---

* ταυτὸν δ'ἐστὶ νοεῖν τὲ καί οὕνεκεν ἔστι νόημα, Trans. Kirk and Raven, *The Presocratic Philosophers*.

it is not so conformed."* Thus the great revolution which Descartes began leaves the Aristotelian definition of truth unshaken.[1]

17. But, if we may believe Windelband, something quite different happened in that other great philosophical revolution which took place in Germany while France was breaking politically with the tradition of her past.

Kant is supposed to have been the one who was then first to reform the Aristotelian, or as Windelband says, the Socratic conception of truth. Kant's great achievement is said to be here—and not elsewhere, as others have thought. "One misunderstands Kant's entire intention", Windelband says in his *Präludien* (2nd edn, p. 149), "and one interprets his doctrine as wrongly as possible if one thinks that he has shown that science can gain a picture of the world of 'appearances', and that, on the other hand, it cannot know anything of things-in-themselves. . . . The truth is . . . that, for him, it makes no sense to speak of a picture which copies reality." This concept retains a meaning only for the Socratics who preserved the conception of truth as correspondence of presentation and thing (or, more accurately, judgement and thing). And therefore it retains this meaning for the French philosophers of the eighteenth century who, with a kind of resignation, and a smattering of scepticism, deny man's ability to know things as they are in themselves. Kant does not know of any such barrier to our knowledge. What he did, rather, was to recast the concept of truth. According to him truth is what corresponds with the norm of our mind; not what corresponds with the object (unless one understands by the object nothing but the rule). Moreover, according to Kant, truth is not restricted to judgements or to thought; it may be found equally well in all the other areas of mental activity, in volition and in feeling, provided only that they conform to certain norms or rules.

* Trans. Thomas Spencer Baynes, 10th edn. The French text reads: "Les propositions se divisent encore selon la matière en vraies et en fausses. Et il est clair, qu'il n'y en peut point avoir, qui ne soient ni vraies ni fausses; puisque toute proposition marquant le jugement que nous faisons de choses est vraie, quand ce jugement est conforme à la vérité (*si judicium rebus convenit*), et fausse, lors qu'il n'y est pas conforme."

9

18. And so, at last, we have the ultimate reformation of the concept for which the world has long been waiting! What could divide philosophers more than to look for different concepts of truth—concepts which are nominally the same, but which in fact serve quite different aims? Accordingly, Windelband classifies all philosophers as being either Socratics, who have been left behind, or Kantians, who are the party of progress. It is to the latter that victory belongs; the others are already non-existent. "All of us who philosophize in the nineteenth century", he says in his Preface, "are pupils of Kant."

19. Now, gentlemen, if you are generous enough to count me a philosopher, you may recognize the exaggeration of this pronouncement. I consider Kant's entire philosophy a confusion, and one which gave rise to even greater mistakes, and which, finally, led to complete philosophical chaos. I do believe that I learned a great deal from Kant; I learned, however, not what he wanted to teach me, but, above all, how seductive for the philosophical public, and how deceptive, is the fame which the history of philosophy has tied to names. Every man who has made history must have had a powerful personality; but in any particular case the question will remain whether the influence of the personality was beneficial or disastrous, and whether we do well to make him our ideal and our master.

20. But there are other things which make us suspect Windelband's historical accuracy.

How so? Did not Kant teach that there were things in themselves which remain theoretically unknowable for us? Did he not believe that God belonged to these things in themselves—and that this belief was grounded in a practical motive and was undemonstrable only from a theoretical point of view? Did he not believe that he had established a limitation of our knowledge when he said that, since our intuitions are purely sensuous and not intellectual (as they might be for for some other being) we could have knowledge of appearance only? Need I say again that the opposite of what Windelband reports has been maintained most emphatically by everyone who knows Kant, as well as by Kant himself?

21. Must we not doubt the views of an author (apparently compelled to make innovations and piquant assertions) who reports Kant's main doctrines in so inventive a manner? And when he comes to Kant's conception of truth, should we not suspect him of entertaining us with a fairy-tale? We may ask whether he is not presenting his own brilliant doctrine in the name of Kant. And were we to accept this doctrine, we should not count even Kant among the Kantians, and we should have to classify philosophers, not as Socratics and Kantians, but as Socratics and Windelbandians.

22. The *Critique of Pure Reason* is before us; since Windelband himself says that he has considered this work exclusively, we shall appeal to it for a decision.

And now listen, and be amazed at the way a German historian of philosophy is capable of offering a German philosopher to the public—that philosopher, moreover, whom he declares to be the greatest, and who, in any case, is nowadays most celebrated.

a) Where, according to Kant, is truth in its primary sense to be found? Windelband says: In all regions of mental activity; not only in thinking, but also in volition, and the like.

But what does Kant himself say? In the Second Division of the Transcendental Logic, which he calls "Transcendental Dialectic", we read on the very first page: "Truth or illusion is not in the object, in so far as it is intuited, but in the judgement about it, in so far as it is thought. It is therefore correct to say that the senses do not err—not because they always judge rightly, but because they do not judge at all. Truth and error, therefore, and consequently also illusion as leading to error, are only to be found in the judgement, i.e., only in the relation of the object to our understanding. In any knowledge which completely accords with the laws of understanding there is no error."*

No further word, I daresay, need be spent on the first question, viz. the question where, according to Kant, truth is to be found.

b) And now, what is this truth which Kant says is to be found solely in judgement?

Does he part from the ancients and no longer understand by it the correspondence of judgement with its object? We heard

* Kant's *Critique of Pure Reason*, trans. Norman Kemp Smith, New York 1933, p. 297.

Windelband's remarks on this topic: let us also hear what Kant has to say.

"What is truth?" he asks in the Introduction to the Transcendental Logic, Chap. III, p. 93, and he answers: "The nominal definition of truth, that it is the agreement of knowledge with its object, is assumed as granted; the question asked is as to what is the general and sure criterion of the truth of any and every knowledge."

What indeed does Kant teach here? Perhaps that it is false to say, as was said at one time, that truth is the correspondence of a judgement with its object? On the contrary, he presupposes this as generally known, and certainly in the familiar sense. But let us hear what follows immediately (p. 94): "If truth consists in the agreement of knowledge with its object, that object must thereby be distinguished from other objects; for knowledge is false if it does not agree with the object to which it is related, even though it contains something which may be valid of other objects." Windelband says that Kant had altered the traditional definition, at least as far as its meaning is concerned, by understanding something different by object, namely a rule of the mind. But doesn't this passage indicate that Kant is explicitly rejecting Windelband's imputation?

On Windelband's interpretation, what would be the meaning of the expression: "even though it contains something which may be valid of other objects"? Of other *rules*? Of rules perhaps that are valid for another mind? Who is tolerant enough to stand for such tricks of interpretation?—But Kant has not yet finished. He continues by talking just about rules, distinguishing them from objects (p. 94). "Now a general criterion of truth must be such as would be valid in each and every instance of knowledge, however their objects may vary. It is obvious, however, that such a criterion [being general] cannot take account of the [varying] content of knowledge (relation to its [specific] object). But since truth concerns just this very content, it is quite impossible, and indeed absurd, to ask for a general test of the truth of such content. A sufficient and at the same time general criterion of truth cannot possibly be given. Since we have already entitled the content of knowledge its matter, we must be prepared to recognize that of the truth of knowledge, so far as its matter is concerned, no general criterion can be demanded. Such a criterion would by its very nature be self-contradictory", and he continues in the same vein to the passage containing the words, "however uninstructed we may be with regard to its content" (p. 96).

After this decisive evidence, no one, surely, would require additional confirmation. Nor would we have time to cite it all. Let me therefore simply append one or two passages indicating that Kant does not think of the object as being that which, in the manner of a rule, guides and influences the function of thinking.

"All presentations have, as presentations, their object, and can themselves in turn become objects of other presentations. Appearances are the sole objects which can be given to us immediately, and that in them which relates immediately to the object is called intuition. But these appearances are not things in themselves; they are only presentations, which in turn have their object—an object which cannot itself be intuited by us, and which may, therefore, be named the non-empirical, that is transcendental object = x.

"The pure concept of this transcendental object, which in reality throughout all our knowledge is always one and the same, is what can alone confer upon all our empirical concepts in general relation to an object, that is, objective reality."*

"*Understanding* is, to use general terms, *the faculty of knowledge*. This knowledge consists in the determinate relation of given representations to an object; and an *object* is that in the concept of which the manifold of a given intuition is *united*. Now all unification of representations demands unity of consciousness in the synthesis of them. Consequently it is the unity of consciousness that alone constitutes the relation of representations to an object, and therefore their objective validity and the fact that they are modes of knowledge; and upon it therefore rests the very possibility of the understanding."†

23. There is not the slightest doubt! Kant, too, retained the Aristotelian definition of truth as correspondence of judgement with reality. And so we can assert that all epoch-making thinkers after Aristotle, however revolutionary their procedure when tackling other questions, found no reason to make any change here.

* Trans. Kemp Smith, p. 137.
† Trans. Kemp Smith, p. 156.

24. But, as Windelband's own case makes clear, there have been attempts to replace the Aristotelian conception. There have been others who have tried to find a substitute for the conception of correspondence with an object—if not, with Windelband, in the notion of rule-direction as such, then in that of a rule-directed, normative act of judging.[2] We find such a view in Sigwart, for example, although he occasionally has recourse to the old conception of truth. The whole of Sigwart's *Logic* is muddy on this point.[3]

25. This attempt to reform the older conception is easily refuted.

If truth were no more than judging according to rule, then every judgement which is made on insufficient grounds or which is completely blind would have to be erroneous. But this is certainly not the case. Insight (*Einsicht*) must always be true; but a frivolously made assumption, a mere prejudice, or a view adopted by mere appeal to authority or because it is fashionable, may turn out to be true or may turn out to be erroneous. Aristotle himself points out that one frequently obtains true conclusions from false premises. If I should happen to reason in this way, my conviction has not been framed according to rule, and thus, on the view in question, is to be disallowed—and yet the conviction is true.

26. And so, of the traditional definitions, there would seem to be only one that can claim our assent: the ancient one which the founder of logic had already given us.

27. But we cannot deny that this definition is burdened with major difficulties.

28. There is, above all, a consideration which is essentially that of the ancient Gorgias.

Correspondence, where this is understood in the fullest sense, is identity. And this, it would seem, is just what must be meant. Some kind of correspondence, a correspondence of certain features, obtains between, say, Peter and Paul. If the judgement asserting Peter's existence corresponded no more closely to Peter than Peter corresponds to Paul, then it would not be true, or at least it would not be a truth about Peter. But if the judgement

14

completely corresponded to Peter, it would be identical with him and would be Peter himself. Yet Peter is outside my mind, not in it. Thus Professor Dilthey of Berlin uses this position to argue against the possibility of our knowledge of the external world as it really is. In his *Einleitung in die Geisteswissenschaften** he justifies this thesis in the following words: "For an idea or presentation [Dilthey conceives judgement as a connection of ideas] can never be identical with a thing, inasmuch as the thing is conceived as a reality independent of the idea. The idea is not the thing brought inside the mind, and it cannot be made to coincide with an object. If one weakens the concept of sameness to that of similarity, then this concept too, in its precise meaning, cannot be employed: thus the idea of correspondence vanishes into the indefinite."

But, surprisingly enough, Dilthey does not deny the possibility of our knowing the intentions and convictions of others, as these are in themselves. A critic has shrewdly remarked that, in order to remain consistent, Dilthey would have to maintain the impossibility of the knowledge of someone else's error.[4] "In order to recognize the error of another person, this error would have to be put into my mind. But this is impossible. And even if it were possible, we could hardly notice the error, since we would have participated in it ourselves." If this reasoning were correct, it would be better to reject altogether the definition of truth in terms of the correspondence of thought and its object. As a matter of fact, if Sigwart in his *Logic* seems prepared to reject the definition, he is compelled by a consideration of this sort—one which seems to have influenced Windelband himself.

29. But the argument is completely fallacious. It stems from a failure to recognize the distinction, which Descartes had described as the distinction between formal and objective reality, but which had been brought fully to light long before by Aristotle, who used it in overcoming the absurdities and sophistries of Parmenides, Gorgias, Protagoras, and others.

If I believe something, then this belief is "formally" in me. When I later recall the belief, then, according to Descartes' way of speaking, the value is "objectively" in me. In each case the same particular act of belief is involved; but in the one case it is my act itself and in the other it is only the immanent object

* Dilthey's *Gesammelte Schriften,* Leipzig 1922, Vol. I, p. 318.

of my remembering. Similarly for every other mental function—volition, desire, aversion, and the like. Every mental act, in itself given formally, has its immanent object which, in Descartes' terms, is given objectively. To avoid misunderstandings, we might express this better by saying that the immanent object is given intentionally. It is obvious that no contradiction is involved in saying that something is in me intentionally but not formally, or vice versa, a fact that can be illustrated by the example of remembering, and by thousands of others. A mistake on this point would be a relapse into the crudest stages of the development of the theory of knowledge.

30. But there are other problems which may seem less easy to dispose of. Some of these are due to the particular features of Aristotle's own formulation, stemming from the fact that his conception of judgement is not complete. When the relevant corrections are made, these difficulties disappear. There is another type of case, however, which will not yield to such treatment.

31. First a word about the problems that stem from Aristotle's theory of judgement. Aristotle states in the *De Interpretatione* that judgement is a combination of thoughts or concepts (συμπλοκὴ τῶν νοημάτων), that it is a synthesis (σύνθεσις). He says that the synthesis consists either in taking one thing to be combined with another, thus forming a unity, or else in taking one thing to be separated or cut off from another. One judges truly when one takes as combined things that really are combined, or when one takes as separated things that really are cut off from one another. One judges falsely, on the other hand, if one judges in a way that is contrary to the way in which the things are related.

32. But this should give us pause. Consider above all the assertion that the separate or distinct existence of the things, which correspond to the subject and predicate in a judgement, is a condition for the truth of the negative judgement and a condition for the falsity of the affirmative judgement. If I say of a dog that he is a cat, then it is indeed the case that the subject (dog) and predicate (cat) have separate existence, and that in taking the dog to be a cat I am judging falsely. But the falsity of my judgement does not lie in the fact that a dog and a cat exist separately; if there were no

cat at all—neither united with nor separated from the dog—my judgement would be still false.

33. We may clarify this point, if it is necessary, by considering other cases. For example, if I judge that a certain tone *"c"* is a twentieth octave *"a"*, my judgement is certainly as false as if I had considered it a first octave *"a"*; the latter tone has a separate existence from the *"c"*; but the former tone is wholly imaginary. And instead of saying of a negative judgement that it is true provided that the predicate exists *separate* from the subject, we ought rather to say that the negative judgement is true provided the predicate does *not* exist *combined* with the subject.

The definition of truth would now become: a judgement is true if it attributes to a thing something which, in reality, is combined with it, or if it denies of a thing something which, in reality, is not combined with it.

34. This change provides us with an essential correction, but the definition is still unsatisfactory. Is it really the case that our affirmative judgements are always concerned with the combination of real determinations? Clearly not: If I believe, of a certain real thing, that that thing is a dog or a physical body, or if I believe that it is round or red, then indeed I do combine real determinations. But consider those cases in which I do not believe of a thing that it is a dog or that it is a physical body, but believe simply in its existence—those cases in which I judge that a particular thing exists. There have been philosophers who really supposed that attributing existence to a thing is a case of combining. But when asked what they meant by this existence, they would simply answer that "an existent" means no more than "a thing", taken in an entirely indeterminate and general way. From this explanation it would follow that to say "Something or other exists" is to say no more than "Something or other is a thing".

Aristotle was quite aware that this strange conception could hardly be correct. Indeed he says in the ninth book of the *Metaphysics* that in such a case there is no belief in anything "being-combined", and certainly no combination of several different thoughts; here the act of thinking is perfectly simple.[5]

35. Thus, according to Aristotle, God in apprehending himself

as a perfectly simple entity does so by means of a thought which is perfectly simple and which does not combine a subject with a predicate.

36. But let us leave the realm of metaphysics, retaining just the general results it has yielded for the theory of judgement. Evidently we must make a substantial modification. As I think I have shown in my *Psychologie vom empirischen Standpunkt,* the result will be a significant improvement in our theory of judgement.[6]

37. We have noted that what Aristotle said about combining and separating continues to be influential; the result is particularly unhappy in the theory of judgement. While he conceded that affirmative belief is not always belief in a combination, he felt certain that negation must always involve belief in a separation; hence, according to him, the affirmation of a predicate is opposed to the denial of a predicate, but simple affirmation is not opposed to simple denial. And thus we read in the *De Anima* that while truth is to be found in simple thought, error can be found only in complex thought. And in the *Metaphysics* he states explicitly that what is opposed to a simple, true judgement is not error, but simply ignorance (ἄγνοια).

38. I shall not take the time to show how this mistake is connected with the earlier one. However glaring the present mistake may be, we have ample reason to judge Aristotle more leniently when we consider the obscurity which has surrounded the conception of existential judgements in the views of virtually all philosophers up to the present time.[7]

39. If now we go on to correct the mistake just considered, we arrive at the following modification of the Aristotelian definitions of truth and error.

The truth of a judgement consists in this: either the judgement attributes to an object some thing which is combined with the object, or the judgement denies of the object some thing which is not constituent of the object; or, if the judgement is of the simplest sort, it asserts of some object that exists that that object exists, or it asserts of some object that does not exist that that object does not exist. And here we have what it is for a true judgement to correspond with reality.

40. But new difficulties emerge. For there are cases to which even this definition does not satisfactorily apply. I shall restrict myself to the two principal ones.

41. Above all, the definition would seem to be inadequate to *all* negative judgements—among these being, of course, those judgements which simply reject or deny the object, or (as this is usually, but not very happily, expressed) "deny the existence" of the object. I say "not very happily", because no one really supposes that in such cases we are still dealing with some object that may subsist but without existence.

42. The difficulty is especially clear in the case of simple denial.

If the truth of "There is no dragon" were to reside in a correspondence between my judgement and an object, what would the object be? Certainly not the dragon, since there isn't any dragon. Nor is there any other real thing which *could* count as the corresponding reality.

43. A similar situation holds when, instead of denying a thing simply, the judgement denies it only as being a real determination of some other object. Suppose I say, "Some man is not black". What is required for the truth of the statement is, not that there *is* black separated from the man, but rather that on the man. There is an absence or privation of black. This absence, this non-black, is clearly not an object; thus again there is no object given in reality which corresponds to my judgement.

It is quite obvious, therefore, that in the case of every true negative judgement—and unmistakably so when the judgement is simple—the correspondence which is supposed to hold between true judgements and reality is not to be found.

44. The other case, which seems to lead to a similar result, may be seen by noting the area in which the affirmative function is exercised.

We find, of course, that the affirmative judgement often does apply to things; but we also find—I shall make the point clear with examples—that it often applies to objects to which the word "thing" should not be applied at all. Now whenever a true affirmative judgement *does* apply to a thing—whether the judgement be one which simply accepts or affirms the thing or one which attributes to it some further determination—we can indicate a correspondence between the judgement and the thing. But how are we to do this when the judgement does *not* apply to a thing?

45. A true affirmative judgement may, of course, apply to a single thing. But it may also apply to a collection of things,[8] or to a part of a thing, or to the limit or boundary of a thing, and the like—all these latter being objects which are not themselves things.[9] Or, if there were someone who ventured to say of such objects that they are really *things*, would he want to say the same of an object that I know to have perished a long time ago, or to exist in the distant future? Here we are not dealing with any *thing* that exists external to me.[10]

And still more! What if I affirm the absence or the lack of a thing? Will it then be said that this absence, this lack of a thing, is itself a thing?[11] Or if I were to say that there is a certain impossibility, or that there are certain eternal truths (the laws of mathematics, for example), would it then be supposed that there are eternal things, perhaps similar to Platonic ideas, which exist in, or outside of, the world? Certainly not![12] The whole idea of the *adaequatio rei et intellectus* seems to go completely to pieces.[13]

46. And so we realize: the proposition that truth is the correspondence of judgement and thing (or however one may wish to put it) must either be completely false, or else it must be given an interpretation quite different from the one offered by those who think there is a relation of identity, or of sameness, or of similarity, between a true thought and a thing.

47. Of these last two possibilities, the second is the one which is correct.[14] And now it should be easy for us to give the proper sense of that formula which has been so long unclear.

To do this we must pay proper attention both to the limits of the area to which judging is applicable, and to the contrast between those judgements which affirm and those which deny.

48. The area to which our judgements may be applied is unlimited, and the content of judgement may be as we like. But our
judgement always pertains to some entity or other. And what does
"entity" signify? It is a term that can be applied to God or to the
world, to anything whatever, and to any non-thing.[15]

49. Now this limitless area can be divided into two parts. The
opposition between the affirmative and the negative judgement
implies, as we know, that in any given case one, and only one, of
the two modes of judging is appropriate and that the other is
inappropriate.[16] This fact is ordinarily expressed by saying that,
of two contradictory judgements, one and only one is true and the
other false.

50. Let us say that the area to which affirmative judgement is
appropriate is the area of the *existent*, a concept to be sharply distinguished from that of *thing*; and that the area to which the
negative judgement is appropriate is the area of the *non-existent*.

51. Following Aristotle's statement that a judgement is true if
it takes as combined what is combined, and so on, we can say: a
judgement is true if it asserts of some object that is, *that* the object
is, or if it asserts of some object that is not, *that* the object is not—
and a judgement is false if it contradicts that which is, or that which
is not.[17]

52. And this is all there is to the correspondence of true judgement
and object about which we have heard so much. To correspond
does not mean to be the same or to be similar; but it does mean to
be adequate, to fit, to be in agreement with, to be in harmony with,
or whatever equivalent expressions one may choose to apply.[18]

53. We may make this concept clearer by drawing another
obvious parallel. In the area of emotion we also find an opposition
—that between loving and hating. Of everything that may be
considered, one of these two attitudes may be said to be appropriate
and the other inappropriate. Accordingly, everything that can be
thought about belongs in one of two classes—either the class of
things for which love is appropriate, or the class of things for
which hate is appropriate. Whatever falls into the first class we

call good, and whatever falls into the second we call bad. Thus we can say that love and hate are correct if we love what is good and if we hate what is bad, and that love and hate are *not* correct if we love what is bad and hate what is good. We can also say that in those cases where our attitude is correct the emotion corresponds with the object, that it is in harmony with the value of the object, and that in those cases where our attitude is incorrect, the emotion contradicts the object and is not in harmony with its value.[19]

54. We have thus an exact analogue to the correspondence which holds between a true judgement and its object, or between a true judgement and the existence or non-existence of its object. And in this case we are not dealing with a being in the sense of that which may be said to be a *thing*.[20]

55. In the light of all this, if we now ask about the relation between truth and reality, we find a very simple answer.

(1) For one class of true judgements, there is, so to speak, a direct relation between their truth and some *thing* or other; these are the judgements which are such that the idea or thought which is at their basis has a *thing* as its object. Clearly the truth of the affirmative judgement—and, in the inverse sense, that of the negative—depends upon the existence, the coming into being, or the passing away, of the thing to which the judgement pertains. The judgement itself may not undergo any change; but it will become true if the thing in question comes into being, and it will cease to be true if the thing is destroyed.[21]

(2) For the other class of judgements, those which are such that the underlying thought or idea does not have a *thing* as its object, there are two possibilities.

(a) It may be that, so far as truth is concerned, the judgement is not at all dependent upon any thing. This may be said of those judgements whose objects are in themselves necessary or impossible. The law of contradiction, and with it all analytic judgements, belongs to this category.[22]

(b) It may be that the judgement is not directly dependent upon a thing, but is *indirectly* dependent upon a thing. The object of the presentation or thought underlying the judgement is not *itself* a thing; yet it may be said to exist, or not to exist, as a result of the fact that a certain thing (or things) happens to exist, or did exist, or will exist. Consider an empty space, any kind of lack, deficiency, or deprivation, a capacity, an object of thought, or the like: these exist, and come into being and pass away, as the result of alterations among objects that *are* things.[23]

56. Thus I think we have the essential points involved in clarifying the definition of truth as correspondence of judgement with the object—a definition which has been the occasion of so much misunderstanding.

57. I can imagine that many will be disappointed with such a result.

For it may seem that very little is expressed by this definition, no more than would be expressed by saying that a judgement is true if it judges an object suitably or appropriately—if it says of something that is, that it is, and of something that is not, that it is not.

The expressions "to judge truly" and "to judge appropriately" would seem to be tautologically equivalent* and the rest to be only an explication in terms of correlative expressions. If we explicate the conception of the truth of an affirmative judgement by reference to the correlative term "existence of the object", and if we explicate the concept of the truth of a negative judgement by the correlative term, "non-existence of the object", our procedure is like that of one who defines the concept of effect by reference to that of cause, or the concept of the larger by reference to that of the smaller. What does this accomplish? The one expression is just as well known and just as much in use as is the other.

58. Nevertheless there are respects in which our investigation should be instructive.

(1) The fact that we will no longer look for more than is really given in the definition is itself of considerable value. Tautological expressions, even without conceptual analysis, may be of considerable use in the task of explication, if one of the two synonymous terms is less subject to misunderstanding than the other. But the expression "correspondence with an object" had no such advantage, and we took precautions against going astray by noting the analogue between appropriate affirmation and denial and the kind

* "Wahr beurteilen" und "antreffend beurteilen" scheint einfache Tautologie.

of appropriateness which applies in the sphere of loving and hating.[24]

And thus we are protected from conceptual confusions and from the blunders to which so many have been led as a result of misunderstanding the definition.

(a) For example, we will not separate formal truth from material truth, as some have done; we see that what is sometimes called formal truth (the lack of inner contradiction) is truth, not in any proper sense, but only in an entirely improper sense—similar to the way in which we sometimes say, of something which is not a judgement at all, that it is true.[25]

(b) Nor are we likely to think, as so many foolishly do, that whenever one is aware of the truth one must *compare* a thing with a judgement. People who think in this way do not realize that our judgements are not always concerned with things that are real. And they do not realize that when our judgements *are* concerned with what is real, we could not compare the judgement and the thing unless the thing were already known to us. The theory would thus lead to an infinite regress.[26]

And finally we shall not be tempted, as so many have been, to confuse the concept of a *thing* with the concept of an *existent*. It is a few thousand years since Aristotle investigated the manifold senses of Being; it is regrettable that even today there are so many who have not learned from his investigation.[27]

59. (2) Our results are significant in still another respect. We spoke earlier of equivocations, and noticed how, at the outset, Aristotle had recognized the extent to which failure to consider them may impair the success of our intellectual efforts.

Indeed, we gain a clearer picture of the significance of this danger when we see that, because of the equivocal expression "Being", a formula which has been used again and again may yet confuse the most important thinkers and keep them from being clear about something which is, basically, quite simple.

60. (3) Finally, we can derive still another lesson from our investigation, and forever impress it upon our minds. We have been concerned with a definition, i.e., with the elucidation of a concept connected with a name. Many believe such elucidation always requires some general determination, and they forget that the ultimate and most effective means of elucidation must always

consist in an appeal to the individual's intuition, from which all our general criteria are derived. What would be the use of trying to elucidate the concepts red or blue if I could not present one with something red or with something blue? All this has been disregarded by those who were concerned with the nominal definition of truth, whose history we have pursued.

If, as I hope, we have succeeded in clarifying this muddled concept, we have done so only by focussing primarily on examples of true judgements. In so doing we came to see that no such relation as that of sameness or equality could be identified with truth—if only because of the fact that affirmation and negation frequently do not pertain to things. Even now, after the elimination of confusions and misunderstandings, our definition would convey nothing to one who lacked the necessary intuition.[28] These are our rewards; they are adequate enough if we keep in mind that our modest problem was only that of explicating an expression which, in its ordinary use, is familiar to us all.

II

BEING IN THE SENSE
OF THE TRUE

(Fragment. Written not later than 1902)

1. In distinguishing the various senses of being, Aristotle contrasts a being in the sense of a thing—a substance and its properties—and being in the sense of the true, of that which *is* the case.

2. The latter concept requires clarification.

3. The two concepts do not exclude each other. Quite to the contrary: a thing *has* being only if it *is* the case that there is such a thing.

Every object that there is, to the extent that it is, is a being in the sense of the true; there can be no thing which is not a being in the sense of the true. . . .

4. There are those who doubt whether there *are* any objects other than *things*. But this doubt is easily set aside.

In thinking about things, our mind forms various concepts of which a part are fictions, to which nothing corresponds—for example, when we form the concept of a golden mountain or, even more to the point, the concept of a wooden flat-iron. There is no golden mountain, and it is completely impossible that there be such a thing as a wooden flat-iron. But to another part of these concepts, something does correspond. For if we consider the concepts of being golden, or of a mountain, or of being wood, or of a flat-iron, we may say that there actually are mountains and flat-irons and things which are golden and things which are wood.

One might think this: that since the mind has formed these concepts in its concern with things, every concept to which something corresponds must be the concept of some thing.

But we can readily see that this is not the case throughout. Consider the following example. We form with respect to ourselves the concept of a thinking being whose thought is directed upon a certain object A. The concept of this object A, like that of the person who is thinking, is the concept of a thing. We may also say of this thing A that it is an object which is contemplated or thought about. It is just as true that this A is a contemplated A [*ein gedachtes* A] as it is that this A is an actual A, existing in reality. A can cease to be actual and yet continue to be thought about—so long as the thinking person does in fact think about it. And conversely it can cease to be thought about—if the person stops thinking about it—and yet continue to be actual.

In contrasting the A which is contemplated or thought about with the A which is actual, are we saying that *the contemplated* A is itself nothing actual or true? By no means! *The contemplated* A can be something actual and true *without* being an actual A. It is an actual contemplated A and therefore—since this comes to the same thing—it is an actual contemplated A which may be contrasted with a mere *contemplated* contemplated A. (One may *think* that someone is thinking about an A.)

There cannot be anyone who contemplates an A unless there is a contemplated A; and conversely. But we must not infer from this fact that the one who is thinking about the A is identical with the A which he is thinking about. The two concepts are not identical, but they are correlative.[29] Neither one can correspond to anything in reality unless the other does as well. But only one of these is the concept of a thing—the concept of something which can act and be acted upon. The second is the concept of a being which is only a sort of accompaniment to the first; when the first thing comes into being, and when it ceases to be, then so too does the second.

Thus it is incorrect to say that there are only things. For we may also form a concept of something else to which something in reality corresponds. But in the example we have considered (and the same would be true of any other example) the assertion of this something else affirms nothing which may not also be expressed in judgements which do refer to things.

For the judgement "There is a contemplated A" is equivalent to "There is something which thinks about an A".[30]

III

DESCARTES' CLASSIFICATION
OF MENTAL PHENOMENA

(From the notes to *Vom Ursprung sittlicher Erkenntnis*, 1889)

Descartes writes in the third Meditation: "It is requisite that I should here divide my thoughts (all mental acts) into certain kinds. . . . Of my thoughts some are, so to speak, images of the things, and to these alone is the title 'idea' properly applied; examples are my thought of a man or of a chimera, of heaven, of an angel, or of God. But other thoughts possess other forms as well. For example, in willing, fearing, approving, denying, though I always perceive something as the subject of the action of my mind, yet by this action I always add something else to the idea which I have of that thing; and of the thoughts of this kind some are called *volitions* or *affections*, and others *judgements*."*

Despite this clear statement, we find Windelband saying that, according to Descartes, to judge is to will.† What misled him is Descartes' treatment, in the fourth Meditation, of the influence of the will in the formation of our judgements. After all, scholastic

---

* Nunc autem ordo videtur exigere, ut prius omnes meas cogitationes in certa genera distribuam. . . . Quaedam ex his tanquam rerum imagines sunt, quibus solis proprie convenit ideae nomen, ut cum hominem, vel chimaeram, vel coelum, vel angelum, vel Deum cogito; aliae vero alias quasdam praeterea formas habent, ut cum volo, cum timeo, cum affirmo, cum nego, semper quidem aliquam rem ut subjectum meae cogitationis apprehendo, sed aliquid etiam amplius quam istius rei similitudinem cogitatione complector; et ex his aliae voluntates sive affectus, aliae autem judicia appellantur. [English trans. from the *Philosophical Works of Descartes*, trans. E. S. Haldane and G. R. T. Ross, Vol. I, p. 159.]

† *Strassburger Abhandlungen zur Philosophie* (1884), p. 171.

philosophers—Suarez, for example—have attributed too much to this influence, and Descartes himself exaggerates it to the point of considering every judgement, even those which are evident, as the product of an act of will. But it is one thing to *produce* the judgement and quite another thing to *be* that judgement. The view that judgement is a product of the act of will does appear in the passage cited above, and it is probably what led Descartes to assign judgement to the third place in his classification of psychological phenomena. And yet he can add, quite consistently, concerning such phenomena, "Some are called volitions and *others* are called judgements".

There are two passages in Descartes' later writings which are more likely to lead us astray. One of these appeared in the *Principles of Philosophy* (Part I, Principle 32), written three years after the *Meditations*, and the other three years after that, in the *Notae in Programma.** It is strange that Windelband did not appeal to the passage from the *Principles,* instead of to the one in the *Meditations,* for the former could easily lead one to suppose that Descartes had changed his views. The passage reads: "All the modes of thinking that we observed in ourselves may be related to two general modes, the one of which consists in perception, or in the operation of the understanding, and the other in volition, or the operation of the will. Thus sense-perception, imagining, and conceiving things that are purely intelligible, are just different modes of perceiving; but desiring, holding in aversion, affirming, denying, doubting, all these are the different modes of willing."†

This passage, which could easily be taken to conflict with what Descartes says in the third Meditation, may tempt one to suppose that he has abandoned his threefold classification, thus giving up Scylla for Charybdis. Has he avoided the older mistake of confusing judgement and idea only now to confuse judgement and will? A closer examination will show that this is not the proper inter-

* "Notes directed against a Certain Programme, published in Belgium at the end of the year 1647, under the title 'An Explanation of the Human Mind or Rational Soul: What it is and What it May be'."

† Ordines modi cogitandi, quos in nobis experimur, ad duos generales referri possunt: quorum unus est perceptio sive operatio intellectus; alius vero volitio sive operatio voluntatis. Nam sentire, imaginari et pure intelligere, sunt tantum diversi modi percipiendi; ut et cupere, aversari, affirmare, negare, dubitare sunt diversi modi volendi. [Trans. Haldane and Ross, Vol. I, p. 232.]

pretation and that Descartes has made no such mistake. Let us note the following points. (1) There is not the slightest indication that Descartes was ever aware of abandoning the views he had expressed in the third Meditation. (2) Moreover, in 1647—three years after the publication of the *Meditations* and shortly before the conception of *Notae in Programma*—Descartes published his revised translation of the *Meditations,* and he made no change whatever in the crucial passage in the third Meditation.* (3) In the *Principles* (Part I, Principle 42), just after the passage we have cited, he says that all our errors depend upon the will, but instead of saying that our errors are themselves acts of will, he says that there is no one who would err voluntarily ("there is no one who expressly desires to err"). And there is an even more decisive indication of the fact that he views our judgements not as inner acts of will comparable to our desires and aversions, but as only the effects of the acts of will. For he immediately adds: "There is a great deal of difference between willing to be deceived and willing to give one's assent to opinions in which error is sometimes found." He says of will, not that *it* affirms or assents, in the way in which it desires, but rather that it *wills* assent. Just as he says, not that it is itself true, but that it desires the truth ("it is the very desire for knowing the truth which causes . . . judgement on things").†

There can be no doubt about Descartes' real view; in the respects concerned it did not undergo any change at all. But we do have to explain the fact that he did alter the way in which he expressed his views. I think the solution is clearly this. Although he recognized that will and judgement are two fundamentally different types of mental phenomenon, he also saw that they have one feature in common which distinguishes them both from ideas. In the passage from the third Meditation, he notes that both will and judgement *add* something to the ideas on which they are based. And in the fourth Meditation he refers to another common character: the

* Entre mes pensées quelques-unes sont comme les images des choses, et c'est à celles-là seules que convient proprement le nom d'idée; . . . D'autres, outre cela, ont quelques autres formes; . . . et de ce genre de pensées, les unes sont appelées volontés ou affections, et les autres jugements.

† Nemo est qui velit falli. . . . Sed longe aliud est velle falli, quam velle assentiri iis, in quibus contingit errorem reperiri. . . . Veritatis assequendae cupiditas . . . efficit, ut . . . judicium ferant. [Trans. Haldane and Ross, Vol. I, pp. 235–6.]

will decides with respect to both—it can initiate and withhold, not only its own acts, but also the acts of judgement. It is this feature which seems to him to be all-important in the first part of the *Principles* (numbers 29 to 42) and thus he contrasts ideas, which he takes to be operations of the understanding ("operationes intellectus"), with both judgement and will, which he takes to be operations of the will ("operationes voluntatis"). In the *Notae in Programma*, he again describes the acts of both judgement and will as being determinations of the will. "When I saw that, over and above perception, which is required as a basis for judgement, there must needs be affirmation, or negation, to constitute the form of the judgement, and that *it is frequently open to us to withhold our assent*, even if we perceive a thing, I referred the act of judging which consists in nothing but assent, i.e., affirmation or negation, not to the perception of the understanding, but to the determination of the will."* Indeed, he does not hesitate to say in the *Principles* that both of these "modes of thinking" are "modes of willing", but from the context it is clear that he wishes only to say that both fall within the *domain* of the will.

We find additional support for this explanation if we consider the scholastic terminology with which Descartes had been familiar in his youth. It was customary to designate as *actus voluntatis* not only the motion of the will itself, but also anything that is performed under the control of the will. Hence there were said to be two kinds of acts of will—*actus elicitus voluntatis,* the acts of the will itself, and *actus imperatus voluntatis,* the acts that are performed under the control of the will. In the same way Descartes includes under one category both the *actus elicitus* of the will and what, according to him, can only be an *actus imperatus* of the will. But his classification must not be taken to imply that the intentional relation is the same in the two cases.

This explanation is clear enough if we consider all sides of the matter; yet we find Spinoza anticipating Windelband's misconception of the Cartesian doctrine. (It is more likely that Spinoza

* Ego enim, cum viderem, praeter perceptionem, quae praerequiritur ut judicemus, opus esse affirmatione vel negatione ad formam judicii constituendam, nobisque saepe esse liberum ut cohibeamus assensionem, etiamsi rem percipiamus, ipsum actum judicandi, qui non nisi in assensu, hoc est in affirmatione vel negatione consistit, non rettuli ad perceptionem intellectus sed ad determinationem voluntatis. [English trans. from Haldane and Ross, Vol. I, p. 446.]

was misled by the passage in the *Principles* than by the one which Windelband cites from the *Meditations*.) In Proposition 49 of the Second Book of the *Ethics*, Spinoza himself interprets affirmation and negation as being, in the strictest sense, "volitions of the mind" ("volitiones mentis"), and then, as a result of still further confusion, he abolishes the distinction between the class of ideas and that of acts of will. The thesis now reads, "Will and understanding are one and the same"*, so that the threefold classification of Descartes and the twofold classification of Aristotle are both discarded together. Here, as usual, Spinoza has served only to corrupt the doctrine of his great teacher.

* Voluntas et intellectus unum et idem sunt.

IV

WINDELBAND'S ERROR WITH RESPECT TO THE CLASSIFI-CATION OF MENTAL PHENOMENA

(From the notes to *Vom Ursprung sittlicher Erkenntnis*, 1889)

All conscious phenomena fall into one or the other of these groups: (i) the mere contemplation of something, having the thing before the mind, (ii) judging, and (iii) the feelings or emotions.* I will not say, however, that there is now general agreement on this point. After all, if we had to wait for universal agreement, we could not even be sure of the law of contradiction; and in the present case there are some old prejudices that are not easily given up. Nevertheless it has not been possible to bring forward a single serious objection to this conception of psychological phenomena, and this fact itself is a significant confirmation.

There are some—for example Windelband—who concede that judging and mere having before the mind should not be thought of as constituting one and the same type of phenomenon, but who do contend that judging and the feelings or emotions should be classified together. They make the mistake that Hume had made in his discussion of belief. The act of affirming is taken to be an instance of approval, or valuing or prizing, on the part of the feelings, and the act of denying is taken to be an instance of disapproval, a rejection on the part of the feelings. There is some analogy, to be sure, but it is difficult to see how this confusion could be made. There are people who affirm the goodness of God and the wickedness of the devil—the being of Ormuzd and that

* Brentano's terms are *Vorstellen, Urteilen,* and *Gemütstätigkeiten.*

33

of Ahriman—and who affirm these things with the same degree of conviction, but they value and prize the being of the one, while feeling nothing but aversion and repulsion towards that of the other. Or again: we love knowledge and we hate error; hence it is entirely proper that we approve those *judgements* which we hold to be correct—and every judgement we make, after all, is one that we hold to be correct. Judging is related to feeling, then, in that we do thus approve of the judgements we make. But why would one confuse the judgement, which we may thus be said to approve, with the activity or feeling which is the approval itself? It is as though a man who loves his wife and child and material possessions were led to confuse these objects with the love that he feels for them. (Compare again what I have just said about Windelband's mistake in ascribing such a doctrine to Descartes. One might also compare Sigwart's note about Windelband, which, to an extent at least, is very much to the point.* If one needs further ground for distinguishing the second and third of these basic types of phenomena, perhaps I may be permitted to refer to my forthcoming *Deskriptive Psychologie*. This work, which is almost completed, will be a further development, and not just a continuation, of my *Psychologie vom empirischen Standpunkt*.[31]

I will now add the following remarks in opposition to what Windelband has to say.

(1) He writes, on page 172, that according to me "love and hate" is not an appropriate designation for this third class of psychological phenomena; indeed, he attributes to me a quotation to this, effect. But he is entirely mistaken and has made a serious oversight—as he could verify for himself if he were to re-read Volume I, page 262, of my *Psychologie*.†

(2) On page 178, he says that, according to me, the only classification of judgements which pertains to the act of judging itself is the classification according to *quality*; but this too is a mistake and one which is entirely unjustified. My own belief is just the contrary. Thus, unlike Windelband, I believe that the distinction between assertoric and apodictic judgements and the distinction between evident and blind judgements both pertain to the act of judgement itself, and that these distinctions are of basic importance.

* Sigwart's *Logik*, 2nd edn, Book I, pp. 156 ff.
† [Second edition, Vol. II, p. 35 ff.]

And there are still other distinctions—for example, the distinction between simple and compound acts of judgement. [32] For it is not possible to resolve every compound judgement into entirely simple elements. The same can be said of certain compound concepts, as Aristotle had seen. What is it to be red? To be coloured red. What is it to be coloured? To have the quality of being coloured. In each case the concept of the genus is contained in that of the specific difference; the separability of the one logical element from the other is thus one-sided. And we find the same situation, I believe, with respect to certain compound judgements. J. S. Mill said that to classify judgements as simple and complex would be like classifying horses as single horses and teams of horses.* But Mill is quite wrong in ridiculing this traditional classification; for his argument would apply equally well to the distinction between simple and compound concepts.

(3) Still another mistake—which almost everyone has made and which I too had made in the first volume of the *Psychologie*—is that of supposing that one's "degree of conviction", so-called, is a kind of intensity analogous to the intensity of pleasure and pain. Were Windelband to accuse me of *this* mistake, his accusation would be entirely just. Instead, however, he criticizes me because I say that the so-called intensity of conviction is only analogous, and not equivalent, to the strict sense of intensity which applies to pleasure and pain, and because I say that the supposed intensity of conviction and the real intensity of feeling are not comparable with respect to magnitude. This is one of the consequences of what Windelband takes to be his improved theory of judgement!

If a man's belief that $2 + 1 = 3$ had a degree of conviction which was literally an intensity, consider how powerful it would be! And if, as Windelband would have it (p. 186), the belief were a *feeling* in the strict sense of the word, and not merely something bearing a certain analogy to feeling, consider the havoc and violence to which the nervous system would be submitted! Our doctors might well tell us that, for the sake of our health, we should avoid the study of mathematics.[33] (Compare what J. H. Newman has to say about the so-called degree of conviction in *An Essay in Aid of a Grammar of Assent*—an interesting work which has received but little notice in Germany.)

(4) Windelband wonders how I could think that the word "is"

* J. S. Mill, *Logic*, Vol. I, Chap. 4.

E

has one and the same meaning in such sentences as "There is a God", "There is a human being", "There is a deprivation", and "There is something which is true" (p. 183). Referring to my *Von der mannigfachen Bedeutung des Seienden nach Aristoteles*, he says that anyone who thus writes on the manifold significance of being ought to take account of this manifold significance himself (p. 184). I can only say that if Windelband cannot see what my theory of judgement obviously implies in this case, then he has not understood the theory at all.[34] Aristotle, in treating this question, divides being (ὄν) in the sense of what is a thing into different categories and into actuality (ὄν ἐνεργείᾳ), and potentiality (ὄν δυνάμει), but it never occurs to him to do the same with "is" (ἐστίν), which transforms the expression of an idea into that of a judgement, or with what he calls being in the sense of the true (ὄν ὡς ἀληθές). Such a thing could be done only if, like Herbart and so many after him, one failed to distinguish the concept of being, in the sense of the true, and being in the sense of a thing.[35] (Compare the following discussion of Sigwart's doctrine.)

(5) I have said above that there are simple and compound judgements, and that there are some compound judgements which cannot be resolved without remainder into judgements which are simple. We must consider this fact when we try to reduce to existential form those judgements which have a different linguistic formulation. For it is obvious that only simple judgements—those which are truly unitary—can be so reduced. It goes without saying that this qualification should be made, and therefore I did not mention it in the *Psychologie*. And if the qualification holds generally, it also holds for the categorical forms of traditional logic. The A, E, I, and O statements are interpreted by the formal logician as expressions of judgements which are strictly unitary and therefore they can be reduced to existential form.* But such reduction is not possible when the ambiguity of our language allows us to use a single categorical statement to express a plurality of judgements.† The existential formulas which can be used to express categorical judgements which are unitary do not adequately express those which are compound.[36]

Windelband should have taken these facts into consideration when, on page 184, he asks whether the statement "The rose is a

---

* See my *Psychologie,* Vol. I, p. 283, and Vol. II, pp. 53 ff.
† See Vol. II of my *Psychologie*, p. 183 and pp. 158 ff, esp. pp. 164 ff.

flower" can be put into existential form. He is quite right in saying that the statement cannot be formulated as "There is no rose which is not a flower", but he is mistaken in thinking that I would disagree. I have never said—in the passage cited or anywhere else—that it *could* be so expressed. "The rose is a flower" cannot be expressed in *this* way, nor can it be expressed in the way in which Windelband and so many others would have it. For the statement expresses *two* judgements, one of which consists in the acceptance or affirmation of the subject of the judgement—which could be "the rose", in the usual sense of these words, or "that which is called a rose", or "that which is understood as a rose". But, as we have remarked above, there are statements of the form "All A are B" which do *not* express judgements in which the subject is thus accepted or affirmed.[37]

Unfortunately Land also overlooked this point.* But he is the only one of my critics who has understood what Windelband has called my "mysterious" suggestions for reforming elementary logic; he has seen their necessary connection with the principle which I have used and he has been able to derive them correctly from this principle.[38]

Let me call attention finally to a certain curiosity which Steinthal has recently provided for us, in his *Zeitschrift für Völkerpsychologie* (Vol. xviii, p. 175). Here I am amazed to read: "Brentano completely separates judgements from ideas and from thinking [!], and classifies judgements, as acts of acceptance or rejection, with love and hate [!!]—a confusion which is instantly dispelled, if one interprets any such judgement [?] as being simply a matter of taking an aesthetic [!] stand or position." Probably Steinthal read only Windelband's review, and did not look at my *Psychologie* itself. But he read the review in such a cursory fashion that perhaps he will appreciate my forwarding his lines to Windelband for correction.

* See J.P.N. Land, "On a Supposed Improvement in Formal Logic", *Abhandlungen der königl. Niederländischen Akademie der Wissenschaften*, 1876.

V

CRITIQUE OF SIGWART'S
THEORY OF THE EXISTENTIAL
AND THE NEGATIVE
JUDGEMENT

(From the notes to *Vom Ursprung sittlicher Erkenntnis*, 1889)[39]

Sigwart's monograph, *Die Impersonalien*, attacking Miklosich, has recently appeared.* There is a penetrating criticism of the monograph by Marty in the *Vierteljahrsschrift für wissenschaftliche Philosophie* (Marty had previously criticized the relevant portions of Sigwart's *Logik*).[40] Quite unreasonably, Sigwart seems to have been considerably annoyed. "Il se fache," as the French would say, "donc il a tort." Steinthal burns thick clouds of incense on behalf of Sigwart in his *Zeitschrift* (Vol. xviii, pp. 170 ff.), and in the fore-word to the fourth edition of his own *Ursprung der Sprache* we find him approving what any true friend of the deserving Sigwart can only regret; yet even Steinthal admits that Sigwart's view is mistaken in its essentials. After the high praise with which he begins his review, one finds oneself somewhat disillusioned at the end. Steinthal (pp. 177–180) rejects the grammatical implications of Sigwart's theory; hence the only real achievement of the mono-graph would be its contribution to psychology. But psychology is not the area in which Steinthal's estimate is authoritative. If it

* Miklosich, *Subjektlose Sätze*, 2nd edn, Vienna 1883. If the reader wishes to acquaint himself with this valuable work, I may suggest that he read the notice of it which I prepared for the *Wiener Abendpost*. Through a misunderstanding it was published as a *feuilleton* in the *Wiener Zeitung*. Certainly no one would look for it there, and so I include it here [in the *Vom Ursprung sittlicher Erkenntnis*] as an appendix.[41]

were, one would even have to be serious about the following remark: "On hearing the lines 'Da bückt sich's hinunter mit liebendem Blick' (from Schiller's *Taucher*), one can only think of the daughter of the king. It is not she who comes before the mind, however; it is only a subjectless bow or curtsey. And now I feel for her all the more. According to my [i.e., Steinthal's] psychology, the idea of the king's daughter hovers in the background, but does not enter consciousness." The wise man knows when he has had enough.

I.

The limitations of Sigwart's psychological theory are apparent when he tries to come to terms with the concept "Existence". Aristotle had seen that this is a concept we acquire through reflection upon the affirmative judgement.* But Sigwart, like most modern logicians, fails to follow the lead of Aristotle on this point. He does not say that the existent comprises everything of which the affirmative judgement is true. Instead of this, he goes

---

* The concepts of existence and non-existence are correlatives to the concepts of the truth of (simple) affirmative and negative judgements.[42] The judgement is correlative with that which is judged; the affirmative judgement with that which is judged affirmatively, the negative judgement with that which is judged negatively. So, too, the correctness of the affirmative judgement is correlated with the existence of that which is affirmatively judged, and that of the negative judgement with the non-existence of that which is negatively judged. One may say that an affirmative judgement is true, or one may say that its object is existent; in both cases one would be saying *precisely the same thing*. Similarly for saying that a negative judgement is true, and saying that its object is non-existent. We may say that, for every (simple) affirmative judgement, either it or the corresponding negative judgement is true; and we may express precisely the same logical principle by saying that, for every such affirmative judgement, either its object is existent or its object is non-existent.

The assertion of the truth of the judgement, that there is a learned man, is thus correlative to the assertion of the existence of its object, viz., a learned man. The assertion of the truth of the judgement, that no stone is alive, is similarly correlative to the assertion of the non-existence of its object, viz., a living stone. Correlative assertions, here as elsewhere, are inseparable. Compare such correlatives as "A is greater than B" and "B is less than A", or "A produces B" and "B is produced by A".

into a lengthy discussion of the concept of being and the existential proposition. But Sigwart is on the wrong track altogether and his views on these questions—which he sets forth again in the second edition of his *Logik* (pp. 88–95)—do not throw light on anything at all.

"To be", according to Sigwart, expresses a relation (pp. 88, 95). What kind of a relation? At first consideration (see p. 92), one might suppose it to be a "relation to me as one who is thinking". But this will not do, for the existential proposition is said to assert precisely the fact that "that which has being exists apart from its relation to me or to any other thinking being". But if the relation in question is not "a relation to me as one who is thinking", what could it be? We do not find out until page 94. Here we are told that the relation is (to be sure, Sigwart adds: "in the first place") an "agreement of the thing thought about with a possible perception"; he also says it is an "identity" of the thing thought about with something "perceivable", or with "something which can be perceived by me" (pp. 94, 90n.).

We can see at once that his concept of existence is too narrow. For much of what exists cannot be perceived; for example, a past and a future, an empty space, any kind of deprivation, a possibility, an impossibility, and so on.[43] It is not surprising, therefore, that Sigwart himself makes an effort to widen his concept. But what he does is very difficult for me to understand. First, he seems to say that, in order for a thing to be counted as existing, the thing need not be capable of being perceived by me; it is necessary only that it be capable of being perceived by someone or other. At least this seems to be what he means when, after saying that existence is an agreement between the thing thought about and a possible perception, he goes on to say: "*That which exists bears *this relation* not only to me but also to everything else that has being.*" Surely Sigwart does not mean to say that everything that there is has the capability of perceiving everything. Perhaps he means only that everything that exists stands in the relation of existence to every other being, in which case his empty-sounding phrase might be taken to say that existence expresses the capability of acting and being acted upon. (Thus he tells us that "what exists . . . stands in causal relations to the rest of the world", and, in a footnote on page 91, that the existent is that which "can exercise effects upon me and others".) Finally, however, there is some ground for supposing that what Sigwart wants to say is something like this: the existent is that which can be perceived or that which can be inferred as capable of being perceived. For he adds that "in consequence" [i.e., in consequence of this causal relation] "a merely *inferred* existence may be ascribed to that which is *capable of being perceived*".

But it is plain to see that these various assertions are equally unacceptable . . .

For (1) "to infer the existence of something" does not mean the same as "to infer that it is capable of being perceived". Thus if we were warranted in inferring, say, the existence of atoms and empty spaces, we would not thereby be warranted in inferring that these things could be perceived by us or by any other creature. Or if one infers that God exists, but resists the temptation to "enliven" his concept anthropomorphically, one will not thereby suppose that God can be perceived by any of his creatures or even by himself.[44]

(2) Given Sigwart's point of view, it would be absurd for one to say: "I am convinced that there are many things the existence of which can never be perceived or even inferred by anyone."[45] For one would be saying only: "I am convinced that many of the things which can be perceived, or which can be inferred to be perceivable, can never be perceived or even inferred by anyone." Who could fail to see that Sigwart has left the true concept of existence far behind!

(3) Or would Sigwart extend his concept of existence in such a way that what exists could be said to be that which is either capable of being perceived, or that which can be inferred from that which is capable of being perceived, or that which stands in some sort of causal relation to that which is capable of being perceived? It might well be asked whether such a monstrous determination of the concept of existence even requires refutation. But in any case, the concept is still too narrow. Suppose I say, for example: "Perhaps there is an empty space, but this can never be known with certainty." I would be saying that perhaps empty space exists, but I would be denying that it is capable of being perceived, or that it can be inferred from what is capable of being perceived. An empty space (since it is not itself a thing) cannot be related as cause or effect to anything that is capable of being perceived. And so Sigwart's view, once again, would transform a

perfectly sensible assertion into one that is utter nonsense.[46]

The extent of Sigwart's error, in his analysis of the concept of existence, may be indicated very simply by the following: no real centaur exists; but a *contemplated* or *thought-about* centaur [*ein vorgestellter Zentaure*] does exist, and indeed it exists as often as I think of it. If there is anyone who fails to see, in this instance, the distinction between the ὄν ὡςνἀληθές (*being* in the sense of the true or of the existing) and the ὄν in the sense of the real (thinghood), I am afraid that he would be unable to appreciate the abundance of other illustrations to which we might also appeal.[47]

But let us also consider the following. According to Sigwart, knowledge of the existence of anything must consist in the knowledge of an agreement between the content of an idea and something else. I do not clearly understand what this something else is, so let us call it simply x. What, now, is required in order to know that one thing is in agreement with another thing? It is necessary, first, that there be the one thing, secondly, that there be the other thing, and thirdly that there be a relation of agreement holding between them; for that which is not can neither agree nor disagree with that which is. But the knowledge of the first of these three items is itself already the knowledge of an existence.[48] Hence it is no longer true that the knowledge of the other two is required in order that there be any knowledge of existence; and therefore Sigwart's theory leads to a contradiction. (Compare what is said here with Sigwart's polemic against my *Psychologie,* Book II, Chapter 7, in his *Die Impersonalien,* pp. 50 ff., and his *Logik,* 2nd edition, Volume I, pp. 89 ff, See also Marty's polemic against Sigwart in the articles "Über subjektlose Sätze", in the *Vierteljahrsschrift für wissenschaftliche Philosophie,* Vol. VIII.[49] *

* I had already written my critique of Sigwart's concept of existence when my attention was called to a note in his *Logik,* 2nd edn, Vol. I, p. 390. The note does not make it necessary to change anything, but I shall add it here for purposes of comparison. " 'Being' in general", Sigwart says, "cannot be regarded as a true generic concept which applies to particular individuals; conceptually regarded it is only a common name. Since 'being' is for us a relational predicate, it cannot be a common characteristic; it is necessary to show, therefore, that this predicate is rooted in a determination which is common to the concept of everything that there is." I am afraid that, so far as Sigwart's concept of existence is concerned, this passage will be no more enlightening for the reader than it is for me; it may help to show, however, why all my efforts to understand his concept have been in vain.

II

If Sigwart misconceives the nature of judgement in general, then we can hardly expect him to understand the nature of the negative judgement in particular. And indeed he goes so far astray that he refuses to regard the negative judgement as being a species of judgement on equal footing alongside the positive or affirmative judgement. No negative judgement is direct, he says; its object is always some other judgement or an attempt to make some other judgement. (*Logik*, 2nd edn, Vol. I, p. 150.)

With this assertion, Sigwart contradicts certain important psychological theses which I have defended.[50] It seems to me appropriate, therefore, to counter his attack. I wish, then, to show three things. (1) Sigwart's own theory is without adequate foundation. (2) It leads to hopeless confusion: for Sigwart's affirmative judgement is negative; his negative judgement—if it *is* a judgement and not merely the lack of a judgement—is positive; his positive judgement strictly involves a negative judgement; and such confusions are compounded. Finally (3) I wish to show the genesis of Sigwart's mistake; Sigwart's detailed discussions make it possible to do this.

(1) The first question that arises, then, in the face of such a novel and outlandish assertion, would be: What kind of basis does it have? Sigwart emphasizes above all else (p. 150) that a negative judgement would have no meaning unless it were preceded by the thought of the positive attribution of a predicate. But what is this assertion supposed to mean? Unless it is a simple *petitio principii*, it tells us only that a connection of ideas must have preceded the negative judgement. If we suppose for the moment that the latter is true (though I have shown in my *Psychologie* that it is not true), then the thesis in question would still not be established. For Sigwart himself (p. 89n. and elsewhere) realizes that no such "subjective connection of ideas" constitutes a judgement; there must be in addition (he would say) a certain feeling of compulsion.

Sigwart subsequently formulates another argument (p. 151), but I find it equally difficult to follow. He notes, quite correctly, that there are countless predicates which we have the right to deny of any given thing; and he adds, equally correctly, that we do not in fact make all of these negative judgements. But now—

what are we to infer from these premises? Perhaps this: the fact that a given negative judgement is justified is not itself sufficient to account for the fact that the judgement is made?[51] And this, of course, we may well admit. But what Sigwart infers is quite different. A necessary condition for making a negative judgement, he says, is that we first attempt to make the corresponding positive judgement; hence if we do not make the attempt at the positive judgement, we do not make the negative judgement. This is a bold leap indeed, which *my* logic at least is unable to follow. What if we were now to ask, "And why is it that all the corresponding positive judgements are not attempted?" Sigwart's examples ("This stone reads, writes, sings, composes verses", "Justice is blue, green, heptagonal, moves in circles") would require the following answer: the reason that we do not attempt the positive judgement is that we have already made the negative judgement, having found it to be evident and certain. This is what would best explain why there is no "danger" of "anyone wanting to attribute such predicates to the stone or to justice". One might also answer our question by saying this: the reason we do not attempt all the relevant positive judgements lies in the fact that our consciousness, after all, has its limitations. I could accept this answer too. But why didn't Sigwart appeal directly to this fact earlier in his discussion? He says himself that there is an "unlimited number" of possible negative judgements.

Sigwart makes still another curious mistake (as Marty has already noted). Affirmative judgements, he says, differ from negative judgements in that "only a finite number of predicates can be affirmed of any subject". How so? Aren't we justified in saying, for example, that a whole hour is greater than a half an hour, greater than a third of an hour, greater than a fourth of an hour, and so on, *ad infinitum*?[52] If now I do not in fact make each one of these judgements, there must be a good reason. After all, the limitations of consciousness would hardly permit it. But these same considerations may be applied equally well to negative judgements.

We find a third argument somewhat later on. We may treat it briefly here, for I have already answered it in my *Psychologie* (Book II, Chapter 7, Section 5). Sigwart reasons as follows (p. 155 f.): suppose the negative judgement were direct and, as a species of judgement, co-ordinate with the affirmative judgement; then, if one thinks that the affirmation of the subject is involved in an affirmative categorical proposition, one should also think that the denial of the subject is involved in a negative categorical proposition; but this is not the case. The latter observation is correct (the denial of the subject need not be involved in the affirmation of a negative proposition). But the observation that precedes it (viz., if one thinks that the affirmation of the subject is involved in an affirmative categorical proposition, one should also think that the denial of the subject is involved in a negative proposition) is entirely untenable and, indeed, self-contradictory. Precisely because of the fact that the existence of a whole involves the existence of each of its parts, all that is needed, if a given whole is *not* to exist, is that only one of its parts be lacking.[53]

There is, finally, a linguistic consideration which Sigwart believes will confirm his view. He says that we symbolize a negative judgement by adding a certain complication to the way in which we symbolize an affirmative judgement; we add the word "not" to the copula. To evaluate this, let us for a moment consider the emotions. Sigwart agrees with me, and with everyone else, that pleasure and displeasure, rejoicing and sorrowing, loving and hating, and the like, are co-ordinate with each other. Yet we have a large group of expressions which are such that the names for feelings of disinclination are dependent upon the names for feelings of inclination. Thus we have: "inclination" and "disinclination"; "pleasure" and "displeasure; "fortunate" and "unfortunate"; "happy" and "unhappy"; "agreeable" and "disagreeable"; and in German "*lieb*" and "*unlieb*", "*schön*" and "*unschön*" and even "*ungut*". I believe that the psychologist will not find this fact difficult to explain, despite the fact that we have here two co-ordinate species of emotive phenomena. But if this is so, why should there be a difficulty in reconciling the corresponding fact, about the way in which negative judgements are expressed, with the fact that there are two co-ordinate species of intellectual phenomena?

If a thinker of Sigwart's calibre must take refuge in this type of argument to defend an important and unorthodox doctrine, then his case must be very poor indeed!

(2) There is no tenable basis, then, for Sigwart's theory of the negative judgement. And this is as it should be. One should not expect to be able to demonstrate a theory which seems to plunge everything into the greatest possible confusion.

Sigwart now finds himself compelled to distinguish a *positive* judgement and an *affirmative* judgement. And he goes on to say (the new terminology will be dumbfounding) that the *affirmative* judgement is, strictly speaking, a negative judgement! Thus we have his own words on page 150: "The original and primordial judgement should not be called affirmative; it would be better to say that it is a positive judgement. The simple assertion, that *A* is *B*, should be called *affirmative* only in opposition to a negative judgement and only *insofar as* it may be said to *reject* the possibility of a negation." Insofar as it "rejects"? What can this mean other than "insofar as it *denies*"? And so it really is true that, given this strange new use of words, only denials are to be called affirmations! But all this—especially if one is also going to say that the assertion, *A* is *B*, is sometimes such a denial (compare the words cited above) —multiplies linguistic confusion beyond necessity and beyond endurance.

Not only does the affirmative judgement turn out to be strictly negative, on Sigwart's account; we also find, paradoxical as it may be, that his *negative* judgement, when closely examined, is a *positive* judgement. He does protest against the view of Hobbes and others, according to which negative judgements are really positive judgements with negative predicates. On *his* view, however, they have to be positive judgements with positive predicates; for he says that the subject of a negative judgement is always a judgement and that its predicate is the concept "invalid". Thus he says (p. 160n.) that negation serves to cancel out a supposition and to reject it as invalid (*spreche ihr die Gültigkeit ab*); these words would suggest that Sigwart does suppose that there is a special function of rejecting which is contrary to that of affirming. But no; according to him (see p. 153) there is no such thing as a negative copula. How on earth are we to interpret his "rejection", then? Could it be the simple "cessation" of the positive judgement about the corresponding subject-matter—and thus (on Sigwart's view) the disappearance of the feeling of compulsion which had previously existed along with a joining of concepts? This could not possibly be; for if the feeling of compulsion disappears, then, on Sigwart's view, there remains only a joining of ideas without any affirmation or negation. Consider how often it happens that something previously certain becomes uncertain—without our thereby rejecting or denying it. What is it, then, to reject or deny? Could we say that just as, for Sigwart, affirmation is a feeling of being compelled to posit, denial or negation is a feeling of being compelled to cancel out? In this case we should have to say that, whenever we make a negative judgement, we have found ourselves frustrated in a previous attempt to make the corresponding positive judgement. But one who simply finds that there is no ground for the positive judgement has a similar state of mind. Whenever we find that there is no ground whatever for believing a given thing, do we *ipso facto* attempt to believe it? Certainly this is false on Sigwart's own definition of judgement; such an attempt would always end in failure. And so we have not yet been able to get the negative judgement clearly before us. If there is no negative copula, then rejection or denial would have to be a matter of attributing the predicate "false" to something, or, in Sigwart's terms, a matter of inserting this predicate into a judgement having the judgement in question as its subject. But this "false" cannot be said simply to mean the same as "not true". For we can say of countless things that they are "not true", where it would hardly be appropriate to say of them that they are "false". If judgements are the only things that can be said to be true, then "not true" applies to everything that is not a judgement; but "false" does not at all apply to everything that is not a judgement.[54] Thus "false" must be conceived as a positive predicate. Hence, given Sigwart's point of view, which is inherently wrong, just as we must say that negation or denial is something other than mere failure to be convinced, we must say that every negative judgement is a positive judgement with a positive predicate. And thus we have a paradox which is even more striking than the first one we encountered.

But there is a third paradox, which serves to make the confusion complete. If we consider the way in which Sigwart conceives the nature of judgement in general, we can easily see that his simple positive judgement involves, again, a negative judgement. According to him, every judgement involves, not only a certain connection of ideas, but also a consciousness of the necessity of our putting them together and of the impossibility of the opposite (see in particular p. 102) and, indeed, it involves the consciousness of such a necessity and impossibility for every thinking being (pp. 102, 107)—which, incidentally, is just as much mistaken as is Sigwart's whole concept of the nature of judgement. Because of

47

this characteristic, then, Sigwart says that *every* judgement without exception is apodictic; there is no valid distinction, according to him (see pp. 229 ff.), between assertoric and apodictic judgements. I would ask, therefore: Do we not have here that which obviously involves a negative judgement? Otherwise what sense could we give to Sigwart's "consciousness of the impossibility of the opposite"? And there is still more! I have already shown in my *Psychologie* (p. 233) that every universal judgement is negative; for to be convinced of universality is no more nor less than to be convinced that there is no exception. Without this latter negation, no accumulation of positive assertions, however extensive, would be sufficient to constitute a belief in universality. Hence when Sigwart says that every judgement involves the awareness that such-and-such a way of thinking must be universal, we have additional confirmation for our contention that, according to Sigwart's theory of judgement, even the simplest positive judgement has to involve a negative judgement.[55] Are we really supposed to believe, then, that the negative judgement shows up relatively late (as we are told on pp. 159 ff.) and that, on the basis of these and other considerations, the negative judgement should be thought unworthy of being placed on an equal footing with the positive judgement as being an independent species of judgement? The more one considers Sigwart's views the clearer it becomes that they do involve the implications developed here; surely Sigwart would never have maintained such things had he thought them through. There are passages, of course, in which he contradicts one or another of these theses which I have shown his views to imply. But what else are we to expect when everything is in such great confusion and when the attempt to clear up things serves only to uncover a multiplicity of contradictions?

(3) We have, then, a highly respected logician, misconceiving the nature of judgement, and then becoming entangled in hopeless confusion with respect to a relatively simple question. What is the origin of the error? The *proton pseudos* consists of a mistake which has been handed down from the older logic; it is the mistake of supposing that a relation between two ideas is essentially involved in the nature of judgement. Aristotle had described the relation as being one of combining or separating (σύνθεσις καὶ διαίρεσις); he realized, however, that the terminology is not entirely appropriate and he noted that there is a sense in which both

48

relations could be said to be a matter of combining (σύνθεσις); see *De Anima*, III, 6. Scholastic logic and modern logic have retained the two terms "combining" and "separating", but in grammar both relations are called "combining" and the symbol for combining is called the "copula". Now Sigwart takes these expressions "combining" and "separating" literally. Hence a negative copula appears to him (see p. 153) to be a contradiction; and the negative judgement is said to presuppose a positive judgement. For how can we separate any two things unless they have first been combined? Thus we find that, according to Sigwart (p. 150 and the passages cited above), it makes no sense to speak of a negative judgement which does not presuppose a positive judgement. The consequence is that all the efforts of this distinguished thinker turn out to be in vain; the negative judgement is no longer even comprehensible.

There is a note, beginning on p. 150, in which Sigwart tells us what finally confirmed him in his endeavours. What we have here is a remarkable description of the process by means of which we are supposed to arrive at the negative judgement. The attentive reader will be able to see the whole series of errors in succession, and he will find that the negative judgement is actually presupposed long before the point at which it is finally supposed to emerge.

Sigwart proceeds from the correct observation that our first judgements are all positive. These judgements are evident and made with complete confidence. "But now", he says, "our thought goes out beyond the given; as a result of recollections and associations, other judgements are formed, also with the thought that they express what is real." (This means that the ideas are connected with a consciousness of objective validity, this being of the essence of judgement, according to Sigwart; sect. 14, p. 98.) These other judgements, he continues, might be exemplified by our "expecting to find some familiar thing in its usual place, or our assumption that we will be able to smell a certain flower. But now some part of what we thus suppose comes into *conflict* with what it is that we immediately know". (Sigwart does not attempt to show how we are able to recognize that something "conflicts" with what we know, if we are not yet able to make negative judgements and are not in possession of negative concepts. The difficulty becomes even more apparent as he continues.) "In such cases, when we do *not find* what we had expected, we become aware of the

49

difference between what is *merely* thought about and what is real."
(What does "not find" mean here? The phrase is one which, prior
to this point, is not to be found. Clearly what I find, in the cases
in question, is that something which I had expected to be accompanied by something else is in fact *without* that something else;
but this is possible only to the extent that I am able to affirm the
one and deny the other—i.e., affirm that the other does *not* accompany the one. And how are we to interpret the term "difference"?
To be aware of a difference is to be aware, with respect to two
things, that one of them is *not* the other. And, finally, what is the
meaning of the phrase *"merely* thought about"? Clearly: something which is thought about but which is *not* at the same time real.
Sigwart does not seem to realize that he has already allowed the
negative judgement to come into play.) He continues: "What we
are immediately certain of is something *other* than that which we
had expected." (Something other—i.e., something which is *not*
the same, something which cannot possibly be the same.) "And
now" (because of the fact that we have already made so many
negative judgements) "negation finally enters into the picture,
cancelling out the assumption in question and rejecting it as invalid.
With this we have something *entirely new*; the subjective combination is separated from the consciousness of certainty. This subjective combination is contrasted with one that is certain and we
recognize the difference between them; out of this the concept of
invalidity arises." The final sentence would seem to be sheer
carelessness. If the word "invalid" is to mean *false*, and not merely
uncertain, then the concept of invalidity cannot be acquired by
comparing a combination of ideas which is certain with a combination of ideas which is uncertain; what we need is a contrast between
a combination which is accepted and one which is rejected. But
actually the conflicting affirmative judgement is not at all required.
The conflict—the incompatibility of certain characteristics—is
already apparent from the relation between the concepts of the conflicting characteristics. Even Sigwart himself, if I may be permitted
to repeat it, is aware that his conflict cannot be grasped by any
attempt at a positive judgement (see p. 89n. and pp. 98 ff.). It may
well be that we often make negative judgements as a result of having
first made the opposing positive judgement, but this is by no means
the way in which negative judgements *always* come about. Suppose,
for example, I am asked: "Is there a regular figure with a thousand

angles and a thousand and one sides ?" It will have occurred to me previously, as may be the case with most people, that I cannot be at all sure that there is such a thing as a regular figure with a thousand angles. Hence I may make the negative judgement, on the basis of a conflict of characteristics, that there is no such figure—*without* having previously made an attempt at a positive judgement. It is not at all necessary, as Sigwart thinks it is, that I must first make a "confident assumption" that there is a regular figure with a thousand angles and a thousand and one sides.

The application of negation or denial is by no means restricted in the way in which Sigwart says it is. Sigwart betrays the fact that he realizes this too (see, e.g., p. 152 and even p. 150), despite his insistence that there can be no negative copula which performs a function of judgement on the same footing as affirmation or acceptance. It is false that, whenever a thing is denied, what it is that is denied is always the property "valid". Even in the case of a judgement, we can deny not only its validity, but also, among other things, its certainty, or its being *a priori*. The subject of the judgement may be treated in a similar way. One can deny certainty or validity of a judgement; one can deny modesty of a request; and, more generally, one can deny, of any A, a B. Sigwart himself makes such denials, just as everyone else does. Indeed, he often speaks with far more correctness than his theory would allow, thus giving instinctive witness to the truth. According to his theory, the only thing that can be denied is validity, and this is always denied of judgements; but he tells us, on p. 151 for example, that "of *any* subject, an *unlimited number of predicates* may be denied". This is certainly correct, and it is precisely for this reason that we are justified in retaining the ancient doctrine that there are two co-ordinate species of judgement.

VI

ON THE EVIDENT

Critique of Descartes and Sigwart

(From the notes to *Vom Ursprung sittlicher Erkenntnis*, 1889)

The distinction between judgements which are evident and judgements which are blind is much too striking to have escaped notice altogether. Even the sceptical Hume is far from denying the distinction. According to what he says in the *Enquiry Concerning Human Understanding* (Section IV), the *evident* comprises analytic judgements (which are supposed to include the axioms and proofs of mathematics) and certain impressions; but these latter do not include the so-called inferences from experience. Inferences from experience, according to Hume, are not the effects of reason, but the effects of a habit or custom which is entirely unreasonable (see Section V).

It is one thing, however, to take note of a fact, and another thing to provide a clear and distinct account of its nature. If the nature of judgement has been almost universally misconceived until very recent times, it is hardly to be expected that the nature of the evident would be properly understood. Even Descartes' usual discernment fails him here. He was very much concerned with the problem, however, as we may see from the following passage taken from the third of his Meditations: "When I say that I am so instructed by nature [he is referring to so-called external perception], I mean merely a certain *spontaneous inclination* which impels me to believe in this connection, and a *natural light* which makes me recognize that it is true. But these two things are very different. For I cannot doubt that which the *natural light* causes me to believe to be true; as for example, it has shown me that *I am* from the fact that I doubt, or other facts of the same kind. And I

possess no other faculty whereby to distinguish truth from falsehood, which can teach me that what this light shows me to be
true is not really true, and no other faculty that is equally trust-
worthy. But as far as natural impulses are concerned, I have
frequently remarked, when I had to make active choice between
virtue and vice, that they often led me to the part that was worse;
and this is why I do not see any reason for following them in what
regards truth and error."*

It is clear from this passage that the concept of the evident
had not escaped Descartes and that he took note of the distinction
between an insight (*Einsicht*) and a judgement which is blind. Yet,
despite the fact that he took care to distinguish the class of judgements from that of ideas, he misplaces the distinguishing characteristic of the evident which pertains always to the insightful
judgement, and classifies it with ideas instead of with judgements.
What he called the *idea*—the presentation, that which is before
the mind—is the basis of the judgement, and Descartes assumes
that the idea is that which is evident. He even goes so far as to
call this idea a "cognoscere"—an instance of knowing. A matter
of knowing something and yet not a judgement!

One might say that what we have here are vestigial organs in
the development of psychology. After the great advances which
Descartes himself has made in the theory of judgement, they
survive to remind us of a stage long since past. There is one
point, however, with respect to which this phenomenon is to be
distinguished from similar phenomena in the evolution of species.
In the present case, the vestigial organs, not having adapted themselves to the stages that follow, become highly troublesome, with
the result that Descartes' additional efforts on behalf of the theory

---

* Cum hic dico me ita doctum esse a natura intelligo tantum
spontaneo quodam impetu me ferri ad hoc credendum, non lumine
aliquo naturali mihi ostendi esse verum, quae duo multum discrepant.
Nam quaecunque lumine naturali mihi ostenduntur (ut quod ex eo quod
dubitem sequatur me esse, et similia) nullo modo dubia esse possunt,
quia nulla alia facultas esse potest, cui aeque fidam ac lumini isti, quaeque
illa non vera esse possit docere; sed quantum ad impetus naturales jam
saepe olim judicavi me ab illis in deteriorem partem fuisse impulsum
cum de bono eligendo ageretur, nec video cur iisdem in ulla alia re
magis fidam. [English translation from the *Philosophical Works of
Descartes*, trans. E. S. Haldane and G. R. T. Ross, Vol. I, pp. 160–161.]

of knowledge turn out to be in vain. To quote Leibniz, Descartes remains in the "antechamber of truth".[56] It is only from this point of view that we are to understand the peculiar hybrid character of Descartes' *clara et distincta perceptio*, of which it is so difficult to obtain a clear and distinct idea. If we are to find that which distinguishes insights from all other judgements, we must look for it in the inner peculiarities of the *act of insight* itself.

To be sure, there are those who have looked in the right place without having found what they were looking for. We have seen how Sigwart misconceives the nature of judgement. Judgement, according to him (*op. cit.*, sections 14 and 31, esp. 4 and 5), involves a relation between ideas and also a feeling of compulsion, or an irresistible impulse, which pertains to the ideas. This feeling, according to him, is to be found even in connection with the most blind of prejudices. In such cases it is not normative, but (Sigwart says explicitly) it is taken to be normative and universal. How do these cases differ, then, from insights? Sigwart says (see section 3, for example) that the evident character of a genuine insight is constituted by such a feeling. But the feeling which pertains to the insight is not merely one that is *taken* to be normative and universal; it must be one that *is* normative and universal.

The untenability of this theory seems to me to be obvious; there are more reasons for not accepting it.

(1) The peculiar nature of insight—the clarity and evidence of certain judgements which is inseparable from their truth—has little or nothing to do with a feeling of compulsion.[57] It may well be that, at a given moment, I cannot help but judge in the way in which I do judge. But the clarity in question does not consist in any feeling of compulsion; no awareness of a compulsion to judge in a certain way could, as such, guarantee the truth of the judgement. One may reject indeterminism and thus hold that every judgement, given the circumstances under which it is made, is necessary; and yet one may deny, with perfect right, that every such judgement is true.

(2) In trying to locate the consciousness of an insight in the feeling of a compulsion to believe, Sigwart asserts that the consciousness of one's own compulsion is at the same time a consciousness of a similar necessity for every thinker to whom the same grounds are present. If he means that the one conviction is indubitably connected with the other, then he is mistaken. Given

that on the basis of certain data one thinker is compelled to make a certain judgement, why should it be that every thinker on the basis of the same data would have a similar compulsion? One may be tempted, in this connection, to appeal to the general causal law according to which, if all the relevant conditions are the same, the effects will also be the same. But this general law is not applicable in the present case. For the relevant causal conditions will include all those psychical dispositions which may not enter directly into consciousness at all but which will exercise their effects upon one's judging; and these dispositions are different for different people.

Misled by paralogisms, Hegel and his school have even denied the law of contradiction; and Trendelenburg, who opposes Hegel, has at least restricted its validity (see his *Abhandlungen über Herbarts Metaphysik*). Hence we can no longer say, as Aristotle did, that it is impossible for anyone inwardly to deny the principle. But for Aristotle himself, to whom the principle was clearly evident, its denial was certainly impossible.

But it is true that anything that is seen to be evident by one person is certain, not only for him, but also for anyone else who sees it in a similar way. Moreover, any judgement which is thus seen by one person to be true is universally valid; its contradictory cannot be seen to be evident by any other person; and anyone who accepts its contradictory is *ipso facto* mistaken. What I am here saying pertains to the nature of truth: anyone who thus sees into something as true is also able to see that he is justified in regarding it as true for all.[58] But it would be a gross confusion to suppose that this awareness of something being true for everyone implies an awareness of a universal compulsion to believe.

(3) Sigwart entangles himself in a multiplicity of contradictions. He says—as he must if he is not to give in to scepticism or to abandon his entire logic—that judgements which are evident may be distinguished from judgements which are not, and that we can make the distinction in our own consciousness. Thus the one class of judgements, but not the other, must appear as normative and universal. But he also says that both classes of judgements—those which are evident and those which are not—are made with a consciousness of universal validity. The two types of judgement, therefore, would seem to present themselves in precisely the same way. If this were true, then one could make out the distinction

between the two types of judgement only by means of reflection—supplementary and possibly later than the judgement itself—in the course of which one would appeal to some *criterion* or other which would then be a kind of measuring rod. There are actually passages in which Sigwart says that there is an awareness of agreement with universal rules and that this awareness accompanies every perfectly evident judgement (*op. cit.*, 2nd edn., Section 39, p. 311). But this is hardly in agreement with our experience—it was possible to reason syllogistically with perfect evidence long before the discovery of the rules of the syllogism. And in any case, we cannot be content with what Sigwart is here saying, for the rule to which he appeals is itself something that must be assured. Given Sigwart's view, such assurance would require either an infinite regress or a vicious circle.

(4) Sigwart is involved in still another contradiction (but one which, it seems to me, he could have avoided even after arriving at his erroneous conceptions of the nature of judgement and of evidence); this concerns his view of self-awareness. What is expressed by "I exist" is said to be *just* evident and *not* to be accompanied by any feeling of compulsion or of universal necessity. (At any rate, this is the only way I am able to interpret the following passage from his *Logik*, 2nd edn., Vol. I, p. 310: "The certainty that I exist and that I think is basic and fundamental, the condition of all thought and of all certainty. Here one can speak only of direct evidence; one cannot even say that the thought is necessary, for it is prior to all necessity. Equally direct and evident is the conscious certainty that I think this or that; it is inextricably interwoven with my self-conscious in such a way that the one is given with the other.") Given the doctrines previously considered, this would seem to be a *contradictio in adjecto* and thus incapable of defence.

(5) Still more contradictions are to be found in Sigwart's extraordinary—and unacceptable—theory of "postulates", which he contrasts with axioms. The certainty of axioms is said to lie in the compulsion we have to think in a certain way. But the certainty of postulates, according to Sigwart, is based upon our practical needs and not upon any purely intellectual motive (*op. cit.*, pp. 412 ff.). Thus the law of causality, on his view, is a mere postulate and not an axiom; we take it to be certain because we find that, if we were not to accept it, we would be unable to investigate

nature. But consider now the consequences, for Sigwart, of his accepting the law of causality in this way: out of sheer good will, he decrees that like conditions produce like effects; thus he is taking something to be true without any consciousness of being compelled to do so; but to say this is to contradict Sigwart's theory of judgement—unless, of course, taking something to be true is not the same as making a judgement. So far as I can see, Sigwart has only one way out: he ought to say that he does *not* believe any of the postulates, such as that of causation in nature, which he assumes to be "certain". But in such a case, he could no longer be serious.

(6) The doctrine of postulates becomes even more questionable if we consider it along with what we have discussed under (2) above. The consciousness of a universal necessity to think in a certain way, according to Sigwart, is an axiom and not a postulate. But this universal necessity to think in a given way is obvious to us only if we apply the law of causality to our own compulsion to think in that way. Now the law of causality is said to be a mere postulate and hence to be without evidence. The mark of axioms, according to Sigwart, is that they involve a universal compulsion or necessity to believe; hence it is only a postulate that there are such axioms. And therefore what Sigwart calls axioms are deprived of what they must have, according to him, if they are to be distinguished from his postulates. All this accords with Sigwart's remark (section 3) that the belief in the reliability of evidence is a "postulate". But given his interpretation of "postulate", I cannot imagine how such a remark is to fit in with the rest of the theory.

(7) Sigwart denies that there is any distinction between assertoric and apodictic judgements (section 31); for, he says, every judgement involves the feeling of necessity. This assertion must also be attributed to his erroneous conception of judgement; he would seem to identify the feeling, which he sometimes calls the feeling of evidence, with the nature of apodicticity. But this is to overlook the *modal* characteristic which distinguishes some evident judgements from the evident judgements of self-awareness; the law of contradiction would be an instance of the former, the judgement that I exist an instance of the latter. The former exemplifies what is "necessarily true or necessarily false", the latter what is only "actually true or false". Both are evident, however, and

in the same sense of the word, and they do not differ with respect to certainty. It is only from judgements of the former sort, not from those of the latter sort, that we acquire the concepts of impossibility and necessity.

Despite his polemic against conceiving apodictic judgements as a special class of judgement, Sigwart occasionally bears witness to the contrary view, as is clear from what was discussed under (4) above. The knowledge expressed by "I exist", according to him (see p. 312), is to be contrasted with our knowledge of axioms in that it pertains to a simple factual truth. Here he speaks more soundly than his general theory would allow.

Sigwart's theory of the evident, then, is essentially wrong. Like Descartes, he certainly took note of the phenomenon; and it must be said to his credit that he exercised great zeal in trying to analyse it. But like many others who have been concerned with the analysis of psychological phenomena, he seems not to have stopped at the right place in his eagerness to complete the analysis; the result was that he attempted to reduce one set of phenomena to another set of entirely different phenomena.

Obviously any mistake about the nature of the evident can be disastrous for the logician. We could say that Sigwart's theory of the evident is the basic defect of his logic—were it not for his misconception of the nature of judgement in general. Again and again we find the unhappy results of his theory; an example is his inability to understand the general causes of error. The principal cause, he says in his *Logik* (Vol. I, 2nd edn., p. 103n.), is the imperfection of our language; and this, surely, is a one-sided account.[59]

Many other prominent logicians, of recent years, have fared no better than Sigwart with the theory of the evident. The views of the excellent John Stuart Mill—to cite only one example—are discussed in note 73 of *Vom Ursprung sittlicher Erkenntnis*.

The fact that the nature of the evident is almost universally misunderstood explains why it is that we often hear the expression "more or less evident". Even Descartes and Pascal spoke in this way; but the expression is completely inappropriate. What is evident is certain; and certainty in the strict sense of the term knows no distinctions of degree. In a recent issue of the *Vierteljahrsschrift für wissenschaftliche Philosophie*, we are even told (the author is serious) that here are *evident presumptions* which, despite their evidence, may well be *false*. Needless to say, I regard this as nonsense. I regret that my own lectures, given at a time when I took degrees of conviction to be a matter of intensity of judgement, seem to have been the occasion for such confusions.[60]

Part Two

TRANSITION TO THE LATER VIEW

I

GRAMMATICAL *ABSTRACTA* AS LINGUISTIC FICTIONS

(From a letter to A. Marty of March 1901)

Your question has occupied me for several days now.[1] I have asked myself whether it is not necessary to give up my view that general concepts are correlative pairs (a view which is required if we think of the so-called abstracta such as "redness", "evidence", etc., as being something—a "divisive" or a "form"—which inheres in things). Should we not say instead that there is *nothing whatever* that corresponds to these abstracta (and not merely that there is no *thing* that corresponds to them)? In other words, that we are here confronted with a widespread error which may be attributed to language? Even Aristotle was infected with this error, for he frequently took language as his point of orientation; he was over-conservative in his approach to language, just as I have been over-conservative in my approach to him.

My earlier train of thought had been this: the theory of concepts as correlative pairs is based upon an analogy with the *parts* of a physical thing. Consider the tail, for example. We seem to have as correlative concepts "A thing which has a tail" (*Geschwänztes*) and "A tail which is had by a thing" (*gehabter Schwanz*). In the thought of "a tail", the animal is considered with regard to a *physical* part and is therefore not conceived completely; similarly, in the thought of "redness", a body is considered with respect to a *logical* part and is therefore not conceived completely. The only difference is that the tail may exist separately; hence "tail" and "tail which is had" are not identical concepts. But "redness" and "redness which is possessed by something" are one and the same concept.

63

It now seems to me, however, that this analogy is false. The idea of the redness of a thing, I should now say, is not the idea of a *part* of the thing; it is the idea of the *whole* thing but of the thing considered in an incomplete way. What does this mean? Perhaps that just a single part of the thing is considered? Not at all. For this would imply that universals are *parts* of things, which is not at all the case. There is nothing universal in the things; the so-called universal, as such, is only in the one who is thinking. It is not a *part* of any of the things he is thinking about, for otherwise these things would have this part in common. And if it were a part of any such thing, then, since the object of the thought is the entire thing, the object would *be* the part.

The truth of the matter is this: the whole object is thought of by means of an indefinite concept, and this is all there is to be said. There is no redness to be found and singled out in the red object. One can say of the object only that "it is red", i.e., that "red" or "being red" can be predicated of it, or that the object falls under the definite concept of a red thing. But we speak in this way only after secondary reflections. If we were to speak in ordinary language of a redness which is inherent in the thing, or to speak with Aristotle of a λόγος, or an ἐνέργεια, or a μορφή, which belongs to the thing in so far as the thing is red, or which makes it a red thing, we would misunderstand the remarkable property of general concepts, which is revealed only in experience, and we would become entangled in erroneous conclusions.

Here, then, is the new thesis. I am aware that it is far-reaching, for all abstracta are now to be counted as delusions. They are useful as ways of speaking. Even Copernicus, for all his enlightenment, found it convenient to speak in Ptolemaic terms of the rising and setting of the sun. And in mathematics, it is convenient to be able to speak of infinitesimals, imaginary quantities, negative quantities, irrational numbers, and improper fractions, despite the fact that mathematicians are fully aware of the intrinsic absurdity of these products of the mind.

Even space and time, then, would not be anything real (to this extent we are with the Idealists), and virtue would be only an empty word (despite our adherence to that which serves the ethical good).[2] A concession should be made to Nominalism; not that Nominalism is correct, however, but only that certain errors can be purged from the opposing theory.[3]

II

THE EQUIVOCAL USE OF THE
TERM "EXISTENT"

(September 1904)

1. We speak in sentences.

2. And we do this in order to indicate that there is something about which we have certain thoughts or feelings.[4]

3. "To indicate" is to make known to another person.

4. Only primary sentences are sentences in the logical sense.

5. These are the genuine sentences.[5] If I were to represent others dramatically, by quoting them directly, then what is grammatically the primary sentence would be logically only a subordinate sentence.

6. And on the other hand, particles such as "Yes" and "No", which are neither subordinate sentences nor primary sentences from the point of view of grammar, may yet be sentences in the logical sense.

7. Just as we call "this" a pronoun, we might call "Yes" a prosentence.

8. From a logical point of view, the primary sentences are of two kinds: those which express one's judgements, in the purely intellectual sense, and those which express one's feelings. The latter are imperatives in the widest sense of the word. "Be it so!" "Do this!"

9. A sign of a judgement about one's feelings or emotions may also serve indirectly as a sign of these feelings or emotions themselves.

10. Every part of even the smallest complete and meaningful utterance is a "particle" in the widest sense of the word.[6]

11. So, too, for the letters, syllables, and words constituting the structure of any complete sentence. And these, not only when they are names, but also when they are verbs, adverbs, *casus obliqui*, pronouns, prepositions, and conjunctions. Nouns, adjectives, and numerals are names.[7]

12. The particles are synsemantic.

13. But one may ask whether the particles do not also, in a certain sense, signify something by themselves or indicate something by themselves.[8]

14. Strictly speaking, this can even be said of letters. In pronouncing the letter "L", one makes known that this sound was in one's thought.[9]

15. The same is true of syllables.

16. Also of every complete word, whether it be univocal or equivocal.

17. When the word is equivocal, then it is a sign which provides some degree of probability but not certainty. The listener knows that *either* this *or* that is my thought.

18. If we restrict ourselves to univocal words, we may readily infer what applies to equivocal words.

19. I am saying, not only of the completed speech, but also of each of its constituent words, that it yields some information about what is going on in the intellect or mind of the speaker.

This is true of the names of things. These names enable me to know that the speaker has something as the object of his thought (he considers the thing positively, though perhaps without accepting it and possibly even under the conviction that there is no such thing). It is impossible to deny or reject a thing without considering the thing positively.[10] Similarly for love, hatred, and the like.

20. The same thing holds of the *casus obliqui* of the names of things.[11] It is impossible to think of the hat of a man without thinking of the man. The latter thought prepares the way for the former. The thought of the man is fundamental, the thought of the hat of the man is supraposed (upon the thinking of the collective, hat and man).

21. The same is true of those names that are not names of things. Actually such names also indicate that the speaker is thinking of some thing.[12] (Only *things* can be thought.) The term "virtue", for example, indicates that the speaker is thinking of a virtuous person and is concerned with him *as* a virtuous person. The term "necessary" indicates that the speaker is thinking of someone who is making an apodictic judgement. The term "thought" indicates that the speaker is thinking of someone who is himself thinking; "willed" indicates that he is thinking about someone willing.[13]

22. The same is true, as we have said, of any other word or particle. "But" indicates that the speaker is making a contrast; "and" that he is thinking of something as conjoined; "a" or "an" that he is thinking of something in general terms; "of" that he is thinking of something relative. (If the latter were not itself equivocal, it would convey even more precise knowledge.)

23. Since only *things*—in the strict sense of this term—can be thought (I have in mind whatever is such that, if it exists, it is a substance, an accident, or a collective of both), it often happens that words which are names in the *grammatical* sense are not names in the *logical* sense. When a word is a name only in the grammatical sense, it does not denote anything in the way in which the word "man" can be said to denote something and to indicate that the speaker is thinking about a man. But a word which is a name only in the grammatical sense does indicate a thought to which some other

word corresponds as a name. "Necessary", for example, indicates that the speaker is thinking of someone who is judging apodictically (it also indicates in a certain way that the speaker himself is judging apodictically). "Empty" indicates that he is thinking in a negative way of what is filled.

24. But if not all grammatical names are logical names, then the expression "there is", which may be used with either type of name, is equivocal. It is synsemantic in all of its uses, though each time in quite a different sense. Similarly the word *"von"* in German may be used, like "of", to indicate possession, or to indicate something having been brought forth from something else, and also to indicate aristocracy or nobility.

25. "There is" has its strict or proper meaning when used in connection with genuine logical names, as in "There is a God" or "There is a man". In its other uses, "there is" must not be taken in its strict sense. "There is an empty space" may be equated with "There are no physical bodies located in such and such a way"; "There is something which is the object of thought" (*es gibt ein Gedachtes*) may be equated with "There is something which thinks" (*es gibt ein Denkendes*).[14] It would be a complete mistake to interpret "there is" when used with mere grammatical names in the way in which we interpret it in "There is a God" and "There is a man". For there is nothing other than *things*, and "empty space" and "object of thought" do not name things.

26. What holds of "there is" also holds of "there exists" and "there subsists"; these expressions are also equivocal and have precisely the different meanings just distinguished.[15]

27. Shall we now say that the concept of "the existent", or "that which exists", in its strict or proper sense, is the same as the concept of thing or that of substance?

28. Not at all. If "the existent", in its strict sense, is a name, it cannot be said to name anything directly. It comes to the same thing as "something which is the object of a correct affirmative judgement" or "something which is correctly accepted or affirmed". If "existent" is a name in the logical sense, i.e. a word which

names a thing, a thing that is judged affirmatively, it is a relational word. I use it to indicate that I am thinking of some thing as corresponding to my thinking (and also, naturally, that I am thinking of myself as thinking correctly).[16] But *thing*—compare οὐσία and συμβεβηκός—is not a concept of anything which, as such, is relative to someone thinking.

["Substance" and "accident" do not denote that which is relative to someone thinking. If the expression "an existent", in its logical sense, could be thought of as a logical name, then it would designate something relative to a thinking. For it indicates that there is something which is objectively related to the person addressed, as well as to the speaker, in so far as each of us is thinking in an affirmative way. "Existent" refers to this relationship between the thing and the speaker and person addressed. The terms "substance" and "accident" do not refer to this relationship. (It would be advisable to make a thorough study of the following question about the words we use to indicate the relations among the parts of a collective: are these words logical names, or are they merely grammatical names pointing to some logical name of the collective itself, for which they may be substituted in some different use without change of meaning? Just as the sentence "There is redness" may be replaced by "There is something red" without change of meaning, so, too, "This is together with that" may be replaced by "*These two* are conjoined".)]*

29. Perhaps it would be more nearly correct to say: "existent" is not even a logical name. The most natural expression is: "there is an *A*" and not "an *A* is existent"; for in the latter case "existent" has the appearance of being a predicate. If we are to distinguish between "There is an *A*", where "existent" does not appear as a predicate, and "An *A* is existent", then we should not take the latter to mean "*A* answers or corresponds to someone thinking in an affirmative way". It means rather "If anyone should be thinking of *A* in a positive way, *A* corresponds to this thinking"—and if "existent" is to be taken in this way, then it is obviously not a name in the logical sense.[17]

30. The equivocal uses of "there is", "there subsists", "there

* Brentano dictated the paragraph in brackets as an alternative to the one preceding it.

exists" enable us to say in truth: "There is virtue", "There is empty space", "There is an impossibility", and the like. If we had to deny ourselves these expressions, we would find our language extraordinarily impoverished. And once we understand their modified senses, there is every justification for continuing to use them.

31. The rejection of *entia rationis* obviously has important bearing upon the explication of disjunctive and hypothetical judgements. Anyone who says "If there is an *A*, then there is a *B*" expresses the thought that, in contemplating that *A* is and *B* is not, he holds this combination of thoughts to be incorrect.* And anyone who says "There is an *A* or there is a *B* or there is a *C*" gives expression to this thought: in contemplating that *A* is not and *B* is not and *C* is not, he considers such a combination of thoughts to be incorrect.

Some would add that the statement "There is an *A* or there is a *B* or there is a *C*" also indicates this: that it would be incorrect for anyone to think of there being an *A*, there being a *B,* and there being a *C*, and at the same time to think that none of the three members of this combined judgement is correct. But if one were to say, of the statement "If there is an *A*, then there is a *B*", that it has the meaning "There is no being of an *A* without the being of a *B*", either his assertion would be false, or he would be using "there is", in the latter statement, in an entirely improper way. Instead of throwing any light upon anything, his translation itself would have to be clarified.[18]

* The word "not" has been inserted here by the translators. R.M.C.

III

LANGUAGE

(Fragment of 16 November, 1905)

1. Whoever asserts anything gives expression to what he thinks. Language is thus primarily a sign of thoughts, but indirectly a sign of events outside us.

2. This does not mean, however, that for each sound there is a corresponding thought or for each thought a corresponding sound. Individual sounds, and even the combinations of sounds which make up words, often have no meaning by themselves; and often they are signs of a multiplicity of thoughts.[19]

Thus individual syllables, particles, *casus obliqui*, have no meaning by themselves.

But the same cannot be said of statements or of names (substantives, adjectives).

These latter denote objects by means of concepts. They signify that the concepts are being thought and they evoke the same concepts in the one who is listening.

3. But it may well happen that a word which has the grammatical form of a noun or adjective actually denotes nothing at all and is therefore not a name in the logical sense.

For example: the *abstracta* ("colour" and "thinking"), also the *negativa* and *modalia* (such as "the necessary" and "the impossible");

Again, the *objectiva* ("an object of thought", "an object of love").

Again, "good" and "evil", as well as "truth" and "falsehood" and the like. Strictly speaking, there is no concept of the good, or of the beautiful, or of the true.[20]

71

4. Nor is there a concept of a thing's being. One erroneously assumes that there is and defines it thus: "A being is that which is". But what one is thinking when one says "*A* is a being" is an acknowledgement or acceptance of *A*. And when one says "*A* is not a being", one is thinking of a denial or rejection of *A*. If one were to say simply "a being" one would be thinking of a person who is accepting or acknowledging something. But this thought is not itself the concept of being, for if it were, the word "being" would have to denote one who asserts or acknowledges something.

5. But there is a concept of *thing*, even if there is no concept of the being of a thing, or of a thing's having being. And the concept of thing applies to everything.

For everything is a thing or entity—a *Usie*.

6. Here we have the most general concept. But only individual things correspond to it. Everything that does correspond to it must be subject to still other determinations fixing the concept of the thing more precisely.

7. If these more precise determinations specify and individuate the concept of the thing, then they are called "essential".[21]

8. Such essential determinations overlap. Determination is pluriserial.[22]

9. There are also determinations which may be lost and replaced by others without changing the essential individuality of the thing.

These are called accidental.[23]

10. These, too, are often pluriserial with respect to that which gives them individual determination.

11. And these accidental determinations themselves may often have accidental determinations of the second order, and so on. In such cases, the accidental determinations of the second order will be essential in relation to those of the first order (they will be essential determinations of what is an accident of the first order).[24]

12. If a determination is an accident of anything, then that thing is its substratum; the ultimate substratum, which is not an accident in relation to anything else, is called substance.

13. The combination of specifying and individuating determinations is of a purely logical nature. None of these determinations can disappear or change without causing each of the others to become something different.[25]

The combination of that which serves as a substratum and that which is only accidental is partly logical, partly real. That is to say, the former part may continue in its individuality when the latter ceases or falls away; the converse, however, is not possible.[26]

14. But there are also combinations of accidents as well as of substances which are such that any of the parts may continue after the other parts cease to exist. Such combinations of parts make up collectives and whatever is continuous.

In these cases the combination of the parts is real with respect to both aspects.[27]

15. A group of minds or an extended body would exemplify combined realities of this sort; indeed both of these are substances.

A multiplicity of accidents of one and the same substance (or of one and the same accident) and a continuous accident of an unextended substance would be examples of real combinations which are themselves accidental.[28] In the latter case, since the same substance underlies all the parts of the accident, no part of the accident can wholly fall away if the others are to be preserved.

Part Three

THE LATER VIEW AS SET FORTH IN LETTERS

I

ON THE SO-CALLED "IMMANENT OR INTENTIONAL OBJECT"

To Anton Marty[1]

17 March, 1905

Dear Friend,

I have your kind letter. I see that the Roman Congress has also upset you a little. I wasn't disturbed myself, I must say, and I have tried to calm E. as well as K. in a letter sent today. Typographical errors are a nuisance, though, and because there were no offprints, I cannot even send a copy to you.[2]

As for your account of Höfler's comments, I was baffled by the reference to the "content and immanent object" of thought (*"inhalt" und "immanentes Objekt" der Vorstellung*).[3]

When I spoke of "immanent object", I used the qualification "immanent" in order to avoid misunderstandings, since many use the unqualified term "object" to refer to that which is outside the mind.[4] But by an *object* of a thought I meant what it is that the thought is about, whether or not there is anything outside the mind corresponding to the thought.

It has never been my view that the *immanent* object is identical with *"object of thought"* (*vorgestelltes Objekt*). What we think about is *the object* or *thing* and not the "object of thought". If, in our thought, we contemplate a horse, our thought has as its immanent object—not a "contemplated horse", but a *horse*. And strictly speaking only the horse—not the "contemplated horse"—can be called an object.

But the object need not exist. The person thinking may have

77

something as the object of his thought even though that thing does not exist.

Of course it has long been customary to say that universals, *qua* universals, "exist in the mind" and not in reality, and such like. But this is incorrect if what is thus called "immanent" is taken to be the "contemplated horse" (*gedachtes Pferd*) or "the universal as object of thought" (*gedachtes Universale*). For "horse contemplated in general by me here and now" would then be the object of a general thought about a horse; it would be the correlate of me as an *individually* thinking person, as having this *individual* object of thought as object of thought.[5]. One could not say that universals *as universals* are in the mind, if one of the characteristics of the "things existing in the mind" is that they are "objects of my thought".

When Aristotle said the αἰσθητὸν ἐνεργείᾳ is in one's experience, he was also speaking of what you call simply "object". But because we do use the word "in" here, I allowed myself the term "immanent object", in order to say, not that the object exists, but that it *is* an object whether or not there is anything that corresponds to it. Its *being* an object, however, is merely the linguistic correlate of the person experiencing *having* it as object, i.e., his thinking of it in his experience.[6]

Aristotle also says that the αἴσθησις receives the εἶδος without the ὕλη, just as the intellect, of course, takes up the εἶδος νοητόν in abstraction from the matter. Wasn't his thinking essentially the same as ours? The "contemplated horse" considered as object would be the object of inner perception, which the thinker perceives whenever he forms a correlative pair consisting of this "contemplated horse" along with his thinking about the horse; for correlatives are such that one cannot be perceived or apprehended without the other.[7] But what are experienced as primary objects, or what are thought universally as primary objects of reason, are never themselves the objects of inner perception. Had I equated "object" with "object of thought", then I would have had to say that the primary thought relation has no object or content at all.[8] So I protest against this foolishness that has been dreamed up and attributed to me. Just what statement of my views is it that Höfler is attacking? Certain passages in my *Psychologie*?— Or perhaps something I am supposed to have said in my lectures? But where? When? Before what audience? I would indeed like to know. I haven't looked at the *Psychologie* or my notebooks for a long time, but, as I remember, I put the matter in the way I have just described. I would like to have it made clear that, unless something incorrect was said, which I do not believe, I have always held (in agreement with Aristotle) that "horse" and not "contemplated horse" is the immanent object of those thoughts that pertain to horses. Naturally, however, I did say that "horse" is thought or contemplated by us, and that insofar as we do think of it (N.B., insofar as we think of the *horse* and not of the "contemplated horse") we have "horse" as (immanent) object.

But enough for now . . .[9]

F.B.

II

ENS RATIONIS AND *ENS IRREALE*

To Anton Marty

1 March, 1906

Dear Friend,

... You say that by *"ens rationis"* you understand whatever is not strictly a *thing*. Examples would be: an empty space, the impossibility of a square circle; a colour (in contrast to something coloured). And from what you say later, it would seem that you also include such determinations as "brighter than what is red", "smaller than the size of a cubic foot", and so on. All these, in your opinion, could be said to exist, in the strict sense of the term, and even when no one is thinking.[10] But in this case, what justification would there be for the expression *"ens rationis"*? The expression is justified only in reference to "objects of thought", for *"ratio"* has the same comprehension as Descartes' *"cogitatio"*. It is not enough to note that if there were no reason, then such entities would not be grasped in their individuality. This would be to commit the mistake of those "who prove too much". The point is that the understanding does not *produce* such entities.

But if one must speak about such entities, then one should be consistent and affirm that in addition to whatever is a thing, there is a second set of entities, subsisting quite independently of reason, and that these might be called *entia non realia*, but not *entia rationis*. However, I am not prepared to do this, as you are aware. I would say that relations and concepts such as *shape, extension, position* (I am speaking of the concreta in question) are included among things. The mode of conception of these things is a special one, given only in cases of complicated apperception where parts are distinguished within a whole. As for the so-called abstract names, such as "colour", I would say that psychologically they are not true names but are quite different parts of speech. Similarly for "the being of A", "the non-being of A", "the impossibility of A". These ostensible names are actually equivalent to such expressions as "that A is", "that A is not", and "that A is impossible". Obviously the latter are rudimentary locutions which need to be completed, as in "I believe that A is", "I wish that A were not", "I deny that A is impossible", and so on. I am convinced that the doctrine of "reflection upon the content of a judgement" is a complete delusion: there is no ground for saying that the so-called content of judgement might be presented merely as an idea and without involving any kind of judgement. To be sure, one can conceive of a person judging without judging in the same way oneself. But the rest is an absurd fiction. What goes on in the mind when one says "I am supposing (*ich stelle mir vor*) that A is, that it is not, that it is impossible" must be ascertained by means of an exact psychological analysis. Once this is accomplished, then we shall also have some inkling as to what happens when one "supposes that A is good", "supposes that A is bad", and so on. What leads to the *entia rationis* is best recognized in those cases where this term is most appropriate—i.e. in "A as object of thought". If I say "I am thinking of A, who is clever", I am connecting the thought of myself as someone thinking in a specific manner with the thought "A is clever"; that is to say, I am related to "clever" in a wholly different way than I am when, thus thinking, I call myself clever.[11]

Possibly the expression "colour" can be equated with "the coloured *qua* coloured", or "the coloured as such", but this "as such", as Aristotle well knew, is also equivocal. . . .

III

IN OPPOSITION TO THE SO-CALLED CONTENTS OF JUDGEMENT, PROPOSITIONS, OBJECTIVES, STATES OF AFFAIRS

I

To Anton Marty

2 September, 1906

Dear Friend:

I have spoken at length with Bergmann about your view that what there *is* includes not only things, but also the *being*, or the *non-being*, of things, as well as a legion—indeed an infinity—of impossibilities. He writes that he has taken up the problem with you again, finding you intransigent as before, and that he has now made some concessions with respect to my own arguments.

And so, once again, I will try to undeceive you, for I cannot help but regard your theory as a serious mistake. First let us make sure that I understood it correctly.

We are not considering the question whether there are contents of judgement *qua* contents of judgement. We want to consider rather whether there is something subsisting in and for itself, which, under certain conditions, may *become* the content of a judgement, and indeed of a correct judgement. Since one can judge with correctness that there is a tree, then (according to the theory) *that* there is a tree may become the content of a correct judgement.[12]

And this *being of the tree* is itself something which *is*. Similarly there would have to be the non-being of a golden mountain, the impossibility of a round square, and such like, where this little word "to be" is taken in an entirely strict sense.

But, according to my view, we are here confronted only with a figure of speech, which leads to the fiction of new beings and which so deceives us with respect to our psychological activities that we believe we are judging affirmatively when in fact we are denying something.

Of course, a person may say that, in imagining, he has had "the impossibility of a round square", or the like, as an object of his thought. But he is not thinking about *it*; he is thinking only of signs which are meant to be surrogates. He is counting on there being no errors in the final result, as does the mathematician who makes use of absurd fictions—for example, negative quantities, unities divided by multiplicities, irrational and imaginary numbers, polygons with an infinite number of sides, etc., etc.[13] In this way the *ens linguae* becomes the *ens rationis*, i.e. it becomes a fiction *cum fundamento in re*, a fiction which, although erroneous, is so firmly related to truth that it may be of help in leading us to the truth.

The difference between our views is considerable. Let us see what seem to be clear and decisive considerations in favour of mine.

1. It is impossible to have an idea without having an idea of *something*. The term "something" here signifies what is a *thing*. If the thinking is a compound thought, then things are what one has compounded.[14]

It is because of this fact that the concept of an idea—of having something before the mind—is a simple, unequivocal concept.

Every observation confirms the point. No one can be said to think of the being of a tree, of the non-being of a tree, or of the impossibility of a round square, in the way in which one can be said to think of a *tree*. A careful psychological analysis shows that the former cases involve not only ideas but judgements. Suppose, for example, I reject *a* apodictically and that I think of *a* as identical with *b* (merely thinking, but not judging, I predicate *a* of *b*). In such a case, language may mislead one into supposing that the *impossibility* of that *b* is here the object of our thought.[15]

To say that, in the strict sense of the term "thinking", one may think of an impossibility, or the like, is just as much of a mistake as to say that an impossibility may be the object of a correct affirmative judgement, or that there *is* such an impossibility.

2. Confirmation of what I have said may be found in this fact: even you must admit that every assertion affirming your *entia rationis* has its equivalent in an assertion having only *realia* as objects. Thus "There is the impossibility of *a*" is equivalent to the judgement "*a* is impossible", which rejects *a* apodictically. What I have shown, with respect to the temporal modes of thinking, indicates that the temporal *entia rationis* are also no exception.[16]

Not only are judgements about *things* equivalent to your judgements about *entia rationis*; wherever there is an instance of the latter there is also an instance of the former. Hence the *entia rationis* are entirely superfluous and not in accord with the economy of nature.[17]

But all this fits in neatly with my conception of *entia linguae*— that they are fictions resulting from an improper understanding of the multiplicity of linguistic forms which we happen to have.

3. Perhaps you will say: The *entia rationis* corresponding to the contents of correct judgements do have their use. For they render the important service of distinguishing judgements which are correct from judgements which are incorrect. And the correctness of a judgement (you may continue) consists in the agreement of the judgement with such entities and not with any thing: a correct affirmative judgement will agree with the real being of the thing and a correct negative judgement with the real non-being of the thing.

I reply: the distinction between correct and incorrect judgements, so far as I can see, does not provide us with the slightest justification for conjuring up these *entia rationis*.

Where some might say, "In case there *is* the being of *A*, and someone says that *A* is, then he is judging correctly", I would say, "In case *A* is and someone says that *A* is, he judges correctly". Similarly instead of "If there is the non-being of *A* and someone rejects *A*, he judges correctly", I would say "If *A* is not and someone rejects *A*, he judges correctly", and so on.[18]

When does one person believe that another judges correctly?—

When the other person judges in the way in which he judges himself. If a man judges "*A* is not", for example, and notes that someone else rejects *A*, then he believes that the other person judges correctly. Everyone who believes or rejects something, believes of himself that he believes or rejects correctly; if he did not believe this of himself, he would not be judging at all.

Of course, believing is not the same as knowing; one may believe without *knowing* that the judgement in question is correct. To know that a judgement is correct, whether the judgement is mine or that of someone else, I must be able to see that it corresponds, in object, form, tense, and perhaps also modality, to a judgement which is directly or indirectly evident to me.[19]

Doubtless a judgement may change from correct to incorrect by virtue of some change that occurs in reality. But the latter change is a real occurrence and not a matter of an *ens rationis* coming into being or passing away. That is to say, the being of *A* need not be produced in order for the judgement "*A* is" to be transformed from one that is incorrect to one that is correct; all that is needed is *A*. And the non-being of *A* need not come into being in order for the judgement "*A* is not" to be transformed from one that is incorrect to one that is correct; all that is required is that *A* cease to be. If *A* were thus to cease (note that we are concerned here only with *things*), nothing further would be needed for my judgement to be correct; there would be no point in dreaming up other processes, involving ostensible *entia rationis*. After all, it is admitted that, in the cessation of the *thing* which is *A*, we have the equivalent of the supposed coming into being of that non-thing which is the non-being of *A*.[20]

4. The doctrine that such non-things exist, therefore, has nothing whatever in its favour. Moreover, it doesn't even have the authority of Aristotle and the others in his tradition who defined truth as the correspondence of intellect and *res*. They did not consider *res* as an *ens rationis* corresponding to the content of the judgement; they considered *res* as the thing which is the object of the judgement.

5. The case against the view in question becomes even clearer when we consider the absurdity of some of the consequences. Consider, above all, the *regressus ad infinitum* which would be involved if a man wished to know, or to judge with evidence,

that "*A* is". He could not affirm or acknowledge *A* with evidence unless he could also affirm or acknowledge the "being" of *A* with evidence. For if he could not convince himself of the existence of this second object, he would be unable to know whether his original judgement corresponds with it. Did he affirm "the being of *A*" *before* he affirmed *A* with evidence? Surely not. Hence the affirmations were simultaneous. And therefore he had "the being of *A*" as content *and* as *object* at one and the same time. In which case there must also have been a content of the second judgement. And he must have affirmed this second content either at the same time or prior to affirming the being of *A*. This second content would be the being of the being of *A*. And this, too, must have been thought, not merely as content, but also as object, and so on and so forth, *ad infinitum*.[21] This infinite regress, or rather this infinite multiplication of simultaneous affirmations—"There is *A*", "There is the being of *A*", etc., etc.—cannot possibly be avoided. Bergmann writes to me that this infinite multiplication seems to him to be avoidable, just as it is in the case of our apprehension of secondary objects ἐν παρέργῳ. He does not see the dissimilarity of the two cases. The inner consciousness is itself included in the act which is the secondary object.[22] The being of the being of *A*, however, could not be included in the being of *A*. Each must differ from the other, just as the being of *A* differs from *A*.

6. The absurdity of this infinite multiplication may be seen just as easily in still another way. We must suppose that innumerable *entia rationis* have existed throughout eternity, just as God has existed throughout eternity; these include, in particular, an infinity of impossibilities, the beings of these impossibilities, and the non-beings of the beings of these impossibilities, and the non-beings of the non-beings of other impossibilities, as well as of the non-beings of *realia*, or *things*. All the arguments against the infinite multiplication of entities will apply to the present doctrine—a doctrine which renders no service whatever (after all, we can describe all the facts without it) and which obviously creates nothing but insoluble problems and confusion. Direct observation and logical analysis thus join forces in showing that it is entirely unacceptable. And let us rejoice in the result! We have complications enough if we accept things as our sole objects.

The appeal to Plato's theory of ideas will not help. For, as Aristotle remarked, if we have trouble computing with a small sum, we are not likely to solve our problem by adding one that is incomparably greater. And this is what we are doing when we bring in the being of A, the non-being of B, the non-being of the non-being of A, and all the other "*entia rationis*".[23]

F.B.

II

To Oskar Kraus

6 September, 1909

Dear Friend:

The fact that you take Marty's side in our scientific controversy will not affect our friendly relations. But when you write that the old theory can be defended in every respect, I do feel that all the things I have said to you have been in vain. . . . There is, to begin with, the absurdity of an infinite multiplication.[24] And then there is the point that I have made again and again (the last time very recently)—namely, that the theory is contradicted by a universal law. For it is a universal law that, when any given thing is thought about, then everything belonging to its content is thought about as well.[25] Whoever thinks about the *non-being* of a living body would also *have* to think about the non-being of a plant, of an animal, of a man, of a man who is black, of a frog, etc. It is conceded on all sides that we cannot think about the non-being of a frog without thinking about a frog. Consider, then, what a monstrous precondition there would be for the supposed idea of the non-being of a body. I tried to point out to you earlier just what it is that we do, strictly speaking, when we perform that act of thinking in which the thought of the non-being of a body is supposed to be given.[26] And so it is incorrect to say that I have not clearly presented the new theory to you.

I have already indicated, moreover, that I am not objecting to the use of such expressions as "There is a man who is only an object of thought", "There is redness", "There is the non-red", "There is a possibility", "There is an impossibility", despite the fact that these expressions do not refer to a being in the strict or proper sense of the term. If we like, we may even speak about the thought or idea of a non-being, or of the eternal subsistence of a non-being, or of the being of infinitely many possibilities and impossibilities, *provided* we explicate these expressions by reducing them to sentences in which "being" is used in its strict sense. At least we should not suppose that we could dispense with such reductions; for even in the case of "There is the non-being of something", the expression "there is" is not used in its strict or proper sense.

Among the remarkable *aporiae* of Theophrastus on metaphysics which I have been reading these days, I even found this: he speaks of those who believe that the Universe contains many things which are not, never were, and never will be. But this seems to him to go too far and he refuses to take up the question. Indeed Theophrastus says of God that he is all-powerful and thinks not only of the best possible world but also of the totality of lesser worlds which are not, were not, and never will be. These worlds could be said to belong to the universe and to be essential to an understanding of its ultimate ground. You and Marty do not go this far. But you do urge that the universe includes what is merely subsistent, and indeed eternally subsistent; there would be all the eternal possibilities and impossibilities and the eternal non-being of worlds which, through God's decree, have been rejected in preference to the best of all possible worlds.

Finally, I wish to make a point of answering the question which you seem to find unanswerable: "According to you, what is the meaning of the statement 'Only *things* exist'?" The answer is this: "Whoever says, of that which he accepts or affirms, that it is not a *thing* is in error."* I would hope that you will have no difficulty in understanding my answer, since, as I believe, we have the same views about compound judgements and, in particular, about what it is to accept or affirm the subject of a sentence while denying a certain attribute of that subject.[27]

---

* "Es irrt, wer etwas anerkennt und es als real leugnet."

III

To Oskar Kraus

Schönbühel, 24 Sept., 1909

Dear Friend:

. . . What you have to say about our scientific differences is both clear and precise.*

You do not understand my statement that, whenever we think about an object, we think implicitly about each of its parts.[28] May I remind you of the thesis of our logic, according to which the entire content must be the object of a positive judgement. Thus if I affirm or accept a sparrow, I also affirm or accept a bird, because a bird is a *logical* part of the sparrow, and I affirm or accept the beak, because the beak is an essential *physical* part of the sparrow.[29] These parts are *judged* only implicitly inasmuch as they are considered or thought about only implicitly.

Suppose that, in the strict sense of the words, one could reflect upon the *non-being* of a sparrow and accept or affirm it. This thought and affirmation of the non-being of a sparrow would *not* implicitly include the thought and affirmation of the non-being of a bird, or that of the non-being of the beak of a sparrow; but it would implicitly include the thought and affirmation of the non-being of an old sparrow, of a healthy sparrow, of a sick sparrow, of a tame sparrow, of a wild sparrow, of a male sparrow, of a female sparrow, of a nesting sparrow, of a hungry sparrow, of a sparrow that has a mate, and so on and so forth. But obviously, this is not what happens. Even those who say that it does, concede that the mental process—which they mistake for the thought of the non-being of *A*—is a process which actually presupposes the thought of *A*. It would follow, then, that if a person thinks implicitly of all these non-beings when he thinks of the non-being of a sparrow, then he really must have had before his mind an old sparrow, a young sparrow, and so on, just as anyone who thinks of a sparrow must have had before his mind a bird and a beak and all the other parts which are essential to a sparrow. But these

* The date of this letter and the formulation of the first sentence are inaccurate in the German edition.—R.M.C.

89

consequences are all absurd, and therefore the supposition that gives rise to them is false.[30]

And now let me comment on what you say about "correct". According to you, it is generally agreed that the concept of "the correct" presupposes a relation or a relative determination; that the concept is applicable, therefore, only when someone stands in a certain suitable relation to some *other* thing; hence that it cannot be acquired by means of abstraction (and the same thing is supposed to hold of all other reflexive concepts); and therefore that the concept of "the correct", unlike that of red, cannot be elucidated by means of intuition.[31]

Is this, by any chance, the kind of psychology that Marty now accepts? If so, it has become estranged in its essential aspects not only from mine but also from Aristotle's. I'm afraid that it shows a remarkable resemblance to the doctrines of Husserl, who also professes to be acquainted with concepts that do not originate in intuition. All this pertains to your two final comments. My own view is that, in addition to outer intuition, there is also an inner intuition, and that this inner intuition is the source of what are called reflexive ideas.

I would concede this much to you—that whenever we intuit a secondary object, we also intuit a primary object.[32] But I don't see at all how you get from this to the conclusion that, if I apprehend myself as one who is making a correct judgement or as one whose love is correct, I must also know, at the same time, that something *other* than I exists. Indeed I find this assertion extraordinarily baffling, especially when it is applied to the case where I make a correct negative judgement, or where I may love or hate something without believing that the thing exists. There are those who would say that there is a certain entity to which we are related when we make a correct negative judgement and also (if I am properly informed) when we love or hate correctly. But no one who talks in this way would hold that this entity is itself the *object* of the judging, or of the loving or hating. For the object of a correct negative judgement could not possibly exist unless the judgement contradicting the negative judgement were correct. I find it entirely unacceptable, therefore, to say that the concept "correct" signifies the agreement of the judgement with an entity which is not the object of the judgement.[33]

If you tell me now that *everyone* accepts such a view, I feel

I would be justified in making a solemn protest, not only in my name but also in that of everyone else.

Once again, I would urgently warn my young friends in Prague not to become lost in vain fictions, but to return to the long-established psychology.

May I also remind them that the two arguments I have appealed to just now are by no means the only relevant considerations. Still a third is the argument of the promise to marry an *ens rationis*, and this is but one of a long series of arguments.[34] If you say that my present point of view may well change in a number of respects, I am quite ready to agree, but with one reservation. So far as my positive assertions are concerned, various amplifications and modifications may be possible; yet I do not hesitate to say that the criterion of evidence itself assures us for all time in *rejecting* the theory we have been discussing.[35]

And now friendly greetings.

Yours,

F.B.

IV

To Oskar Kraus

25 September, 1909

Dear Friend,

You refuse to understand my reason for saying that there cannot be any thought or idea of the non-being of a cow. You don't see the point of saying that, if there were such an idea, it would include the non-being of cows of all sizes and colours, of every age, and of whatever state of health you like, and that it would also include the non-being of a collection consisting of a cow, an ox, a herdsman, and a meadow.

The explanation is very simple. These various non-beings would have to belong to the very content of the idea of the "non-being of a cow", and not merely to its range or extension. They would be a part of the content: if the supposed concept of "the non-being of a cow" were thought in its *full distinctness*, it would include—also with full clarity and distinctness—the thought of the non-being of a white cow, of a two-year-old cow, of the

91

collection of a cow, a herdsman, and a meadow. This would be necessary, just as it is necessary that in the *distinct* idea of a white horse there would also appear in full distinctness the idea of its white colour, its head, its eyes, its species as horse, its genus as hoofed animal, as well as the higher genera of mammal, vertebrate, animal, living organism, physical substance, and the like—for all these belong to the content of the thought or idea of such a horse. But what belongs to the range or extension—for example, the individual white horse which Napoleon rode—need not be thought as such in order for the thought or idea of the horse to be completely distinct.

Perhaps these remarks are enough to clarify what I had said earlier and to make you see that your reply was not to the point.[36]

Another observation in your letter shows how my words are sometimes misinterpreted. I had been concerned with the question whether all general ideas are derived by means of abstraction from individual ideas, or whether all or some of our intuitions show a certain indeterminateness, and I had decided in favour of the latter alternative. But this is quite different from supposing that we have ideas which are not intuitions and which are not acquired by means of abstraction from intuitions. There is a view about the nature of intuition, handed down from Aristotle, which must be set right in this regard. Actually Aristotle himself takes sensible intuition to be a kind of abstraction, for he says that the senses grasp the form without the matter. And if you consider that, according to him, accidents are given individuality by means of substance, and if you compare what he refers to as common sensibles (κοινὰ αἰσθητά), you will find that the principle of individuation does not appear to be contained in the content of sensation.[37] . . .

V

To Oskar Kraus

Schönbühel, 11 October, 1909

Dear Friend,

You suggest that my view about the content of ideas must recently have been revised in essential respects. But I am not aware of having revised it since I introduced the theory of temporal modes, and the latter theory has nothing to do with the present question.[38] I have never doubted that every thought or idea has a content and (with the exception of absurd ideas) a range or extension. Nor have I doubted that the affirmative judgement applies to the total *content* of the thought or idea, whereas the negative judgement applies to its total *extension*. What I wanted to do was to draw your attention to this question: in the supposed thought or idea of the non-being of a horse, what is it that is to be considered as the content and as belonging to the content? Certainly not the non-being of everything that belongs to the content of the concept "horse"; for otherwise all this non-being (for example, the non-being of an animal and of a substance) would also be implicitly accepted. After all, what is thought of is judged according to its entire content.

What would be the alternative? Obviously nothing but a non-being. So which one? Shall we say the non-being of a stallion? Or the non-being of a mare? This sort of answer is contradicted by the fact that a clear analysis of the content in question reveals nothing like the non-being of a horse. To make fully clear what this supposed idea really is, we need only the concept of *horse* and of *its falsehood*; both of these must be given if I am to reject the distinctly conceived universal, horse.[39] Hence, there is no justification for saying that the non-being of a white horse or of a black horse belong to the content of the idea of the non-being of a horse. So what *does* belong to it, if I may ask? Anyone who reflects on the question will see that the supposed idea of the non-being of a horse would have to include such characteristics as: animal, vertebrate, mammal, living being, body, not to mention head, heart, and other parts. I hope all this makes it obvious to you just how fantastic it is to suppose that, in the strict sense, there are ideas of the non-being of a horse and of other non-beings and impossibilities. What Aristotle said remains true: we know privation, so to speak, "by means of its contrary" (τῷ ἐναντίῳ).

I hope this is enough to make my own position clear, even if you cannot feel that it settles the whole question once and for all. . . .[40]

VI

To Oskar Kraus

31 October, 1914

. . . Both of us esteemed Marty incomparably more than anyone else—as a person and as a thinker of the first importance.* Let us keep this point in mind when we discuss his criticism of my views, a critique in which Marty's free spirit is so clearly manifest. He was quite right in not sparing the views of his former teacher, for that would not have been consistent with his love of truth, and he would want us to treat his own views in a similar way.

Those of my opinions to which he took exception had developed gradually and only after repeated attempts at self-criticism. It could be, therefore, that it was I who prejudiced Marty against what I had said, for he heard me criticize my own opinions. But perhaps he would have done better had he told himself that only very important considerations could have led to such a deviation from my earlier opinions. One thing was obvious—namely, that I am not infallible—and this very fact might have suggested that my later opinions could also be wrong. It would be worthwhile to keep this possibility in mind and to decide these questions on purely objective grounds and not by any appeal to authority.

I shall try to set forth these grounds for you in letters. I shall begin at once, today, by giving you what I believe to be a simple and rigorous proof of the fact that only *things* can be objects of our ideas and therefore that only things can be objects of any type of mental activity at all.

The proof is based upon the fact that the concept of having an idea—of having something before the mind—is one that is uniform; the term "thought", therefore, is univocal and not equivocal. But it is essential to this concept that thinking be always a matter of thinking *of* something. If the term "something" were ambiguous, then the term "thought" would also be ambiguous. And therefore it is not possible to interpret this "something" as being at one time a thing and at another time a non-thing; for there is no concept which could be common to things and non-things.

* Anton Marty died on 2 October, 1914.—R.M.C.

I would say that this proof is absolutely decisive. One may verify the result, again and again, by analysing those cases in which a non-thing appears to be the object of a person's thought. If you feel that there is any such case that we haven't yet touched upon, please let me know and I will be glad to carry out the analysis. Let us recognize that there are linguistic factors which may mislead us here. And also this: that whenever we do seem to be concerned with a non-thing, we will find—if we are attentive enough—that there is in fact some *thing* with which our thought is also concerned. Our analyses must take these facts into account, and there are many closely connected considerations which must be explicated and clarified, if our thread is to lead us out of this labyrinth. Here too, as before, it is good to remind ourselves of Leibniz's pertinent observation: whenever we put anything into abstract terms, we should be prepared to translate it back into concrete terms, in order to be sure that we have not altered the sense.

VII

To Oskar Kraus

8 November, 1914

. . . As for our philosophical question, I am most grateful to you for letting me know the way in which Marty himself attempted to answer my objection. It is regrettable that he never told me of this reply, for otherwise I might have been able to persuade him that it is untenable. I note with satisfaction that he and I agree on one point: that if the term "something" has no unambiguous meaning in the expression "to think of something", then the term "thought" itself cannot be univocal. The fact that the term is univocal cannot be denied; Marty now believes he can preserve this fact by holding that the "something", as that which is thought, is simply the correlate of the thinking. But it would be easy to show him that this is a mistake. The "something" is the *object* of our thoughts—in the one case, horse; in another, that which is coloured; in another, the soul; and so on. But the term "horse" does not signify "contemplated horse", or "horse which is thought about", the term "coloured" does not signify "coloured thing which is thought about", and the term "soul" does not

95

signify "soul which is thought about". For otherwise one who affirmed or accepted a horse would be affirming or accepting, not a horse, but a "contemplated horse"; or, more precisely, he would be accepting or affirming a person thinking about a horse; and this is certainly false. To see the matter even more clearly, you might want to consider the following. If the "something" in the expression "to think about something" really meant only "something thought about", then the "something" in "to reject or deny something" would mean no more nor less than "something rejected or denied". But nothing could be more obvious than the fact that, if a man rejects or denies a thing, he does *not* reject or deny it as something rejected or denied; on the contrary, he knows it is something which he himself does reject or deny. If a man denies God, for example, he does not deny a denied God, for this would be to deny that anyone denies God. So the uniform concept which relates to "something" in the expression "to think about something" is not the concept of "something thought about"; rather, it is a concept which is common to God and horse and that which is coloured, and so on and so forth.

With this I have said everything I need to say in order to show that Marty's answer is untenable. It doesn't matter at all what word we use to refer to the concept which is common to the things that are thought about. Whether we speak of "thing" or "entity", the essential point is that the highest universal to which we can attain by means of the supreme degree of abstraction is what it is that Marty dared to reject. I cannot forbear expressing my surprise and regret that Marty permitted himself to deviate from long-established usage. He transformed the concept of *thing* into the concept of that which is capable of causal efficacy; in this way, a term which has traditionally been the most simple and the most general of all our terms has been transformed into one designating a sophisticated and complex concept which has been a matter of controversy since the time of Hume. Given Marty's sense of the term "thing", we would have to say that according to Hume and Mill and many others, there are no things at all![41] Could anything show more clearly that Marty has permitted himself to alter terminology in an entirely arbitrary way? And if we go back from modern times to the Middle Ages and to antiquity, we are equally struck by Marty's deviation from what has been a consistent usage throughout all times. Thus, according to

Thomas, the concept of a thing, of being in the sense of the real, is the most general concept to which reason can attain. Could he have imagined that one would think of a "thing" as being equivalent to that which is capable of causal efficacy? And in antiquity Aristotle had declared the concept of thing to be included in the concepts of substance and of accident. Note he would have contradicted himself if he had identified *thing* with the concept of causal efficacy, for he cites ποιεῖν as a special category which falls under the accidental!

I think I may say that Marty's highly irregular deviation from traditional usage has other unfortunate consequences. A good many of the misguided corrections which he was led to make in his views about space and time and contents, and, what I especially regret, in his views about God, would have been avoided had he not revised his terminology in such an arbitrary and misleading way—and in a way which does not correspond at all with our thinking. The drive and zeal with which Marty tirelessly pursued his investigations will continue to make us marvel; and so it is all the more to be regretted that the road leading to the goal has been missed entirely, with the result that each step leads farther away from the truth instead of closer to it.[42]

VIII

To Oskar Kraus

16 November, 1914

I am pleased to note, in connection with my argument appealing to the unity of the concept of thought, that Marty attempted to answer it by taking the concept of "something" to be the concept of "that which is thinkable" rather than "that which is thought". But I would ask you to consider carefully and without prejudice whether this distinction really bears upon our question. Could it be that, after appropriate modifications, my argument will remain just as cogent as before? If it is necessary to concede that our thinking does not have "that which is thought" as its object, then it is equally clear that our thinking does not have "that which is thinkable" as its object. Who would want to take "being thinkable" as a generic characteristic, common to stone, horse, forest?

My comparison with denying or rejecting something may be made to apply equally well here. For if the atheist cannot be said to deny God as something denied, then he cannot be said to deny God as something capable of being denied; in each case he would be contradicting what is intuitively obvious to his own consciousness. A person who denied God would not in the same thought be affirming him as something which is incapable of being denied. If it were not for the bias of those deep-rooted convictions which you have so often expressed to me, you could hardly be satisfied with the type of answer that you have given.

The fact that you have lived so long with this conviction may thus be a disadvantage, but there are compensations. Since you are in the position of one who has nursed a conviction for a long time and who continues to cling to it even after it has been emphatically rejected by others whose judgement he respects, it may be assumed that you have carefully pondered all sides of the matter and that you will have no difficulty in answering a number of elementary questions.[43] May I ask you, then, about one of the simpler examples of your supposed non-things? Let us consider, if we can, the being of a certain particular thing—say, the being of this individual person. If I ask whether the being of this person is to be distinguished from the person himself, then, of course, you will say yes; and similarly you will have to say that the being of this person is distinguished from the being of the being of this person, and then, of course, that this fourth thing is distinguished from still another, and so on *ad infinitum*. And now, since I am dealing with one who is so well-informed about the sort of entity that the being of this particular man is supposed to be, I may ask for still more information. The man himself is made up of head, torso, and extremities, and his head is made up of a nose, a mouth, two eyes, and two ears, and various smaller parts, and a continuity of limits. Do you say, then, that the being of this man, and the being of this being, and the being of this being of the being, are composed, in a similar way, of the being of the being, and of the being of the being of the being, of the particular parts and limits which make up the man? Surely you would have to answer affirmatively. Assuming, then, that you do, I go on to my next question. Would you say, of the being of the man, and the being of the being of the man, that they are extended entities having the same dimensions as the man himself? Would they be included in a primary continuum which is three-dimensional and infinite in every direction—a continuum, however, which is not space, but which in one instance is the being of space, in another the being of the being of space, and so on? Since space is supposed to be a non-thing, there would be no distinction between these innumerable and ever-multiplying infinite primary continua and space itself. I will only intimate here that one could construct an analogous argument with respect to time: one would have to assume that outside time there is the being of each thing, and you would say that the being of the beings of these things exist. Consequently, so far as I can see, you couldn't put these beings in time any more than you could put them in space. But doubtless you have considered all this long ago, in feasting your eye upon the majestic splendour and inexhaustible wealth of infinities which the doctrine of non-things has bestowed upon the world.

A series of other questions arise. If the being of this particular man exists over and above the man himself, then, over and above the man who is thought of only in general terms, there will also exist the *being* of a man who is thought of only in general terms. Indeed, if the sentence "There is this particular man" has a content that exists, then the indefinite sentence "There is some man or other" would also have a content that exists. But now we may ask: How is the existence of the content of "There is some man or other" to be related to the being of this definite man? Marty's views about the universal *man*, so far as I know, are in complete agreement with mine. The universal as universal does not exist. General concepts are realized only in individual things. But what are we to say of the content of an indefinite affirmative sentence such as the one just considered? If this content is supposed to exist, does it have an existence in and for itself, or in the contents of particular things, or perhaps both? You have long considered this area from Marty's point of view, and you continue to feel fortified in the conviction that we are dealing here with what really exists and not with mere chimeras. And so I would like very much to know your answers to these questions. But I hardly dare to anticipate what they might be, for whenever I try to imagine what one might say, I find myself sinking into a chaos of absurd assumptions.

Enough for today. I look forward to the enlightenment I expect to receive from you. It would be distracting at this point if I were to comment on your belief that you know the development of my own views better than I do myself. Perhaps you will understand my doubts if I ask you some questions. Do you have any idea what could have led me to accept such an untenable doctrine as that of the existence of contents, which was so alien to my great teacher Aristotle? And (to leap from ancient times to the present) how could I possibly have abandoned every doubt about taking thought or presentation (*Vorstellung*) as one of the three basic classes, especially after having devoted a long period of time in the attempt to get along without it, and this, once again, only for the sake of arriving at the truth? You speak as though a certain resistance on the part of my students has had some influence here. Nothing could be more inaccurate. The progress of my own psychological investigations enabled me to overcome difficulties which stood in the way of accepting the third category. And it is precisely at this point of progress that I have lost company with those companions who once seemed to be inseparable.[44]

IX

To Franz Hillebrand, Innsbruck

Florence, 25 February, 1911

Dear Friend,
        You have not only given me a sign of life; you have also raised important theoretical and practical questions. And so your letter has a twofold—a threefold—interest.
        . . . You do not touch upon the supreme theoretical question that I would take up in connection with the attempt that you discuss. Instead you speak of Köhler and Kastil and discuss the immanent object, the possible distinction between the immanent object and content, the distinction between *being* (*Sein*) and *being so-and-so* (*Sosein*), and the question of an instinctive belief in outer perception. According to you, there is no such instinctive belief; I would be interested to know how you reconcile your animal psychology with this point.[45] Kastil does not accept Meinong's doctrine, according to which there can be a knowledge of *Sosein* without a simultaneous knowledge of *Sein*—a knowledge of what characteristics a thing has without a simultaneous

knowledge of whether there *is* such a thing. And the fact that Kastil does not accept this doctrine is something we must keep in mind if we are to understand his statement that one can describe a thing without believing that the thing exists. If I do not misinterpret what you attribute to him, he contends that one can say of something, what it *would* be if it *were* to exist: thus one can say that a centaur, if it were to exist, would be a creature whose upper parts are like those of a man and whose lower parts are like those of a horse. We can agree with Kastil on this point without agreeing that it is proper, in such a case, to speak of a description of a *centaur*. The important question concerns the thought itself and not the way in which it is expressed. Kastil would not hesitate to say that a person can speak of what it is that he is thinking about even if that person does not believe that the thing in question exists. Perhaps he would be willing to revise his mode of expression and to concede that, in such a case, it would be better to say that one is describing, not a centaur, but someone who is thinking about a centaur—someone who has a centaur as the object of his thought. For Marty does not deny that a person thinking about a centaur has a centaur as object, and therefore Kastil would not want to deny it either. As for Marty's distinction between object and content, a single example may be enough to illustrate his point of view. If someone judges "There are no centaurs", then the *object* of his judgement is a centaur. But the *content* of his judgement, according to Marty, is what it is that he judges, i.e. *that* there are no centaurs—in short, the non-being of a centaur. Marty then goes on to say that the non-being of a centaur, unlike the centaur, is something that exists in reality. It is precisely here that Marty and I part ways. I admit, of course, that in one good ordinary use we may talk in such a fashion, just as we may say that there is an impossibility, or that there is a past, and so on. But, in my opinion, when we do talk in this way, we are not using the expression "there is" in its strict or proper sense. A psychological analysis of what occurs in such cases will show that "There is the non-being of a centaur" expresses not an affirmation but a negation.

X

To F. Hillebrand, Innsbruck

Zurich, 21 May, 1916

Dear Friend,

Your impression of the work which Kraus has dedicated to Marty agrees with my own.[46] Of the two points you touch upon in particular, the correspondence theory has been the topic of several letters I have exchanged with Kraus, but I have not had any real success. I pointed out that a directly evident judgement is not merely one that is seen to be *true*; it is also one that is seen to be *logically justified*, and in this respect it is to be distinguished from a blind judgement which happens to be true.[47] If a judgement does not happen to be logically justified, we can determine its truth only to the extent that we can compare it with a judgement which *is* logically justified; we then find out whether the two judgements agree with respect to object, tense, quality, and modality. In many cases, the question whether the object of the thought or idea is in agreement with a thing existing in reality is completely beside the point; and in the case of a negative judgement any such agreement would be incompatible with the truth of the judgement. It is a pernicious metaphysical confusion to suppose that, in these cases and in general, the truth of a judgement is a matter of the judgement's content being in agreement with an *ens rationis* subsisting outside the mind. The *ens rationis* relating to the judgement "A tree is green" is supposed to be the existence of a green tree; the one relating to "There is no carnivorous horse" is supposed to be the non-existence of a carnivorous horse. I had asked, then, whether this non-existence of a carnivorous horse is a universal having exemplifications in different places—say, one of them in Prague and another in Zurich—or whether it is itself an individual. I received no definite answer, but I gather that there was some inclination towards the latter view. I was then led to ask whether that individual which is the non-being of a carnivorous horse includes among its parts the non-being of a carnivorous stallion, and whether the latter individual, in turn, includes the non-being of a carnivorous Arab stallion. These questions could be answered only in the affirmative. Then I asked about the nature of these parts. Are they to be thought of as a part of a continuum, or as parts of a definition pertaining to an individual, or as marks which, belonging to a complicated idea, are included in the thought of the whole? Each of these alternatives was patently absurd, and it turned out that one had to appeal to still more fictions, making it obvious that the whole thing is a monstrous confusion. And there are still other difficulties: if there is the non-being of a carnivorous horse, then there is also the non-being of a winged horse, in which case the non-being of a winged, carnivorous horse would have to be a part of each of these two individuals. But it would be childish to press this dialectic any further; half of what has been said is enough to show that one has become lost in a realm of chimeras.

As for the other point you touch upon, I continue to feel that we have not yet understood each other. Neither you nor any other sound thinker would say that, because someone happens to think about a thing, the thing therefore may be said to exist, in the strict or proper sense of "exist". Gorgias refuted the view by saying that, if it were true, then there would be a chariot battle at sea as soon as he thought about one. On the other hand, Marty certainly did not want to deny that there is one ordinary linguistic usage in which we *may* say that, if a person thinks about something, then that thing exists "as thought by him" or "in his mind". But he felt it necessary to warn against confusing the "being" that a thing is supposed to have "in the mind", with "being" in the primary sense. "Being in the mind" is simply "being thought", and what does not exist in the strict or proper sense is capable of being thought, provided that there is someone who thinks about it.

As for relations and relative determinations, Aristotle paved the way for the distinction by means of still another distinction he had made in his theory of relations. He divided relations into three classes: comparative, causal, and intentional. He said of the first two that a real relation corresponds to a real correlative. If Caius is taller than Titus, then there exists not only the taller, but also the shorter; if one thing causes something else, then there exists—in the primary sense—not only that which is causing, but also that which is affected. But when something is merely *thought* of, then the *thinker* exists in the strict sense but that which is thought does not. When Aristotle made these distinctions, however, he did not take note of the following: not only do we compare things in the present with other things in the present; we can also compare things which exist in the present with things which have existed in the past or with things which will exist in the future. I can say, not only that Caius is taller than Titus is now, but also that Caius is taller than Titus was a year ago, and that he is taller than Titus will be a year from now. It is only when I compare Caius now with Titus now that the language allows me to say simply, Caius is taller than Titus. Only in this case does the correlative exist as well as the relative. When we say that Titus *was* smaller than Caius now is, the correlative is something which *formerly* existed; when we say that, in a year from now, Titus will be smaller than Caius is now, the correlative is something which *will* exist. Let us note, moreover, that a thing may be compared with something that is merely thought about, or with something that is judged about, whether truly or falsely, or with something that is hoped or feared. For example: "The damage is less than I thought it was". We have a similar situation when one says that the number of discernible stars is less than a million: here one is thinking, not of a million real things but of a concept which has a familiar place in the decimal system. If the Aristotelian theory of relations is developed in this way, then the difficulty which gave rise to the distinction between relations and relative determinations disappears completely.

In Friendship,

Yours,

F.B.

Part Four

THE LATER VIEW AS SET FORTH IN ESSAYS

I

ON THE EXISTENCE OF CONTENTS AND THE DOCTRINE OF THE *ADAEQUATIO REI ET INTELLECTUS*

(20 November, 1914)

1. In our ordinary language we use such expressions as "to be" and "to exist" in application to what cannot be called *things*. For example, we say "There is the possibility . . .", or "There is the impossibility". We also say that there is something that is the object of a thought, or that there is something that is wanted, and we say that there *is* a law, etc. There are even those who would say that, if a certain thing does not exist, then there *is* the non-being of that thing, and that, if a certain thing does exist, then there is, not only the thing, but also the being of the thing, as well as the being of the being of the thing. And some say that there *are* truths which are eternal and necessary.

2. The question arises, then, whether in cases such as these, the word "is" is being used in the same strict sense as it is used when one says that there is a certain *thing*. Some of those who have answered this question affirmatively have noted, quite correctly, that even when we say, of something, that "the thing is" we are not using the word "is" as the expression of a predication. We are using it, rather, as the expression of an affirmation. They then go on to note that the same thing holds for the other cases: the "is" performs a similar function in such cases, since there, too, it is not being used as a predicate.[1]

3. But this is a hasty conclusion. A word that is synsemantic may still have a variety of uses. The essential question in the present cases is whether the phrase that is being used with "is" really designates something that can be made an object of thought.

4. The expression "to think" (*vorstellen*) is univocal. To think is always to think of *something*. Since "to think" is univocal, the term "something" must also be univocal. But there is no generic concept that can be common both to things and to non-things.[2] Hence if "something" denotes a thing at one time, it cannot denote a non-thing—an impossibility, say—at another time.

5. If, when something A may be said to exist, there may also be said to exist, in the strict or proper sense of the term "exist", the being of A, and the being of the being of A, these as things distinct from A itself, then the infinitude of complications and multiplications would be extraordinarily baffling. For some, the difficulties involved in assuming an actual infinite manifold would be sufficient reason for rejecting the view.[3]

6. And the question arises: How does one arrive at the knowledge of the *being* of A, as distinguished from the knowledge simply of A itself? Is it something that is immediately perceived? Is the being of this being, etc., also perceived at the same time, or is it something that is inferred? No one would accept the first of these alternatives, for the consequences are much too paradoxical.[4] But the other alternative leads to the question: How does one arrive at such a conclusion and what premises does one use? And in this case the general rules of logic would also be of crucial importance.

7. If we have an idea, not only of A, but also of the being of A, then this idea is either an idea that we have *a priori*, or it is an object of intuition, or it is acquired by means of abstraction from intuitions. But the whole doctrine of *a priori* ideas is to be rejected.[5] Intuition of the being of A, alongside that of A, is out of the question. And the idea cannot be acquired by means of abstraction, for "the being of A", in such a case, would have to be a *more general* concept than that of A (since, according to the view in question, "the being of A" is distinct from A itself).

8. Strictly speaking, then, it is obvious that there is no thought of the *being* of *A*. We think only of the *A* itself. If we think of something else along with it, the something else must be a thing, once again. For example, it might be ourselves as that which is thinking of *A*, or accepting or affirming *A*. In giving up the view that there is, in addition to the thought of *A*, the thought of the being of *A*, we thereby rule out any possibility of proceeding from the knowledge of *A* to the knowledge of the being of *A*.

9. We should follow Leibniz's counsel with respect to *nominibus abstractis*.[6] The locution "There is the impossibility of *A*", which seems to be the expression of an affirmation, is identical in content with "*A* is impossible", which is the expression of an apodictic denial; hence the former expression should be reduced to the latter. Similarly "There is the being of *A*" and "There is the non-being of *A*", respectively, should be reduced to "*A* exists" and "*A* does not exist". In this way we rid ourselves of a delusion which provides us with nothing but endless complications.

10. Why would anyone suppose that, if *A* exists, then there is also the being of *A*, and that, if *A* does not exist, then there is in its place the non-being of *A*? Those who accept the view reason in the following way. Truth, they say, consists in an agreement or correspondence between the intellect and a fact: *Veritas est adaequatio rei et intellectus*. Hence there must be something for a true negative judgement to be in agreement with. But (the argument continues) this cannot be the *thing* which the negative judgement correctly rejects or denies. Hence it must be something else, and it may be said, in every case, that there is nothing for this something else to be except the non-being of the thing which is denied.

11. What is meant by the formula *Veritas est adaequatio rei et intellectus*? It is essential that we have an answer to this question, for we do not concede that, in the strict and proper sense of "is", there *is* truth. We cannot interpret the "is" of the formula as having the function that it has in "*A* is" or "There is an *A*". Actually what the formula says is no more than this: if *A* is, then whoever accepts or affirms *A* judges correctly; and if *A* is not, then whoever rejects or denies *A* judges correctly. The formula does not at all require that, if there is no *A*, then there has to be something else—

the non-being of A—to function in its place. A itself is the thing with which our judgement is concerned.

If A is to be affirmed, then the affirming judgement may be said to be true and the negative judgement false, and the one who accepts or affirms A may be said to judge correctly and the one who rejects or denies it to judge incorrectly. Similarly for the case where A is not: the judgement affirming A may be said to be false and the judgement denying it may be said to be true; the one who affirms A judges incorrectly and the one who denies A judges correctly.[7] There is not the slightest justification for supposing that the term *"adaequatio"*, or "correspondence", designates a relation which, in order to hold, requires the existence of two terms. The object of a correct denial or rejection is not something which exists, except in the sense in which one says, improperly, that whatever is thought "exists in the mind". The principle of the *adaequatio rei et intellectus* does not require that a negative judgement correspond to an object (viz., the non-being of something) which *exists*. The *adaequatio* consists precisely in the fact that the object of the judgement does *not* exist and that the one who judges *denies* its existence.[8]

12. Some have even gone so far as to say that, whoever thus rejects the existence of a non-being, is guilty of subjectivism and psychologism.[9] Nothing could be less justified. For the subjectivist, there is no "A is" or "A is not"; one says only, "A is for me (or for someone or other)". Neither acceptance nor rejection of the doctrine that there is the being of A, or the non-being of A, commits anyone to subjectivism. The proponent of *psychologism*, on the other hand, goes wrong in confusing a judgement's being *evident* with the fact that it is natural for all, or almost all, of the members of a certain species to judge in a certain way.[10] He does not distinguish what one "ought" to do from what one is "compelled" to do, and in consequence he plays into the hands of subjectivism. But nothing of this sort is implied when we say that the objects of affirmation and denial are always only things and never the being or the non-being of things. We say, of those who affirm or deny a thing, that some do it, not blindly, but with evidence. Judging with evidence excludes not only the possibility of error, but also the possibility that there be anyone judging to the contrary who is *not* in error.[11] There is no being of A and no

non-being of A, but either A is or A is not; and therefore, of two people who judge that A is, it is not possible that the one is judging correctly and the other incorrectly. And similarly for any two people who judge that A is not.

So the entire objection is based upon a misunderstanding.

13. We have said that those who oppose our view have misinterpreted the statement, "*Veritas est adaequatio rei et intellectus*". If their interpretation were correct, then in order to *know* that a certain thing exists, one would have to know that there is a certain equality or similarity holding between something that is in the mind and something that is outside it. Knowledge of this equality or similarity would then presuppose that one had *compared* the two. But how does one compare something that is in the mind with something that is not in the mind? Our knowledge of what is not in the mind is certainly not acquired as a result of making a comparison. Where such knowledge is immediately given, it is a matter of a simple and evident apprehension.[12]

14. Anyone who says that, in addition to things, there is the being of the things, as well as the non-being of things, is also committed to this: in addition to the individual dog, there exists the being of that dog, and the being of each of its parts, however small, as well as the being of the limits which belong to it as a body; and these, in analogy with the dog itself, form a continuum of *existences* which are located in the *existence* of space, just as the dog is located in space. And then the being of the being of the dog, in turn, would require analogous assumptions. An infinity of complications which has no use at all! But the adventures one encounters with the *non-being* of the individual dog—whether one denies or affirms the dog itself—would be even more bizarre. If one rejects or denies the dog itself, then its non-being would be located, not merely in *one* place in the *being* of space, but in each and every place in the being of space, thus overlapping and intersecting itself in its manifold existence. If one accepts or affirms the dog, then there would be one place in the being of space where the non-being of the dog would *not* be located; but it *would* be found in every other place in the being of space, reaching from all sides and in every possible way into that place where the being of the dog would be. And the non-being of a dog-in-general, or of an

animal-in-general, would be even more extraordinary. The non-being of a dog-in-general would not include the non-being of any of its parts, for a part may well exist even though the whole does not. This non-being of a dog-in-general would be composed of the non-being of every type of dog—spitz, poodle, pointer—and indeed of the non-being of each and every conceivable type of individual dog. And the non-being of an animal-in-general would be more complex, since every conceivable species would have to be taken into consideration. What are we supposed to say now? Are we really to believe that, whoever thinks of the non-being of an animal-in-general, really thinks of such a compound? And that this really subsisting non-being, compounded from such an over-abundance of parts, is to be found somewhere in the "existence of a somewhere", and indeed in every place in space or in every "existence of a place in the existence of space", and so on, *ad infinitum*? And wouldn't we have to say, of this complicated something, which makes one's head so dizzy, that it also exists in four-dimensional and multi-dimensional topoids? For no animal or any other three-dimensional body is to be found there. If all this doesn't bring our philosopher back to his senses, then nothing will.

15. Some of those who accept, not only things, but also non-things and the existences of things and the non-existences of things, would want to say, not that these objects *exist*, but only that there *are* such objects, though in the strictest sense of the term.[13] But this distinction between what *exists* and what *is* is empty; the words in which it is formulated cannot be understood as expressing any thought at all. I will touch upon this curious deviation of the theory only to note that considerations we have just set forth apply as well to those who try to distinguish being and existence as to those who do not. What we have said about the compounds of the being of a thing, and of the non-being of a thing, whether the thing be thought of as an individual or in general, holds also in the present case. These compounds remain the same, and in all their multiplicity, whether one says that they exist, or whether one says that, instead of existing, they simply *are*.

16. It scarcely needs to be added that what I have said about the non-being of things (any thoughtful reader will be convinced

that non-being can never be the object of a thought) may also be applied to other negative expressions, e.g., to "non-red", "non-physical", and the like. For here too we encounter the same bizarre and useless complications.[14]

17. If we want an authoritative verification, we may find it in those philosophers who, at first consideration, may seem to favour the views of our opponents. Aristotle taught that there is a "being in the sense of the true". When asked whether something or other is impossible, one may reply, in the affirmative, "It is"; since Aristotle does not consider the existential statement as a compound of subject and predicate, some have concluded that, according to him, the "is" in this "It is" has the same function that it has in "A man is" or "There is a man".[15] But if we look more closely we see that this is not the case. With the statement, "There is a man", or "A man is", one accepts or affirms a man who exists outside of the mind. But in the case of "It is", one says of something, which exists only in the mind, that it is *true*; and what this comes to is that the one who is making the judgement is judging correctly. But if a man is, then, according to Aristotle, the man is not "true" in the same sense in which a judgement is true. Aristotle says explicitly that the true, unlike the good, is not in the things; he also says that it is only in the intellect. To be sure, Thomas Aquinas seems to give "is", in the statement that "God is", the same sense that it has when it is used to indicate that a judgement is true.[16] This was in connection with his unsuccessful attempt to think of essence and existence as being combined in the case of created things and as being identical in the case of God. Sometimes even the greatest of commentators can make a mistake. It cannot be denied that Augustine believes in the existence of eternal truths throughout eternity; but he makes it clear that, unlike those whom we are opposing, he does not regard them as subsisting on their own. According to him they can exist only in a mind, and for this very reason he believes that, from the supposed eternal existence of necessary truths, one may infer the existence of a divine and eternal intellect. Now that which is merely thought cannot be said to be in the strict sense; what exists is the particular thing that has the thought. Hence Augustine's doctrine actually confirms the view that only *things* can exist. A close examination shows that Leibniz's doctrine also confirms what we

are saying. One might be led to think that he accepts the view that along with things there are certain non-things which exist in the strict sense of the term; for he does speak of the existence of possibilities and says that God necessarily chooses the best of them and thus creates the real world which is the best of all possible worlds. But if we look more carefully, we see that Leibniz allows these eternally subsisting possibilities to exist only within the divine mind and not outside it. And this is similar to the view of Augustine. That which exists in the strict sense is God himself, insofar as he knows these possibilities as true and, one might add, insofar as he is omnipotent (for if it were not for God's omnipotence, no created thing could be said to be possible). So much, then, for the proper interpretation of the view of certain greater thinkers with respect to our question. It is to be expected, of course, that some ancient thinkers would make mistakes similar to those that have been made in our own day. Thus Democritus taught that non-being exists as well as being, for there *is* empty space which is a void or a nothing.[17] And even John Stuart Mill cannot be absolved of the error; for he talks about his possibilities and allows them to produce what is real. His positivistic reluctance to go beyond experience leads him in this case to the most thoroughgoing extravagances. Our awareness that only things can be objects of thought and of affirmation is the best protection we have against the errors considered and, in particular, against those of positivism.

II

ON THE MEANING OF "VERITAS EST ADAEQUATIO REI ET INTELLECTUS"

(11 May, 1915)

1. It has been said that this principle is immediately obvious. Before assenting, however, we should know what it is that the principle says and what is meant by each of its terms.

2. *Intellectus* refers, not to the faculty of thinking (more precisely, the faculty of judgement), but to the activity of thinking, where this activity is considered *in abstracto* and not *in concreto*.[18] No one says that a person thinking or a person judging is true; it is the judging of such a person that is true or that constitutes a truth.

To say that a person judges correctly, and to say that what he judges is true, are one and the same.

The opposite of "true" is "false", "incorrect", "erroneous". And thus truth is the opposite of error.

3. *Res* is to be understood simply as *thing*, if we take the term in its most general sense.[19] But one can speak of a thing, and make a judgement about it, even though the thing does not exist, and such a judgement may be true; for negative judgements, as well as affirmative judgements, may be true. Since the time of Aristotle, affirmative judgements have been taken to comprise, not only those which say, of a certain thing, that it is, but also those which say that the thing has been or that it will be. Thus if the thing does not now exist, the judgement that it will be, or that it was, may yet be true.

It is clear that the term "res" has the same meaning in each of these cases; indeed it would be a serious mistake to use a term equivocally in a definition. But this is what we would do if we took "res" to have a different meaning in the case of judgements which are negative or which are temporally modified.[20] For the definition must be one that applies to all true judgements.[21]

4. And, finally, we must ask: What is to be understood by "correspondence" or "*adaequatio*"? Surely it does not mean *aequalitas*, for the judgement and the thing are not homogeneous or *equal*. And certainly the principle is not meant to say that the concept of a thing, uniformly and without exception, determines whether the judgement is true and whether the judgement should be positive or negative, or in the past mode, or in the present, or in the future. How, then, are we to understand this correspondence?

5. This much at least is certain: judgements contradicting each other cannot both be correct; and this holds in general, whether the judgements be affirmative or negative, and whether they pertain to what is past, present, or future. In the case of judgements that contradict each other, only one of them in each case can be said to be the one that corresponds; yet such judgements pertain to the same thing, and in the same temporal mode. Hence a thing which is the object of contradictory judgements will be such that, of the two judgements, one must be said to correspond to the thing and the other *not* to correspond to it.

Suppose I have the answer to a certain question and know, say, that such-and-such a thing happened yesterday. If I know that another person says that it happened yesterday and that some third person says that it did not happen, I may then compare the way in which they judge with what it is that I know about the thing; I shall then find that the judgement of one of them agrees with what I know and that the judgement of the other does not. Since we are supposing that I know that the thing took place, we may say that if someone else tells me what he thinks about the thing, then I have only to compare the way he judges with what I know, in order to be able to say whether his judgement is true or false. If this is all that is meant by the thesis in question, then, of course, the thesis would be obvious to anyone who is aware that the truth is the same for all. Here we would have a criterion by means of which I could decide the truth or falsehood of another man's opinion;

but use of the criterion would presuppose that I already have the truth myself. Clearly, it would be a mistake to suppose that such a criterion would provide me with a way of deciding whether I have the truth. Some would say that I can decide this by comparing my judgement with the thing that I am judging about. They do not seem to see that I cannot accomplish this unless I am already sufficiently acquainted with the thing to be able to know what it is in reality. And this means that I must already be in possession of the truth—something which is not a result of my having compared my own judgement with what it is that I know.[22]

6. The thesis has been misinterpreted in other ways too. According to some it tells us that a true judgement exhibits a kind of similarity with something existing in reality. If a man believes that a tree is green, then his judgement is said to combine tree and green in the way in which these are combined in reality. If we raise the question of negative judgements, we shall be told that if a man says that a tree is not blue, he separates tree and blue in the way in which they are separated in reality, and if he says there is no devil, then he is saying that there is the non-being of a devil. Actually, if I say that a tree is not blue, I am not asserting the existence of a separation of tree and blue. And if I say that there is no devil, my judgement is about the devil and not about the non-being of the devil. The latter is no kind of a thing at all and cannot even be thought about. But if we were to suppose that the non-being of a devil *is* a kind of a thing, it would *not* be the thing with which a negative judgement, denying the devil, is concerned; instead it would be the object of an *affirmative* judgement, affirming the non-being of a devil. For otherwise we would make the mistake of supposing that there are no negative judgements at all, having replaced them by affirmative judgements which have negative things as their objects.

Similar difficulties arise in connection with what is affirmed in the past and in the future tense. Clearly it would be preposterous to say that what the sentence "Caesar is in the past" asserts to be is, not Caesar, but the-being-in-the-past-of-Caesar.

7. Still another attempt at construing the so-called "*adaequatio rei et intellectus*" in terms of a relation between a judgement and some existing thing would be this: One would say that *res*

is to be thought of as the totality of things that exist. Anyone acquainted with this totality would have the means of passing upon the truth of every judgement, negative as well as affirmative— a negative judgement being true if the object which it denies is not to be found in the totality of things, and false if the object is to be found in the totality of things.

And (one might continue) this known totality of existing things would also provide the means of determining the truth of judgements in other tenses, for these things would be related causally to what is past and what is future.

But this interpretation would seem to be entirely forced (one would have to speak of "*rerum*" rather than "*rei*"). The *adaequatio* principle would now have to be made secure by all kinds of explication—for example, it would be necessary to refute indeterminism and to prove that a given state cannot be brought about in a variety of different ways.[23] And in any case the principle would be of no practical value whatever, since no human being has the wealth of knowledge which its application would presuppose.

8. Some of those, who have been unclear with respect to the meaning of the principle and with respect to the fact that its practical significance is relatively minor, have simply rejected it and replaced it by another: truth is now said to consist in the agreement of thought with the *rules* of thought. But this is certainly no improvement.[24] It is well known that false premises, by means of a paralogism, may lead to a true conclusion; but since the conclusion is attained by an improper method, it cannot be said to be known. In such a case, the thinking—though true—does not at all correspond to the rules of thinking.

9. One would have to take the new definition of truth in a different way. "Rules of thinking" could be interpreted by reference to a judgement which is *evident* and which related to the thing in question and in the same temporal mode; thus even a blind judgement, which agrees in content with one that is evident, would be said to be true despite the fact that it is not itself knowledge. Clearly, if it were not for that which is evident, no judgement about the truth of an assertion would be possible to us. And if a man judges with evidence, then he knows his judgement to be true without having made *any* comparison.

And so we may stay with the old thesis.[25] But we must resist the temptation to think of it as a profound truth from which we can draw a wealth of metaphysical consequences. Indeed its most important consequence for psychology and logic was drawn by Aristotle: he pointed out that existential statements should not be interpreted as categorical statements ascribing the attribute of existence to things. An existential statement is concerned with a simple thing, which it affirms or denies; it does not combine things and therefore it does not involve a synthesis of thought (Metaphysics, IX, 10).

III

ON THE THESIS: "VERITAS EST ADAEQUATIO REI ET INTELLECTUS"

(5 March, 1915)

1. To the question, what is to be understood by *truth*, one usually replies: truth is an agreement between the intellect and a thing. And then one tries to draw important metaphysical conclusions. Some have even supposed that we have here a *criterion* of what is true and what is false. But this is to overlook the fact that we cannot possibly know that there is an agreement between things unless we know each of the things between which the agreement holds. Hence if all knowledge were thought of as knowledge of agreement, we would be required to complete an impossible *regressus ad infinitum*. The real guarantee of the truth of a judgement lies in the judgement's being evident; if a judgement is evident, then either it is directly evident or it is evident as a result of a proof connecting it with other judgements which are directly evident. It is possible to distinguish certain classes of evident judgements. By referring to the characteristics which are peculiar to these classes, using them as a kind of rule, we may be able to orient ourselves in those cases, all too frequent, in which the weakness of the human intellect leads us to confuse apparent evidence with real evidence.[26]

2. But what about the definition of truth above? What does it mean? Is it really an adequate criterion, and is it meant to be such? It speaks of an agreement between the intellect and a thing; truth has to do with someone who judges and who, in judging, relates

himself to a *thing*; and this, in my opinion, is undeniable. We can speak of truth only in the case of someone who is judging correctly, and we can speak of falsehood only in the case of someone who is judging incorrectly.[27] In judging we relate ourselves to something, either by accepting it or by rejecting it, and this "something" is to be understood as a *thing*. But although the one who judges must exist, this something need not exist. For the one who judges may refer to the thing either by accepting it or by rejecting it. And there are other cases where the concrete thing need not exist. Some of the things referred to by the person who judges are thought of only in *modo obliquo*, though always in relation to something which is itself thought in *modo recto*; for such an affirmative judgement to be true, the thing that is thought in *modo obliquo* need not exist. Thus I might judge that there is someone who believes that the devil exists.[28] Or, again, I might say that a certain event took place 100 years ago. The event need not exist for the judgement to be true; it is enough that I, who exist now, be 100 years later than the event. If I judge that a thing is impossible, the thing need not *exist* in order for my judgement to be correct. And if I say that a thing is possible, I do not thereby accept or affirm the thing; what I do is to deny, of anyone who apodictically rejects the thing, that he judges correctly.[29] We see, then, that the great variety of ways in which we can refer to things makes it impossible to require that each thing to which a correct judgement refers be something that exists. The requirement holds only in case the thing is thought in *modo recto*, and even here it holds, not for the negative judgement, but only for the affirmative judgement.[30] It is only in this last case, then, that we can speak of an agreement in the sense of any kind of equality. But if we consider the matter more closely, we shall see that even here we cannot speak of equality or sameness in the strict sense of the terms. It is one thing for the person who judges to accept or to affirm a tree and to think of it in the thought which the judgement presupposes; it would be quite another thing for the one who judges to *be* the tree.

3. And so we cannot speak in that sense of an *adaequatio rei et intellectus*. Can we find some other interpretation for "*adaequatio*" which might make the thesis more acceptable? My answer would be that the thesis tells us no more nor less than this: Anyone who judges that a certain thing exists, or that it does not exist, or that

it is possible, or impossible, or that it is thought of by someone, or that it is believed, or loved, or hated, or that it has existed, or will exist, *judges truly* provided that the thing in question does exist, or does not exist, or is possible, or is impossible, or is thought of . . . etc. And what all this comes to, strictly speaking, is the following:

Truth pertains to the judgement of the person who judges correctly—to the judgement of the person who judges about a thing in the way in which anyone whose judgements were *evident* would judge about the thing; hence it pertains to the judgement of one who asserts what the person whose judgements are evident would also assert.[31]

IV

REFLECTIONS ON THE
THEORY OF THE EVIDENT

(8 July, 1915)

1. Some of our judgements are true and some of them are false. But those which are true are often unjustified. A judgement is justified only if it enlightens us.

2. But when does a judgement enlighten us? Some would say: only when it has been *proved* to be true. But every proof proceeds from premises and with the conviction that if the conclusion is unjustified the premises must also be unjustified. If the premises are not enlightening, the conclusion cannot be enlightening either. And if the premises themselves cannot be enlightening unless they have been proven, then they will require further premises which are enlightening, and so on *ad infinitum*.

3. And so if there are any truths which enlighten there must be a truth which is without proof and which enlightens. What is it, then, that distinguishes such an enlightening truth from the judgements that are said to be blind?

4. Some say that the judgements which are thus enlightening— and directly enlightening—are those on which all mankind has agreed. But how would this agreement be ascertained without a vicious circle? And, since each of us is aware of a different and unique self, how, on such a theory, could anyone acquire any unique knowledge of *himself*?[32]

5. Others say that the mark of the judgement which is enlightening, as distinguished from any of those which are not, is simply the

fact that there is an irresistible compulsion which keeps us from giving it up. And they say that we are conscious of this compulsion. When Descartes wanted to construct his philosophy upon an absolutely firm basis, he decided at the outset to count as true and as certain only that which he was plainly incapable of doubting. Hence he would seem to be saying that such a compulsion is the distinguishing mark. But when he attempted to analyse a case of this compulsion more exactly, he believed that he had found clarity and distinctness of perception to be the mark of what is enlightening. His expression is well known: *quod clare et distincte percipio verum est*. If "percipere" is interpreted in the sense of "to judge", and "clare et distincte" in the sense of "to be enlightening", then we have nothing more than an *idem per idem* which doesn't get us anywhere. But in another sense of these terms, "percipere" does not take into account the evidence of negative judgements, and "clare et distincte" does not take into account those cases in which we may think of some complex thing, but in a wholly confused manner, without analysing it into its parts; we may be aware that we are thinking of the thing and we may be thinking about it correctly. This is what happens, for example, when we hear a vowel or a chord consisting of many primary and secondary tones.[33] It would seem, therefore, that the only distinguishing mark with which Descartes is left is the consciousness of an irresistible compulsion.

As recently as Mach, it seems to have been held that evidence is bound up with such a compulsion. Mach tells us that he gave up solipsism on the ground that he finds himself absolutely compelled to believe in an external world. But Helmholtz, in his *Tatsachen der Außenwelt*, says that solipsism is a possible hypothesis and one which cannot be refuted. And Descartes, unlike Mach, found that that compulsion, which one is supposed to feel, *could* be overcome.

If we are left only with this irresistible compulsion, then truth is by no means assured. Sophisms tend to make prisoners. And fools are incapable of freeing themselves from fixed ideas, however absurd. A habit of thought, which has become sufficiently engrained, may deprive a man of his good sense as well as of his freedom. Pascal seems to have thought of evidence, at least in the case of direct judgements, as an irresistible and natural compulsion to make a certain kind of judgement; this led him to the sceptical thought that, as long as we do not know who the author of our nature is, our trust in those judgements which seem to be directly enlightening is entirely unfounded.

6. One may say that these observations are pointless inasmuch as they cannot have any practical results. For if a man is subject to an irresistible compulsion to make a certain judgement, then he will make that judgement, no matter what considerations there may be to the contrary. And therefore—one may argue—this principle will always be valid, so far as he is concerned, as a principle of thought. But this reasoning is clearly unsatisfactory. What if several such principles were to contradict each other? And there actually is such a conflict if, as Pascal supposes, reason tells us it is evident that evident propositions are not to be believed. Here one *must* believe and one must *withhold* belief—and thus fall into despair.

7. It is obvious, therefore, that the evidence of a judgement cannot be identified with any irresistible compulsion forcing us to make the judgement. How are we to interpret the concept, then? The correct method is the one that we use in many other cases where we are concerned with a simple mark or characteristic. We will have to solve the problem by considering a multiplicity of judgements which are evident and then contrasting them with other judgements which lack this distinguishing characteristic. This is what we do, after all, when we make clear to ourselves what is red or not red, and what is coloured or not coloured. The type of case that Descartes considered was a case of something really being evident and one having a great variety of instances. It was that of self-perception—our perception of ourselves as thinking, believing, denying, rejoicing, being in sorrow, and so on. But he should not have restricted himself to this type of case. He should have considered the kind of evidence which is exemplified in the apodictic knowledge we have of axioms. In this way he would have made it possible to make a comparison and thus to single out the common mark of evidence; then there would have been no need for further explications of the mark by reference to other attributes which happen to be associated with it. Indeed, as we have seen, one fares better without such attributes than with the "clare et distincte percipio".

V

THE EVIDENT

(9 July, 1915)

1. One usually says "This is evident" and not "This is evident to me". Probably because of the faith that what is evident to *one* is evident to all. And the exception proves the rule. For in the case of self-awareness, one says "It is evident to me that I exist"; it cannot be directly evident to anyone else that I exist.

2. That which is called evident is a judgement or the content of a judgement. For example, it is evident that $1 + 1 = 2$.

We do not say that the person judging is evident; we say, rather, that he judges with evidence.

Thoughts or ideas cannot be said to be that which is evident, nor can our emotions.[34]

3. What is evident cannot be in error.[35]

And where something is evident there cannot be doubt. But neither freedom from error nor freedom from doubt makes a judgement an evident judgement; an evident judgement has a characteristic in virtue of which the judgement is seen to be correct.

4. "It is evident to me" comes to the same thing as "It is certain to me", "I know this", or "I am aware of this".

The expression "I see into it", however, seems to have a narrower sense. A person may perceive with evidence that he exists, but we do not say that he *sees* that he exists.[36] And the expression "I know that so-and-so" may have a still narrower sense, when it is used in connection with our awareness of something that has been demonstrated. But this is not always so, for linguistic usage often varies in many different ways.

5. To say that an evident judgement is one that is certain is not to deny that a man may know with evidence that there is something which is probable for him. In such a case, of course, the something is not itself certain; but the man does judge with certainty that it *lacks* the necessary conditions of being certain and that there is something to be said both for and against it. Some believe that in such cases a man judges with less intensity. But this is not true; otherwise, when the probability is one-half, the man would have to judge both *pro* and *contra* at the same time and with equal intensity. It is even less reasonable to say that such a judgement, with a suitably lowered intensity, may be a "correct presumption" or an "evident presumption", where correctness and evidence are taken to be compatible with error. Actually some have gone so far as to say that there is such a thing as a *"direct* evidence of presumption" which may be ascribed, for example, to memory. This is to make the mistake of supposing that there is a direct knowledge of probability; but actually, as Laplace observed, every probability is compounded out of knowledge and ignorance, and to know a probability, one must be aware of both.[37]

6. If evidence always pertains to judgements, the question arises whether evidence is related to judgement as a specific difference or as an accident.[38] The latter possibility would be excluded at the outset if, as is generally taught, there can be no accidents of accidents. And the former possibility would be excluded if, as is also generally taught, there can be, for any genus, only specific differences which are opposed to each other; for if there are any opposing specific differences falling under the genus of judgement these would certainly be affirmation and denial.[39] But neither affirming nor denying excludes evidence, for some things are affirmed with evidence and some things are denied with evidence. These two doctrines which, as I say, are generally taught, are often advocated by one and the same person; obviously any such person must be mistaken with respect to one or the other of the two doctrines. And perhaps he is mistaken with respect to both; for two judgements, which judge about different objects, would seem to differ, not merely accidentally, but specifically; similarly for two judgements which are concerned with one and the same object and differ with respect to *quality*. In this case, we are dealing immediately with specific differences which are not opposed. As

for the other view, it may be said that, just as a substance is a subject of an accident, so also an accident may be subject of still another accident. The relation of substance to accident differs from that of genus to specific difference in this respect: the accident includes the concept of the substance, and not conversely, just as the specific difference includes the genus, and not conversely; but the substance remains the same individual if the accident falls away, whereas that which is thought under the concept of the genus could not remain the same individual if it changed its specific difference. If a genus were without the specific difference, it would have to exist in co-ordination with some other specific difference; for no genus can subsist as a universal. But the relation of substance to accident is different. If, now, we compare certain accidents with other accidents, for example, if we compare thinking with affirming or denying, the relation would seem to be analogous to that of substance and accident; for the thinking is included in the affirmation and in the denial, whereas the converse is not true. And the thinking can continue to exist without continuing to be an affirmation or a denial. Just as the soul serves as the substratum for the thinking, it would seem that the thinking, in turn, serves as the substratum for the judging. Is it not possible, then, for the judging itself to be the subject of accidental differences, instead of being specifically differentiated? If we perceive or demonstrate something with evidence and if we continue to adhere to it but without direct or indirect evidence, then we would seem to judge the same as before, even though the evidence has not been replaced by any other differentia which is co-ordinated to it. One could hold, therefore, that instead of serving to differentiate the judgement essentially or to determine it specifically, the evidence is related to it as an accident, just as the judging is related to the thinking and the thinking to the soul.

7. It is not my intention to discuss the details of this particular question here. I would remark, however, that we cannot answer the question unless we note that every thinking includes an awareness of the thinker himself and that this awareness is not accidental to him. And if a person having an evident insight has an awareness of his insight, then he is aware of himself as a person judging with evidence. The question arises whether he must have, beyond this, still another awareness of himself as one who is

judging, but an awareness in which the evidence is not included.

When that which has been perceived with evidence becomes fixed in memory, then, no matter how the problem of the temporal mode is dealt with, what had earlier been given as a secondary subject is now given as a primary object and the accompanying inner perception is directed upon the recollection. And when a theorem which has been proved becomes fixed in memory, but without the proof which conferred the evidence upon it, then the belief in it without the earlier motivation would seem a different object. If I remember that the theorem has been proved, then again the inner perception of this recollection must be distinguished from the earlier inner perception of the mental process itself which I now remember.[40]

VI

ON THE EVIDENT

(Fragment of 12 July, 1915)

1. Every judgement that is evident is either directly or indirectly evident. First of all, it is essential to characterize the directly evident in more detail.

2. Some directly evident judgements are judgements of fact; the others are truths of reason, or insights.[41] The knowledge that *I think* is an example of the first class; the law of contradiction an example of the second.

3. Every *affirmative* judgement that is directly evident belongs to the first class.

4. And all these are inner perceptions. None of them pertains to anything other than the one who is judging.[42]

5. When we recall an earlier experience, we may have a confident belief and judge directly, not indirectly.[43] But the judgement lacks evidence. For it is possible to prove that we could have exactly this recollection even if that of which we are convinced had not occurred. The proof, like that of Descartes, would be based upon the lack of external evidence.[44]

6. If it is asked, then, whether directly evident affirmative judgements must always be made as judgements in the *modus praesens*, the answer must be in one sense affirmative. But we should not overlook the fact that the present is possible only as the end of a past, or as the beginning of a future, or as the transition from past

to future. Hence whatever is affirmed as present cannot be affirmed without being related to a duration of time, which extends into the past or into the future, even though one may not be able to determine exactly just how far the duration extends. The earlier or later existence of our self is necessarily included in the perception of this indeterminate extent.

7. But it is true that our directly evident affirmative judgements are restricted to knowledge of our self, and that they are restricted to the present. No moment of the past or of the future can be said to be assured with the same direct evidence that a moment of the present can be assured. However near such a past or future moment may be thought to be to the present, there is always some other moment which lies between it and the present; hence there will be a lapse of time which does not extend to that past or future moment but which is sufficient to constitute the present.

8. It is certain that we possess a directly evident affirmative knowledge within the narrow confines indicated, and what is more, that within those limits we never lack such knowledge. Whenever we are mentally active, this mental activity is an object of inner perception. And it is perceived with evidence. To be sure, our perceptions are not always equally distinct. The distinctness of a perception will depend upon whether, in our psychical relation to the *primary* object, we are thinking distinctly or indistinctly. Inner perception shows us precisely what this degree of distinctness is. Obviously degrees of distinctness are not to be identified with degrees of evidence.

9. All attacks aimed against the unexceptionable evidence of inner perception rest upon the confusion of inner perception with something which is not inner perception. Mental phenomena can also become the primary object of thinking.[45] Similarly, the assertion that external perception may sometimes be directly evident is a result of taking some fact of inner perception for one of outer perception. It is sometimes said that, in presenting us with an instance of red that does not exist, outer perception shows a red that "phenomenally exists"; but what one should say is that inner perception makes it known that outer perception presents us with a red—a red which, in truth, does not exist.

10. There remains the further question whether we are justified in asserting that what is true of our own experience holds more generally, and without exception, for *all* knowing beings.[46]

The great philosophers of antiquity have indeed affirmed that directly evident affirmative knowledge is limited to self-awareness, even in the case of God's knowledge.[47] And rightly so. The same grounds of proof are valid for all knowing beings.

To be sure, God knows himself, not only as actual, but as immediately necessary, whereas we know ourselves only as actual. But the knowledge God has of himself includes the actual knowledge of himself. Our knowledge of him is in accordance with a general concept; but his knowledge shows him in his individuality and thus in complete independence of any external influence; therefore, since nothing can be absolutely accidental, it shows him as immediately necessary.

A man can be said to have direct, affirmative, and therefore factual evidence concerning the existence of a thing only if it would be contradictory to say that, although he is thinking of the thing, the thing does not exist.[48] And one cannot recognize something affirmative as necessary without also grasping it as a fact. We will understand this, when we turn to the discussion of rational knowledge, or insights. . . .[49]

APPENDICES

ON THE GENERAL VALIDITY OF TRUTH AND THE BASIC MISTAKES IN A SO-CALLED "PHENOMENOLOGY"

I

Brentano to Husserl

Florence, 9 January, 1905

Dear Friend,

I thank you for your cordial letter and good wishes which I warmly return. I have read with great interest what you say about your endeavours, over the long years that have separated us, and about your present point of view.

If I understand correctly, you distinguish a twofold logic. One is an art,[1] the other a theoretical discipline. The latter is supposed to comprise all pure mathematics (geometry apparently being a discipline which is applied only to space). What is its subject-matter?[2] Apparently objects of reason and their combinations. It is supposed to be a part of philosophy and not to be based upon our knowledge of psychology. And this latter seems to you to be the point of greatest importance, for otherwise the validity of logic could be restricted to beings who happen to have the same make-up as we do.[3] This theoretical logic is concerned, not with evidence for us, but with an evidence of truths in themselves, so to speak. You praise Bolzano as your teacher and guide.

I must admit that I have several misgivings and I will not hesitate to mention them. For even if you too should have second thoughts, you need not be discouraged.[4] For it does seem clear, generally speaking, that all or most of the questions which you take up in your so-called theoretical logic will find their proper place in other classifications of the sciences.[5]

I think you may be justified in holding that the task of pure mathematics falls within the sphere of logic. But what seems unclear to me is whether this logic is anything other than the *art* of logic.

We do speak of the "art of calculating", after all. And in mathematics do we not learn to *perform* certain logical operations, such as adding, subtracting, multiplying, dividing, extracting square roots, and so on?

Was not the discovery of the differential calculus, in particular, the discovery of a mathematical procedure, with the result that Leibniz's symbolism, so superior to that of Newton, proved to be a great step forward? Even the invention of calculating machines could be mentioned.

To be sure, not only do we learn how to add, but we also learn certain laws, certain equations stating what adds up to what, as "$2 + 5 = 7$"; not only do we learn to multiply, but we learn the multiplication tables, which are, again, laws, such as "$7 \times 7 = 49$", telling what factors have what product. One could even be taught the Pythagorean theorem for a mathematics of the continuum and in abstraction from its specific spatial character. What is the point of this? Only that such knowledge is required for calculating and measuring; without it any attempt at measurement would be certain to fail.[6]

Every art, to the extent that it is theory and not practice, teaches laws. It goes beyond the spheres of the particular sciences, though in different degrees. A considerable part of the laws of mathematics have the character of the laws just mentioned—i.e., "$7 \times 7 = 49$", and the Pythagorean theorem (considered in abstraction from space). And just what is this character? I answer without reservation: that of the principle of contradiction. We would have a contradiction if there were any 7 which when multiplied by 7 were not to equal 49, or if the square of the hypotenuse of a right-angled triangle were not to equal the squares of the other two sides.[7]

Surely it would also be contradictory to suppose that the tone colour of the vowel *a* might not have the overtones which Helmholtz has established. This particular example shows how much the indistinctness of apperception tends to veil such contradictions. We find many more such veils if we enter the sphere of the theory of numbers and the theory of continuity. There are certain large numbers which we cannot even think of in the strict sense; for we think, not of these numbers themselves, but only of their surrogates. And what are we to say of the parts, and of the inner and outer boundaries, of an infinitely divisible continuum? Small wonder, then, that the imperfection of our powers of conception and apperception necessitates the invention of all kinds of ancillary methods. What might well be an immediately enlightening truth[8] is something which we come to know only by way of a roundabout procedure. Hence the art of calculation and measurement, which is such an important and impressive part of logic that it takes up entire textbooks in its own right. And hence, too, the results of all those analyses which lead to the discovery of contradictions in particular cases and which serve as aids for further procedures.

But though I cannot believe that the art of logic along with that of measurement draws its truths from any *single* discipline, I do not hesitate to maintain, now as earlier, that among the theoretical disciplines *psychology* stands in *closest* relation to it.[9]

What is the general law of contradiction, after all, but this: that whoever (explicitly or implicitly) affirms and denies the same thing, i.e., whoever contradicts himself, thinks absurdly?[10]

And the very thing that gives rise to the search for methods of explication is certainly psychological—for what is it but the indistinctness of certain apperceptions and our inability to group certain things in a distinct concept?

But you fear that such a conception would make the validity of the truths of logic and mathematics conditional on our own make-up. You believe that the laws of thinking which hold for us might be different from those that would hold for other thinking beings. What would be evident for us might not be evident for them, or indeed the contradiction of what is evident for us might be evident for them.

You are certainly right in emphatically rejecting any theory which would thus demolish the concept of knowledge and truth. But you are mistaken if you think that, in giving psychology this position in relation to logic, one has no way of avoiding such an error.

Whoever really makes an evident judgement really *knows* the truth and is certain of it; whoever really knows something with *direct* evidence is *directly* certain of the truth. This is unaffected by the fact that the knower, as a person judging, came into being, is subject to causation, and is dependent upon the particular cerebral organization which he happens to have. To the one who judges with evidence, the truth is secured *in itself*, and *not* by reflection on any such preconditions. If there is anyone who believes that this is contradictory, he is mistaken. If he were to try to make the contradiction analytically clear, he would end up with the discovery that he is guilty of confusing concepts. For it is one thing to say that the person who judges with evidence is caused and conditioned as such a person, and it is an entirely different thing to say that, if he were otherwise caused and conditioned, he might judge the contrary with similar evidence. So there is no contradiction involved in seeing into something directly, acquiring this insight as a result of some cause and under very complicated conditions, and yet having no idea at all of these causes and conditions.

Having the insight is itself sufficient to assure one that no one else could have a contrary insight.[11] Even the omnipotence of God could not make it possible; the very assumption is absurd and inconsistent with the concept of evidence.

There is no need at all to postulate any such thing as a truth in itself or a judgement in itself. There are only particular individuals who judge and only particular individuals who judge with evidence; what there is, no matter what area we are talking about, can consist only of things that are individually determined.

What you call "psychologism" is essentially the πάντων τῶν ὄντων μέτρον ἄνθρωπος of Protagoras. This is anathema to me, as it is to you. But this does not mean that we should countenance a realm of entities of reason. It is unfortunate that a mind such as that of the highly respected Bolzano should have soared too high and lost its way at this point. For the supposition of such a realm can be shown to be absurd.[12]

But I do wish you good fortune in your intellectual contact with this noble and sincere thinker. Even the errors of such a person are more instructive than are the truths which may occasionally be found in the glib talk of others.

This is a long letter, and yet I am afraid it is too short to convince you or to make my position clear in every point. And so I hope all the more that you will be able to appreciate the intention of my remarks. I am confident of your continued good will.

In sincere friendship,

F.B.

P.S. I think I ought to add still another word about the place of mathematics among the various scientific disciplines. Under what *theoretical* standpoint are we to regard the laws which concern the relationships among magnitudes? I would answer:

(1) From the theoretical point of view not every truth is worthy of being an object of scientific investigation. We are forced to practise a certain economy which takes into account the importance of a question in relation to our total understanding of the universe. This point of view may justify neglecting all, or almost all, of the so-called laws of metamathematics.[13]

(2) Otherwise these laws should be classified only as falling within psychology, being special cases of the evident knowledge of what things are contradictory.[14]

(3) Naturally the situation would be entirely different if one were to prove that there is a topoid of four or more dimensions. For then there would be an analogue of our three-dimensional geometry; and such a discipline (if we think of geometry as a science of bodies) would belong with the natural sciences.

There is one point of view from which, even today, the so-called metamathematical considerations might be classified along with geometry. This is the practical one of division of work. It is the one Marty indicated, in his important address as Rector, in order to prove the unity of philosophy. Indeed nothing more is necessary in order to show that, from this practical point of view, knowledge of metamathematics and knowledge of geometry are intimately connected. But it is essential to note that this point of view must be distinguished from the theoretical one. I would refer you to Marty.[15]

A certain economy is also required in logic considered as an *art*; this would seem to me to preclude such logic going into metamathematical doctrines. At least if the logic is a general logic. A logic adapted to the practical discipline just referred to should give detailed consideration to those artifices designed to compensate for the failure of our intuition in connection with the fourth dimension and such like. I have in mind, in particular, the method of projection into a three-dimensional space.

II

Draft of a letter from Brentano to Husserl

Florence, 30 April, 1905

On Pure Logic [16]

If I understand correctly, you would hope to take all those evident truths which are said to be conceptually illuminating and unify them within a special theoretical discipline, and you would call this discipline "logic".

That there are such conceptually illuminating truths is beyond doubt. And it is undeniable that, as such, they have something in common. But you must admit yourself that they cannot possibly be unified.

To what extent you hope to succeed in this is still not sufficiently clear to me.

Nor is the leading thought sufficiently clear. It is not supposed to be a practical one; it is all supposed to be done in a purely theoretical interest.

Anything that is known may well be of *some* theoretical interest. Knowledge, even of the most insignificant kind, is a good. But much of it, from the theoretical standpoint, is relatively worthless. The historian who does not exclude from his account most of the things that he finds to have happened is dull and vapid. But so too for the one who is concerned with general laws. How absurd it would be to prepare a book which contained nothing from beginning to end but multiplications of numbers taken at random. Yet each would express a general law.

What is it, then, that determines the value of certain truths and indicates that they are more worthy than others to be considered for their own sake and to be combined into a purely theoretical discipline?

What Aristotle required above all was this: if we are to be concerned with the necessary properties of some general concept, then there must *be* certain objects which fall under that concept.

This requirement seems justified. Where it is not fulfilled, everything becomes a mere exercise for the wits. And it explains satisfactorily why Aristotle, and those who came after him, never tried to mark off, as a separate theoretical discipline, a science of those truths which merely illuminate concepts and which contain no assertoric, empirical data.

If this is what it is that you want to do now, I can hardly feel that it is reasonable.

The term "logic" in particular is not to be recommended. The term has a fixed and well-established meaning. Why make it ambiguous? The scientific thinker, after all, is concerned to remove those ambiguities we already have.

As for the investigations which some would call "metamathematical", I am certainly aware of their value; I do confess, however, that I regard it as absurd to interpret a continuum as a set of points. Mathematicians allow themselves, within certain limits, to make use of absurd fictions with impunity. And this is highly relevant to a practical logical interest. It was those speculations on possible topoids of more than four dimensions which finally made evident the empirical character of a space of three dimensions. Even Leibniz was found to be in error, having held that Bayle's ideas on worlds of more than three dimensions were impossible *a priori*.

But the most ingenious of mathematicians, such as Euler and Descartes, never considered mathematics as being an end in itself. It is not surprising, therefore, that your Felix Klein, weary of excursions into metamathematics, should turn to the technological applications of mathematics.

These are the reasons which keep me from accepting all the observations in your kind letter, and not a tendency towards what you call "psychologism".

2

ON THE ORIGIN OF THE ERRONEOUS DOCTRINE OF *ENTIA IRREALIA*.

(Notes taken by A. Kastil after a conversation with Brentano. Innsbruck, May 1914)

How I arrived at the erroneous thought of the existence of the non-real.

1. Following Aristotle, I realized that the "is" of the existential statement "*A* is" is not attributive and does not involve a predicate, in the strict sense. "Is", therefore, is a word which is merely synsemantic.

2. Then I noted that "is" may also be used in such statements as "There is the impossibility of a round square" and "That there are no round squares is something that is". These are the cases where, according to Aristotle, the "is" is used for "Being in the sense of the true" (ὂν ὡς ἀληθές).[17]

Hence there is already a temptation to believe that the word "is" has the same function in the two cases (for example, in "A thing is", and in "An impossibility is"); for in the one case as in the other, it is merely synsemantic and not attributive.

3. But perhaps I would not have been led to the view, had I not been confirmed in it by a passage in Thomas Aquinas, whom I then thought of as my teacher. Thomas has the curious doctrine, quite alien to Aristotle, that things are composed of *essentia* and *existentia*—created things, that is, and not God. In the case of God *essentia* and *existentia* are identical.

Now Thomas himself raises an objection. We can know only the existence of God and not his essence; how, then, could his essence and existence be the same? Thomas answers: we do not know the existence of God, in the strict sense; when we say "Deus est", the "is" refers, not to the real existence of God, but to the "being in the sense of the true"—the *ens tamquam verum*.[18]

He thus assumed that the "is" has the same function in both types of case ("God is" and "There is the impossibility of so and so").

But this was by no means Aristotle's view. To be sure, the "is" functions only synsemantically in each case, but from this it does not follow that "is" performs the same function in each case.

If Aristotle holds that "is" in "There is the impossibility of a round square" pertains to being in the sense of the true, he does *not* hold this of the "is" in "Socrates is". In the latter case, it indicates the affirmation or acknowledgement of Socrates; but in the former it says that whoever asserts that the thing is impossible thinks correctly. Hence Aristotle says that this being in the sense of the true is to be found only in our mind. What is accepted or affirmed is not the impossibility of a round square, but, at most, the person who denies or rejects a round square and who does so with evidence.[19] I am aware of myself as someone who rejects correctly. (The one who denies is himself something positive: Leibniz.)

4. The history of all this is tied up with the Aristotelian doctrine that truth is *adaequatio rei et intellectus*. In *De Anima* 6 the question is raised: When is something true?[20] Answer: If a thing has a certain attribute, then I judge truly and correctly if I judge that the thing has the attribute —if I thus combine what is combined in reality. If the thing does not have the attribute, then I judge truly if my judgement denies the attribute of the thing—if I thus separate what is not combined in reality.

But there is also a knowledge which is not compound. For it is not necessary that I combine ideas. What is it that I do in such a case? I simply have an idea and accept or affirm it (θιγγάνειν); Aristotle, *Metaphysics*, Θ, 10, 1051b, 17). And what if I simply reject or deny? Aristotle may have intended to touch on this with the following words: τὸ δὲ ψεῦδος οὐκ ἔστιν.. My own conjecture is that he meant to say this: In the case where a thing is thought about and correctly rejected, there is nothing. In that stage of my thinking, I was not sufficiently clear about this point and assumed that the doctrine of the *adaequatio rei et intellectus* should be extended to apply in the case of negative judgements, as though such a judgement had, as its objective correlate, the non-being of that which is correctly rejected.

NOTES

by Oskar Kraus

INTRODUCTION (References 1 to 10)

[1] There are modern theories of knowledge which are nothing but correspondence theories in disguise—for example, those theories which would rely, not upon evidence, but upon "verification", i.e., upon a comparison between a judgement and a state of affairs (or the facts, or what is actual). A comparison with the empirically given is itself an act of judgement, which can be either false or correct; and one cannot make the comparison unless one already *knows* both the judgement and the fact.

[2] In Brentano's Würzburg lectures on ontology, given prior to 1872, we find the following passage: "One may correctly characterize truth in the following way: Truth (or knowledge) is goodness or perfection in judgement, just as beauty is goodness or perfection of thought or idea (*Vorstellung*) and virtue the goodness or perfection of will (or desire)." This is the way in which Windelband was later to speak.

[3] Wherever there is a belief in ideal and unreal objects, reasons of the sort that Brentano cites may be said to be at work: ordinary language is a practical and not a theoretical instrument; its influence is misleading, for it was not formed for the purposes of philosophy. But the philosopher must make use of ordinary language as long as there is no *characteristica universalis* grounded upon an adequate psychological analysis.

[4] The negative judgement is the source of our apparent references to non-being and to nothing. By denying this fact, one is led to the nonsensical mysticism of Heidegger's "Nichts-theorie", with its delusion that in certain moods and feelings we can "contemplate the essence of nothingness". This is discussed in "Über Nichts und Alles" in *Wege und Abwege der Philosophie* (Prague 1937), by O. Kraus.

[5] This principle is not to be confused with Höfler's thesis (a product of misunderstandings), according to which contradictory judgements cannot be made by the same subject.

[6] According to Husserl (*Logische Untersuchungen,* 2nd edn, Vol. I, pp. 176–177), the law of contradiction, "when properly understood", says that "of two contradictory propositions (judgement-contents), one is *true* and one is *false*". And this, according to him, is to be distinguished from saying: "Of two contradictory judgements, one is *correct* and one is *incorrect*." The latter is supposed to be merely a consequence of the former *strict* formulation. According to Husserl, when we think of the law of contradiction in its strict sense, we need not think of judgements as real acts at all, and in no case are judgements the objects with which the law is concerned. This over-subtle distinction must be rejected as nonsense, if only for the following reason: the term "correct", when it is not used to mean the same thing as "evident", is

not being used as a real predicate which applies to the acts of judgement which we call correct; it functions rather as a mere *denominatio extrinseca,* merely expressing the thought that a judgement contradicting the one called correct cannot possibly be one that is evident, or seen to be correct.

The principle that, of two contradictory propositions, one is true and one is false, tells us no more than this—"when properly understood". The principle of contradiction does not imply that in calling a judgement "true" we are treating the judgement as being the subject of any kind of predication (and to this extent Husserl has a vague notion of what the correct view is); still less is the principle concerned with ideal propositions or contents of judgement. The principle of contradiction is an apodictic denial that there can be an evident judgement which contradicts a judgement called "true". The fictions of our language, however, serve to conceal the results of psychognostic analysis. The errors to which these fictions may lead are illustrated by Husserl's doctrine that "the" judgement that two and two are five (two and two are six, two and two are seven) is of the same sort as "the" judgement that there are dragons. His realm of ideal objects, in other words, is populated not only by every possible "eternal truth" but also by every possible "eternal falsehood". The "pure consciousness" is hardly to be envied, therefore, for the wealth of its *Noëmata.*

⁷ [According to Brentano's theory of judgement, every judgement has an object which the judgement either affirms or denies (accepts or rejects); two judgements have the same object if the object that the one affirms or denies is the same as the object that the other affirms or denies; they have the same quality if they both affirm the object, or if they both deny the object.—R.M.C.] We must distinguish between saying (i) that it is *impossible* for an evident judgement to contradict one that is "true", and saying (ii) that a true judgement is one such that it is *possible* for it to be evident. See Section 14 below.

⁸ See Brentano's *Vom Dasein Gottes* (Leipzig 1929), edited by Alfred Kastil. The editor calls our attention (p. 496) to the *regressus ad infinitum* which is involved if we stress *possibility* at this point. For what does "possible" mean? Simply "not impossible". And what does it mean to say that a thing is "impossible"? Not, surely, that the thing *is* apodictically rejected. It would have to mean that the thing *can be* apodictically rejected—in other words, that it is *not impossible* for the thing to be apodictically rejected; and so on.

⁹ Compare Husserl's *Ideen*: "Everything that may be called a World and a reality must be represented within the sphere of a real or possible consciousness" (p. 278). "Absolute reality is no more tenable than a round square" (p. 106). "Being, reality is . . . only consciousness" (p. 94).

¹⁰ It has been said that Husserl was "able to overcome" Brentano's theory of knowledge. The fact of the matter is that Husserl never went beyond Brentano's *Psychologie* of 1874. In chapter 8 of Book II (Volume II, p. 121, of the second edition), Brentano speaks, entirely in the

spirit of the later Husserl, as though evidence were nothing but the "experience of truth" or a grasping of the truth (compare the *Logische Untersuchungen*, Vol. I, pp. 176 ff., pp. 190 ff.). Brentano even spoke of a grasping of laws. Other parallel citations may be found in the notes for the lectures on logic which Brentano gave at the University of Vienna. Consider the following, for example, from p. 461 of these notes: "Just as the evident judgement is related to the existence or truth of its object, love that is seen to be correct is related to the goodness of its object." On the preceding page Brentano equates existence with the truth of the object and non-existence with the falsehood of the object. Husserl remains faithful to the letter of Brentano's *Psychologie* of 1874 and the lectures on logic and continues to talk in such terms. Thus he argues finally: "Just as it is self-evident that, where there is nothing, there is nothing to be seen, it is also self-evident that, where there is no truth, there can be no true insight—and thus no evidence." We need not consider whether it is in accord with good psychology to say that, where there is nothing, there is nothing to be seen (consider hallucinations, so-called "retinal grey", and the like). Let us ask only what it means to say "Where there is no truth, there can be no true insight." The term "where" obviously should not be taken in its literal, spatial sense; hence what we have is "*If* there is no truth, then an insight is not possible." And what does this mean? According to our analysis it comes to no more than this: "If a given insight, whether affirmative or negative, is impossible, then such an insight is impossible." If "Two and two cannot possibly be other than five" is not a truth, that is to say, if it is impossible as an apodictic insight, then such an insight is impossible. And this, of course, is nothing but a simple *idem per idem*.

PART ONE (References 1 to 60)

[1] The Cartesian definition, "Verum est quod clare ac distincte percipio" contains the germ of correct theory: the true is to be defined in terms of the evident and the correspondence theory is to be rejected. This conception is clearly expressed—in spite of some wavering—by Spinoza (*Ethics*, II, prop. 43).

[2] To do complete justice to Windelband one needs to distinguish between two questions: first, whether his exposition and interpretation of Kant's doctrine is historically correct, and, second, whether Windelband did not come close to a correct view in what he said about "the concept of truth". So far as the first question is concerned, Brentano easily succeeds in proving the inaccuracy of Windelband's interpretation of Kant. As for the second question, Windelband had a notion—however vague—which ought not to be rejected out of hand. Brentano himself (§24) calls the proposed interpretation an attempt to shake off the old correspondence theory; opposing this attempt, Brentano puts forward his own interpretation, which (in the lecture on truth) is a revision rather than a complete repudiation of the correspondence

theory. Windelband, faithful to his slogan "To understand Kant is to go beyond him" (*Präludien*, p. iv), goes far beyond the historical Kant by allowing him neither a Ptolemaic nor a Copernican conception of truth; he would have Kant reject *every* version of the correspondence theory. With a much finer touch than that of the Marburg Neo-Kantians, Windelband would have truth consist in thought which accords with a normative rule (p. 114); "the mind brings this norm to its own awareness."

Windelband writes (*Präludien*, p. 47): "The only thing that philosophy can do is to extract this normative consciousness from the flux of our empirical consciousness and to rely upon direct evidence; it is in this direct evidence that the normative consciousness, once it has been brought to light, has the efficacy and validity which it ought to have for every individual." There is little to quarrel with in this statement, unless one takes too seriously the contention that it is "the *only* thing that philosophy can do".

All this is certainly fraught with confusion, if "judging" is not distinguished from "thinking about", and if the logical ought is identified with the axiological and ethical ought. But this aberration from the intellectual to the emotional, against which Brentano correctly protests in the fourth essay, does show that Windelband looked for the norm—that which is as it ought to be—in consciousness itself. And in doing this he was following the path which, indeed, Spinoza had taken before him (*Ethics*, II, prop. 43); see the review by Oskar Kraus of Cohen's writings on philosophy and the theory of knowledge in *Deutsche Literaturzeitung*, No. 30 (1929). To be sure, one still finds traces of the doctrine of correspondence in Spinoza, but Freudenthal conceives these traces as being no more than a gesture towards the venerable principle. Here too Spinoza bases his thought on that of Descartes.

Unfortunately, Windelband and his circle, having set out in the right direction, soon become lost in the chimerical realm of absolute values and validities.

But Brentano, at the time of his lecture on truth, tried merely to modify the correspondence theory. Later he saw that this would not do either. The theory of the evident, which Brentano was one of the first to revive, has been developed to the point where it clarifies the concept of truth, and removes the attendant difficulties, without resort to the fiction of ideal objects, "eternal realms of value", and the other non-things which serve only to restore the correspondence theory in some form or other.

³ Compare Brentano's criticism of Sigwart's doctrine in Essay V.

⁴ Franz Hillebrand in *Grünhut's Zeitschrift für das Öffentlich- und Privatrecht* (1884, XI, p. 633).

⁵ Cf. Franz Brentano, *Von der mannigfachen Bedeutung des Seienden nach Aristoteles* (Freiburg 1862), p. 22.

⁶ Compare the new edition of Brentano's *Psychologie vom empirischen Standpunkt*, Felix Meiner, *Philosophische Bibliothek*, Vols. I–III, esp. Vol. II.

[7] On the so-called "existential judgement", see Brentano's *Psychologie*, II (pp. 55, 195). Compare also Franz Hillebrand, *Die neuen Theorien der kategorischen Schlüsse* (Vienna 1891); see notes 25 and 38, below.

[8] Brentano later withdrew the assertion that collections of things, and parts of things, are not themselves things. A boundary or limit is indeed not a thing on its own, but it is a thing which exists as part of a continuous thing.

[9] Brentano later attacks the doctrine. Everyone calls a house or a chair a "thing", although it is considered as a joining together of many things (bricks, pieces of wood, etc.). Certainly the old doctrine is correct in holding that a collection—a herd or an army, for example—is not something that may be added to the particular soldiers or sheep as still another entity; it is a real totality in the sense of a sum whose parts likewise consist of real things.

[10] Brentano held at that time that "a past pain", "a former man", "a future man", and the like, are expressions in which the adjective functions as a modifier converting a thing into a non-thing. Most of Brentano's students have remained faithful to this doctrine or have further elaborated upon it, extending the realm of non-things into that of the boundless. Husserl's phenomenology and Meinong's theory of objects both tended to propagate this realm of *irrealia* to an extravagant degree. But Marty and Stumpf were content to defend the traditional stock of *irrealia*—"non-real things", "essences", "states of affairs", "contents"—against Brentano's repudiation of non-things. So far as "past" and "future" are concerned, Brentano's later doctrine was that differences of praeterital and futural thinking are differences not in the objects of thought, but in its modality. (He spoke of "Vorstellungs-modi".) The thing that I think about in the present mode can be thought of at some other time in the past or in the future mode. The modes of thinking or presentation also affect the judgements we make about these things, but in every case what is thought of is itself a thing. When we think of a past or a future man, we are thinking of a thing—a man—in the praeterital or in the futural mode. Compare Brentano's doctrine of time and temporal modes of presentation (*Psychologie*, Vol. II and esp. Vol. III), and also Brentano's published letters to Marty going back to 1895 (*Archiv für Psychologie*, LXXV, Heft 1 and 2, 1930). The latter also contain a discussion of Husserl's later doctrine of modalities.

The question that Brentano raised here—"Does one expect to find, as a *thing* external to oneself, some entity one knows to have perished a long time ago?"—is a question which, at that time, he answered in the negative; he believed that one is here concerned with a non-real entity that once existed, and that one is not concerned with a thing.

[11] Brentano held at that time that, if I say there is a lack of money, then I have affirmed something, acknowledged something in judgement; this something is not a "thing" but is the *lack* of a thing, and the *lack* of a thing is itself an entity—a non-thing. Things as well as non-things are subsumed under the concept of "entity" (cf. ¶ 48). But Brentano later realized that this was a mistake. The statement "There

is a lack of money" is nothing but the linguistic disguise of a denial—
"Money is lacking", "There is no money", or "No money is there",
all of which express my disavowal, or denial, of money. Such expressions
as "lack of money" are not names but pseudo-names. They are syncategorematic (*mitbedeutende*) expressions; their role in the complete statement is that of expressing a denial and not, as the language might
suggest, an affirmation.

[12] Brentano speaks here of "impossibilities", "eternal truths" which
subsist (*bestehen*); he rejects the idea that one might speak here of
"entities" or "things" to which a true judgement corresponds. As may
be gathered from the following paragraphs, however, he does allow
himself to speak of non-things or *irrealia*, and he believes that any non-
thing may be counted as an "entity" which exists and to which our
affirmative judgement corresponds. At the time Brentano did not
consider the "entity" in such cases to be a thing; it was a *non-real* entity.
Thus he considered mathematical truths as something existent, though
he did not consider them to be existing *things*. This is all false; and the
fact that it has been exposed as such by Brentano himself has been
obstinately ignored. Contemporary theory of knowledge and especially
later "phenomenology" (Husserl's *Ideen* and *Transzendentale Logik*)
absorbed these thoughts which had long been surmounted by Brentano
and developed them into a direction from which Brentano himself had
parted.

[13] It seems, Brentano says, that the *adaequatio rei et intellectus* disinte-
grates because there is no *res*, no "thing", among the "eternal truths",
"impossibilities", etc. to which thought would correspond. But in the
following paragraph he holds that entities which are non-real and are
yet capable of existing may serve as that to which thought corresponds.

I repeat that this idea is untenable and that Brentano later rejected
it categorically. But the theory reigns over the whole of epistemological
literature without anyone taking note of Brentano's (later) objections.

[14] Brentano believed, then, that the doctrine of the *adaequatio rei et
intellectus* is not completely false; it is to be interpreted, however, not
as a correspondence of judging with a *res* (a thing or entity, in the strict
sense of the term), but as a correspondence of the affirming judgement
with something existent, and of the denying judgement with something
non-existent. Non-things, *irrealia*, entities of reason, were thus said to
be like things in that they sometimes exist and sometimes do not exist.

[15] In this context "entity" is the most fundamental concept for Brentano,
under which not only every thing but also every non-thing can be
subsumed. Later Brentano rejected this thesis. He attempted to show
that "entity" must be a univocal concept, since the concept of our
consciousness, which always has something as its object, is univocal.
But it would be impossible for "entity" to be a univocal concept if it
were intended to encompass both things and non-things, for these
would not share a single characteristic. Mental and physical things,
indeed *n*-dimensional things, can be subsumed under the concept of
"thing", or "entity"; but what characteristics could a physical thing

or a mental thing have in common with the "impossibility of a round square" or a "past pleasure"? These are not to be subsumed under one concept. Otherwise the word "entity" would be equivocal, sometimes referring to things and sometimes to non-things. The question is discussed in Part IV.

16 The defect in these detailed arguments consists in the following: Brentano proceeds from the concept of correct (*richtig*) or fitting (as he had done in *Vom Ursprung sittlicher Erkenntnis*, Section 22), instead of proceeding from the concept of the evident or insightful (*einsichtigen*) judgement; but the concept of the *correct* can be acquired only by an appeal to a judgement which is seen to be correct, or seen to be evident. Brentano had always held, however, that we can give an account of correct and incorrect only by reflecting on the evident judgement (or, in the emotive sphere, by reflecting on emotions which are, analogously, correct or right, and incorrect or wrong). In *Vom Ursprung sittlicher Erkenntnis*, all reference to "true and false", "right and wrong", is reduced to judging that is seen to be correct and to loving or hating that is seen to be correct.

Elements of different theories are lined up here in a somewhat disorderly manner. An older conception which derives from Aristotle connects the *correct* with the convenient or with the fitting, and a later, more progressive theory reduces the correct to the evident, to that which is insightful.

We must stay with this later doctrine. For it alone sheds light on the question: What is truth?

17 It is clear that Brentano was here trying to improve upon Aristotle's definition of truth—to transform it without completely abandoning it. But this half-way measure is astonishing in view of the fact that, even then, Brentano based the theory of knowledge upon the concept of evident judgement, just as he based the theory of value upon that of correct emotion.

18 We say of a judgement that it fits, corresponds to, or harmonizes with its object provided that the judgement is true; and we say of a judgement that it is true provided that the judgement is evident, or that we believe that it corresponds to an evident judgement with respect to its quality, or that we believe that an evident judgement that is concerned with the same object could not possibly be of a different quality. This is the consequence of Brentano's later doctrine which emerges more and more clearly in the essays that follow, and which we must defend against the older doctrine that was advanced in the lecture on truth. Two judgements are said to correspond qualitatively (or formally) if both are affirmative, or both are negative, and if they have the same temporal mode.

19 What holds of evident judgement also holds of correct emotion. Any discussion of *correct* or *right* in the sphere of emotive phenomena derives its meaning from evident judgement. We call an emotion suitable to its object, or fitting to its object, if it is seen to be correct, or if we believe that no emotion that is seen to be correct and that is directed

upon the same object could possibly have a different quality. In saying of something that it is "good" we mean that no attitude towards the object other than love, or positive evaluation, could possibly be seen to be correct. "Good" is a syncategorematic word, like "being" and "non-being". Compare the Introduction and the Notes to the new edition of *Vom Ursprung sittlicher Erkenntnis* (3rd edn, Leipzig 1934); see also Brentano's *Psychologie*, Vol. II, as well as the later essays in the present volume.

Hence the complete opposite of what is said in the text is true. It is not that the correctness of loving and hating depends upon whether or not we love the good or hate the bad; the truth of the matter is just the other way round. And to say that our emotion *fits* or corresponds to the object again, is only to say, that the emotion is right or correct. The basic point is that the emotion is seen to be correct. We say of an object that it is good or bad if it fits an emotion which is right—a correct emotion. One does not first recognize the value and *then* recognize the emotion as correct; it is, again, the converse that is true. What we call a value or a good is whatever may be the object of a correct emotion; we know that any qualitatively (formally) different emotion directed upon such an object is one that cannot possibly be correct. This was Brentano's later view.

[20] Later Brentano declares this to be false. One can refer only to *things*; for only things can be objects of thought. There is a detailed and complete account of this topic in Brentano's *Psychologie*, Vol. I, Introduction, Vol. II, Appendix 9, and in the later essays in the present book.

[21] Truth is not a real property of judgement unless one understands by "truth" simply the property of being evident or of being insightful (*einsichtig*). Since one cannot take "truth" in the latter way (and it is not so taken in the lecture), it is clear that in speaking of truth one is concerned with an *apparent* attribute or characteristic. Such apparent attributes are what the scholastics called *denominationes extrinsecae*, marks from the outside, so to speak. In referring to the truth of a judgement that is not evident, one has in mind either that this blind judgement corresponds with respect to quality to some other judgement that is evident, or else that an evident judgement could not possibly contradict it. Compare the Introduction.

Brentano says in the text: "The judgement itself may not undergo any change; but it will become true if the thing in question comes into being, and it will cease to be true if the thing is destroyed." Suppose, for instance, I judge that it is raining. The rain stops, I do not revise my judgement, and the judgement is thus transformed from one which is true into one which is false. If "true" and "false" were real predicates, or real properties of the judgement, this would constitute a miracle—indeed a contradiction; something would change its real properties without itself undergoing any change other than a temporal one.

Thus "true" and "false" cannot signify real predicates or attributes. Therefore, one might argue, they must signify non-real predicates.

But the great progress of Brentano's thinking consists in showing that there cannot be determinations other than things—indeed that non-real determinations cannot even be imagined. What, then, does it mean to say "The judgement is deprived of its truth without its being changed in any way"? I believe the answer is roughly this: "The judgement 'It is raining' ceases to be true." And what this means, when put clearly and explicitly, is: "From now on a judgement which affirms rain cannot possibly be evident." Our statement is an apodictic rejection of evident judgements affirming rain.

22 One must object to the view that analytic judgements, and specifically cognitions *a priori*, refer to objects devoid of real content. The principle of contradiction, for instance, no matter how it is formulated, refers to *things*.

23 At the time Brentano's view was as follows: The coming into being or passing away of something that has "no real content" (*Gehalt*) and is thus not a thing is always tied to the coming into being and passing away of that which *is* a thing. A deprivation, for instance, comes into being when some thing passes away, and a deprivation passes away when the corresponding thing comes into being. Thus an empty space comes into being when certain bodies pass away or change their location. And an empty space passes away if certain bodies come into being or change their location. An object of thought comes into existence when one thinks, and it passes away when one stops thinking. It is noteworthy that Brentano had always held that the coming into being and the passing away of the so-called non-things is bound up with the coming into being and passing away of *things*. He did believe, at the time of the lecture on truth, that "An empty space comes into being" conveys something other than "Some physical object passes away", and that "My lack of money begins today" conveys something other than "Today I am devoid of all money", or "Today the last of my money is gone". He took the statements to be logically equivalent and yet he considered them psychologically and conceptually different. According to the later doctrine, however, the statements express the same thought but in different ways; in each case there is a relation to a thing, in the one example a relation to matter that changes or moves, in the other example a relation to money which changes its owner, and so on. See additional details below and Brentano's *Vom Dasein Gottes*, p. 42.

The germ of Brentano's later view, which rejects *irrealia*, even as possible objects of thought, is contained in this doctrine of the dependence of non-things upon things.

24 What Brentano is doing here is essentially this: he replaces the doctrine of correspondence between thought and object (*rei et intellectus*) by that of the adequacy (fittingness, propriety) of thought to the existent *or* non-existent. This is what most of his students designate as adequacy to an "objective" or "state of affairs" (the state of affairs *that* something *A* is, or that it is not). The analogue holds true in the case of the correspondence between valuation and value, states-of-value, value-contents, and the like. Brentano had not yet become completely aware of the fictitious character of these modes of speaking.

[25]Instead of speaking of a "correct inference" from false premises, one should speak of the correct conception of the so-called "rule of inference". To call the inference itself formally correct or formally true is inadvisable and misleading. Compare Hillebrand, *Die neuen Theorien der kategorischen Schlüsse*; compare also notes 7 and 38.

[26] From this point on, the entire correspondence or "adaequatio" theory is capable of refutation. Any such theory, including the one presented in the text, is untenable, because it is absurd, indeed ridiculous, to hope to compare the thing with the judgement in which the thing is known. For the thing in question would have to be known before the comparison could be made. Yet every theory intending to trace back the concept of the "true" to the concepts of being "appropriate", "fitting", "suitable", or the like, tacitly implies that such a comparison must be made.

[27] The concept of a *thing* is not to be confused with that of an *existent*. We derive the concept of *thing* from any intuition of outer, or inner, perception; "thing" is the most general concept that there is. But we speak of "the existent" or of "that which has being" only when we assert of some thing that it is; "existence" and "existent" are thus related to the judging attitude and to affirmation in particular. We will not discuss the ways in which some recent philosophers have played with the words "Being", "*Dasein*", and "Existence", except to note that, if a theory has anything new to offer, it should not be expressed in words which have traditionally been used in other senses.

[28] The principle according to which any conceptual investigation must ultimately go back to intuition is what finally enabled Brentano to dispose of the doctrine of *irrealia*.

[29] Brentano here expressly states that to every thought (*Denken*) there corresponds, as a correlate, that which is thought about (*das Gedachte*). Brentano always insisted that when we think about a horse, we think about the horse and not about the idea of the horse; but he is saying here that there is a correlation between the thinking-of-a-horse and the horse as something which is thought about. I mention this because by the time he wrote the letter of 17 March, 1905, which is printed below, the latter doctrine had become so foreign to him that he questioned whether he had ever enunciated it. According to his later views, the "*A*-as-something-which-is-thought-about" is a *linguistic* and not a *conceptual* correlate of "That which is thinking about *A*".

[30] The fragment breaks off with the additional phrase, "And similarly in the case of judgement, 'There is . . .' " The manuscript was written certainly not after 1901, and most probably long before. This is confirmed by the fact that the handwriting does not yet show any indication of diminishing eyesight and, even more strongly, by the fact that the general train of thought is the same as that of the lecture on truth.

[31] The *Deskriptive Psychologie* which Brentano announces here exists up to now only in the form of unpublished lectures. In 1911 Brentano prepared a new edition of Book Two of his *Psychologie vom empirischen*

Standpunkt and added supplementary material; see Chapter VII, "On the Impossibility of Regarding Judgement and the Emotions as forming a single basic category" (Vol. II, p. 152).

[32] Concerning those compound or double judgements, see Volume II of the *Psychologie*, p. 183, and "Miklosich über subjektlose Sätze" published in 1883 and translated as "Miklosich on Subjectless Propositions", in the appendix to *The Origin of the Knowledge of Right and Wrong* (London 1902), Cecil Hague's translation of Brentano's *Vom Ursprung sittlicher Erkenntnis*.

[33] On the concept of intensity, see Brentano's *Vom sinnlichen und noetischen Bewusstsein* (Vol. III of the *Psychologie*) and his *Untersuchungen zur Sinnespsychologie* (Leipzig 1907).

[34] Brentano would now approach Windelband's doctrine somewhat differently. Windelband had said that the statement "There is freedom" does not ascribe to freedom the kind of being that "There is a God" ascribes to God. He had also held that substances do not have the same type of being as do properties or activities. But Brentano never accepted any such distinction between modes of being; he held instead that the word "is" has a single meaning in the statements "There is a God", "There is a substance", "There is a property or quality". But at the time he wrote the criticism of Windelband he did believe that such words as "deprivation", "possibility", "truth", and "freedom" are categorematic, and hence that one could think about a deprivation, and accept or reject it, just as one may think about a physical thing, or about a man, or God. But later investigations (see the appendix of Vol. II of the *Psychologie*) indicated that the words in question have only a syncategorematic use. The lecture on truth, at the beginning of the present book, implies that the statement "There is a deprivation, or absence, of gold" affirms an "irreal" object of thought—that it affirms the "absence of gold" or the "non-existence of gold". But according to Brentano's later view, the statement rejects or denies something; "There is an absence of gold" is only another way of saying "There is no gold". And what is denied or rejected is always some *thing*, whether it be gold or water or whatever. Brentano would also add this: if we are to express ourselves strictly, we should not speak of the *meaning* of the expressions "is" and "is not"; we should speak rather of the synsemantic uses of such words. And these uses may be very different: in the sentence "There is a God" the word "is" is used to express an affirmation, but in "There is an absence or deprivation" and "There is an impossibility" it is used to express a denial or rejection, which in such cases happens to have the linguistic form of an affirmation. Brentano's criticisms of his own earlier doctrine are set forth very clearly in a letter which I have included in my introduction to the *Psychologie* (Vol. I, pp. xliv-liv).

[35] Brentano is here calling attention to the fact that when the word "is" is used syncategorematically as a copula, in order to express an affirmation, it has nothing to do with that sense of "being" which is synonymous with "object" or "thing" and which *does* function as a

genuine name. It would be well if this equivocation in the term being could henceforth be avoided.

[36] A simple *thetic* judgement, according to Brentano, is adequately expressed in the forms "There is an *A*" or "There is not an *A*", or even in the forms "There is an *AB*" or "There is not an *AB*". A compound predicative judgement (a "double-judgement") would be put as "*A* is *B*" or "*A* is not *B*". The traditional logic misconceives the nature of the latter judgements; it takes them to be single judgements (as Brentano had done at first) and not as consisting of two judgements. Thus it takes "*A* is *B*" and "There is *AB*" to be different verbal expressions of the same judgement; just as Brentano had taught, in 1874, that "Some man is sick" has the same meaning as the existential statement "There is a sick man". But if there are "double-judgements", then the proper way to express them is in the form "*A* is *B*"—"Some man is sick". In the latter judgement a man is accepted or affirmed and it is said of him that he is sick. But "There is a sick man", on the contrary, is the proper expression for a simple thetic judgement, in which the object of a synthesis of ideas—"sick man"—is simply acknowledged.

[37] According to Windelband, the statement "The rose is a flower" may be thought of as being like the statement "All roses are flowers" and consequently he believed it to mean the same as "There is no rose which is not a flower" or "There is no rose which is a non-flower". Brentano says, on the contrary, that "The rose is a flower", as well as "All roses are flowers", expresses a twofold judgement: one judgement which accepts or acknowledges a rose, and a second judgement which rejects or denies roses which are non-flowers. In other words, one must take account of the fact that statements beginning with "all" may have two different senses. Sometimes they may express what is merely a negative judgement. For example, the judgement expressed by "All triangles are such that the sum of their angles is 180 degrees" is a purely negative apodictic judgement which does not assert that there *is* such a thing as a triangle; the judgement is true, and yet there cannot be anything that is actually made up of three absolutely straight lines. But when one says "All men are mortal" and "All roses are flowers", one is expressing the judgements (1) that there are men and that there are flowers and (2) that there are no men who are not mortal and that there are no roses which are not flowers. It was in 1883, so far as I know, that Brentano first published this interpretation of "all" statements.

[38] Windelband had written: Brentano "proposes in a very mysterious way that the traditional theory of inference may be revolutionized on the basis of a theory of the nature of judgement, but he has lifted the veil only enough for us to see some of the paradoxical consequences of this theory." Meanwhile, however, Brentano's suggestions enabled Hillebrand to write the book on *Die neuen Theorien der kategorischen Schlüsse* (Vienna 1891). J. P. N. Land, who was not at all close to Brentano as a philosopher, understood the new theory of judgement and inference much better than Windelband did. See J. P. N. Land,

"Brentano's Logical Investigations", *Mind*, I (1876), pp. 284–292; compare also Anton Marty's *Gesammelte Schriften*, Halle a. S. 1916–1920.

Brentano discussed Land's criticism in a letter dated 15 April, 1876, which is reproduced in large part in Vol. II of the *Psychologie* (p. 288). Land had said that all categorical statements—and hence those beginning with "all"—presuppose the existence of a subject. Brentano had originally held that *A*-statements have only one possible interpretation and that this is purely negative, as explained in the previous note. He conceded to Land, however, that there are also *A*-statements which may be interpreted as affirming the existence of their subjects, in which case such moods as *Bamalip* and *Darapti* remain valid. But Land was entirely mistaken if he intended to deny that there are *A*-statements which serve only to express pure and often apodictic denials. Geometric statements in no way presuppose the existence of the structures or forms with which they are concerned. For further details see Vol. II of the *Psychologie*, p. 248 and the notes on pp. 284–6 of that work.

Land had defended his view in this way: When we say "No stone is alive" or "All men are mortal" we presuppose the existence of stones or of men; in making these statements we are not concerned with the possible properties of purely problematic men or stones (op. cit., p. 291). It is true, as indicated above, that in the natural sciences statements of this sort do include an affirmation. "All men are mortal" says (1) that there are men and (2) that there is nothing which is a man and not mortal. Similarly for those statements of geometry which are concerned with the three-dimensional space in which we live, but such statements— e.g., those that speak of ideal tetrahedrons—can be applied only approximately. But we are also acquainted with geometries which are concerned with manifolds having more than three dimensions, and we do not know, and cannot know, whether such manifolds are actual; the objects of non-Euclidean geometry, moreover, are entirely problematic.

Brentano had added the following lines to the letter referred to above: "And what of statements which contradict each other—'Some angels are damned by God' and 'No angel is damned by God'? According to all logic up to now, one of these must be true. But if there are no angels, then, according to Land's view, both would be false."

It should be noted that it is Land's view and not Brentano's which conflicts with the traditional doctrine that, of two contradictory statements, one must be true. According to Land's view the statement "No angel is damned by God" would be false if there were no angels, for on his interpretation the statement is equivalent to "There are angels and none of these is damned by God".

[39] Except for the footnote on Miklosich, I have omitted the critique of Sigwart from the second edition of *Vom Ursprung sittlicher Erkenntnis*; for the critique has no direct relevance to the problems of value theory with which the *Ursprung* is concerned and, as will be seen in what follows, Brentano was later to give up some of the views which the note expresses. The note is not without value, however, for it contains a telling criticism of Sigwart's doctrine and it is essential for under-

standing those earlier views of Brentano which still survive in the writings of most of his followers.

⁴⁰ Now republished in Anton Marty, *Gesammelte Schriften* (Halle 1918), edited by J. Eisenmeier, A. Kastil, and O. Kraus, Vol. II, Part I.

⁴¹ Brentano's remarks are taken from note 25 of the first edition of *Vom Ursprung sittlicher Erkenntnis*; this part of the note does not appear in the second edition, for reasons that are explained in the Introduction to that edition. What is said in the note is not relevant to the context of that work, nor does it correspond to Brentano's later point of view. But it is relevant to the present work.

⁴² Brentano here defines the "existent" as that in relation to which the affirmative judgement is true or correct. His later theory gives us a more exact formulation of the thought behind this definition.

According to Brentano's later theory, such expressions as "existence", "being", "existing", are synsemantic, having no meaning by themselves; that is to say, "existence" and "being" do not name any kind of a thing, and "existing" and "having being" are not predicates, referring to any kind of attribute; each of these words is only a *denominatio mere extrinseca*. (This is not true, of course, of such expressions as "an existent", or "a being", which are used, not to refer to being in the sense of *existing*, but to refer to *thing* or *res*, in the Aristotelian sense.) Compare Vol. II of the *Psychologie*, Appendix XVII, "Vom ens rationis", and see the index under "Sein", "Seiendes", "Existenz", etc.

⁴³ Brentano is certainly right in saying that "A thing exists" does not imply the perceptibility of the thing. His examples, however, are unfortunately chosen, for they presuppose that such expressions as "deprivation", "possibility", "future", and the like are not synsemantic but have a meaning of their own. He might better have cited, as examples of what exists without being "perceptible", the inner, unconscious structure of the soul (*habitus*, as a permanent property) or the process of being affected or coming into being, in the case of physical bodies.

⁴⁴ I. e. one can infer that there is a necessary being, without thereby supposing that such a being must be "perceptible", in the usual sense of the word, by itself or by anything else.

⁴⁵ Strangely enough, there are many physicists and *Naturphilosophen* who would now say nothing can exist unless it is at least "in principle" observable.

⁴⁶ Brentano here says that the statement "Perhaps there is an empty space" is not at all absurd. He also says explicitly that empty space is not a thing. Hence he seems to have classified empty space among the *irrealia* which he was later to reject. The question turns upon how we are to understand "empty space". If it is intended to refer to a Newtonian, *irreal*, infinite empty space, then, according to Brentano's later view, the concept is contradictory (see *Psychologie*, Vol. II, pp. 262 ff., and "Raum und Zeit", in *Kantstudien*, Vol. 25, 1920, pp. 1–23). This infinite empty space pertains to the so-called possibility of places, but the latter comes to nothing more than the fact that spatial things

as such are not absurd or impossible. (For a more precise statement, see the *Psychologie*, Vol. II, pp. 254, 266.) But one might also take "empty space" to refer to a real spatial object having no qualitative determination. In such a case, empty space would be an extended thing and its stages could be regarded as physical conditions; the non-qualified space would then become under certain circumstances the bearer of such states. Empty space, in this latter sense of the term, is not a contradictory concept. One could doubtless say of such empty space that it is a thing and that it exists, even though it is not perceptible. (Compare Brentano's *Uber die Zukunft der Philosophie*, Leipzig 1929, ed. O. Kraus, pp. 137, 175.)

[47] This passage is now of historical interest. It makes clear that in 1889 Brentano interpreted the doctrine of intentionality in terms of the mental existence of the object, thus saying of the contemplated centaur (*den vorgestellten Zentaur*), the centaur that is an object of thought, that it exists as a correlate of the act of thinking about a centaur (see the second selection in this book and note 29). But he was soon to submit these ideas to criticism. By 1905 he was so far away from this doctrine that he even expressed doubts, in a letter to Marty, that he had ever held it. Thus he wrote: "It has never been my view that the immanent object is identical with the 'object of thought'. What we think about is the object or thing and not the 'object of thought'. If, in our thought, we contemplate a horse, the object of our thought is not a 'contemplated horse'; it is the horse itself which is the immanent object—the only thing that can strictly be called an object." (See the first letter in Part III of the present book.) But the passage in the paper on Sigwart cites the so-called immanent object as an example of a non-thing, an entity which is not an ὄν in the sense of the categories, but is an ὄν ὡς ἀληθές and thus something which may be said to exist. Marty also rejects the immanent object in his *Untersuchungen zur Grundlegung der allgemeinen Grammatik und Sprachphilosophie* (Halle 1908), but he replaces it by another untenable doctrine—that of consciousness as a "process of assimilation (*Verähnlichungsprozess*)" with the object. Husserl too seems inclined to reject the doctrine of the immanent object in his *Logische Untersuchungen*, but he is not entirely consistent, for he also seems to regard the objects of his sensuous intentions as being "real components (*Bestandstücke*) of consciousness" (Vol. II, pp. 238, 244). The older doctrine still haunts the *Ideen* (sections 88, 91) and appears in the correlative fictions of *Noema* and *Noese*. The Rehmke school, independently of Brentano, takes a strong stand against any distinction between object and content.

[48] This critique constitutes a definite rejection of the correspondence, or "adaequatio", theory; Brentano now seems to be preparing the way for the transition from the lecture on truth to his later views. In any case, he here anticipates a criticism of Marty's later version of the correspondence theory. This passage is also of interest in connection with Leonard Nelson's "Unmöglichkeit der Erkenntnistheorie", in *Abhandlungen der Fries'schen Schule*, Vol. III (Göttingen, 1911).

[49] Now reprinted in Marty's *Gesammelte Schriften*, Vol. II, Part I.

[50] Brentano here refers to the views which he defended in the main text of *Vom Ursprung sittlicher Erkenntnis*.

[51] Instead of saying "the fact that a given negative judgement is justified . . .", it would have been better to have said, "the fact that a given negative judgement would be justified if it were made . . ."

[52] One might doubt whether these comparative judgements are real predications, in which case another example would have been preferable. But this is of minor significance in relation to the question at issue.

[53] Sigwart contends that if we think of the negative judgement as a species co-ordinate with the affirmative judgement, we are committed to this consequence: since the affirmation of a man is included in the proposition "Some man is sick", the denial or rejection of a man should be included in "Some man is not sick". But Brentano replies: in the affirmation ("in the existence") of a sick man (which follows from the assertion that some man is sick) the affirmation of a man and of something sick is included. Hence to deny the whole it suffices either to deny that there is anything sick or to deny that there is a man. For if there is nothing sick, then there is no sick man. Therefore the subject of "Some man is sick" need not be denied in order to deny the whole. The proposition "Some man is not sick" would be false if there were no men, but if there are men, then "Some man is not sick" would be true provided there is nothing that is sick.

[54] What we have here is an *argumentatio ad hominem*, not an explication of the terms "true" and "false".

[55] In my opinion, Brentano's criticism of Sigwart at this point is correct insofar as it is directed against the contention that every positive judgement must be accompanied by a negative judgement which is an "awareness of the impossibility of the opposite". It is certain that such negative judgements do not always accompany positive judgements; consider in particular the positive judgements of inner and outer perception. But one may still ask whether our assertions of the form "*A* is", "*A* is not", "*A* is *B*", "*A* is not *B*", do not in fact express certain convictions in addition to the judgements directed upon *A* and upon *B*. It would seem to be the case that these linguistic formulations also contain the assertion of the correctness of the judgements about *A* and about *B*. Any such assertion of correctness, as Brentano shows here, is a negative judgement, which denies the possibility of the contradicting judgement being correct. What Sigwart thought to hold of *judgements* themselves actually holds only of the *linguistic expressions* of judgements; these linguistic formulations do bring several judgements to expression, of which one is necessarily negative. Thus if I say "There is a God", not only do I express my belief in God, but I also express my belief that it is correct to believe in God; in other words, I express my belief (as will be seen more clearly later) that a judgement contradicting my belief cannot possibly be correct. Analogously for the negative assertion "There is no God". In this case, the negative judgement that there is no God is the primary judgement; the secondary judgement is a second

negative judgement to the effect that there cannot possibly be a correct judgement contradicting the primary judgement. But from the fact that this second judgement in every case is apodictic, Sigwart is not entitled to infer that the first judgement is always apodictic. If I say, for example, "I am thinking", my assertion expresses an assertoric judgement the correctness of which may also be affirmed in an apodictic judgement. For further details, see George Katkov, "Bewusstsei n, Gegenstand, Sachverhalt', in *Archiv für Psychologie*, Vol. 75 (1930). It may be that Felix Weltsch has something similar in mind in saying that every *judgement* contains the "intention of its own correctness"; in "Kann die Evidenz Sanktion der Ethik sein?", *Ruch Filosoficky*, Vol. III.

[56] Compare the second edition of *Vom Ursprung sittlicher Erkenntnis*, Note 34, p. 59. Brentano here criticizes those modern philosophers who contend that every evident judgement depends upon the application of some criterion. If this contention were true, then the criterion itself would first have to be given in some way or other. It would be necessary to assume either that the criterion may be found in some property of ideas, in which case the criticism offered in the text is valid, or else that the criterion is known in some other way, in which case there would be an infinite regress. Conventionalists, such as Dingler, are aware of this fact; but they go wrong when they say that it constitutes a *reductio ad absurdum* of a properly conceived theory of the evident and when they speak of the resulting "collapse of science".

[57] Husserl's polemic against construing the evident in terms of a feeling (*Logische Untersuchungen*, Vol. I, Section 49, and Vol. II, Section 39) may be traced back to these observations. See the Introduction to the present book.

[58] This entire passage is of fundamental importance in connection with the theory of truth and the theory of the evident. See note 55.

[59] Brentano is far from wanting to deny that the defects of language have had unfortunate results upon theorizing about logic. His logic note-books contain a voluminous chapter about the dangers of language in its effect upon our thinking. The remark in the text is concerned only with cases that Sigwart discusses, which are not appropriate examples.

[60] Meinong defended the concept of "evident surmises". See Brentano's *Versuch über die Erkenntnis*, p. 209.

PART TWO (References 1 to 28)

[1] In the course of his correspondence on the problem of the formation of general concepts, Brentano had attempted to formulate a law which would indicate the relative nature of all simple concepts. He had accepted the traditional doctrine which holds that such words as "Size", "Redness", "Equality", etc., are logical names, i.e., that they signify concepts. But since redness cannot be conceived except as the redness of something, Brentano taught that "redness" (*Röte*) and "thing having redness" (*Röte-Habendes*) are correlative pairs of concepts. Since

"Redness", "Colour", "Size" and the like are nothing but the Aristotelian forms ("it is by virtue of their largeness that large things are large"), the theory could be considered only as one type of attempt to justify the Aristotelian theory. Each of the Aristotelian forms has as its correlate that which has the form. A set of questions raised by Marty caused Brentano to revise this theory. The result appears in the text. See also Brentano: *Aristoteles und seine Weltanschauung*, pp. 46 ff. ("Ursprung der Ideen"), and A. Marty: *Die "logische" usw. Kasustheorien*, pp. 93 ff. Compare Part III, note 44 below.

The *sprachkritische* reform, initiated by this letter of 1901, is one of the most significant achievements in epistemology and should be capable of settling the conflict between nominalism and realism. See the references to Vaihinger's radical theory of fictions in the index of the *Psychologie*, Vol. II.

² In other words, there is no such thing as "space" or "time"; there is only "the spatial" and "the temporal". And there is no "virtue", but there are "the virtuous". See Vols. II and III of the *Psychologie*, and section 21 of the following selection.

³ "Man", "animal", "stone", "house", and the like, signify concepts; but the grammatical *abstracta* and *synsemantica* ("humanity", "size", "form", "justice", "beauty") do not. See the appendix of Vol. III of the *Psychologie*.

⁴ "Indicating what we have in mind" (*Anzeigen, was wir im Gemüte hegen*) is what Marty called the "secondary intention" of the speaker. He took the "primary intention" to be that of producing a certain mental event in the listener. The primary intention of using a name would be to call up an idea; that of making a statement would be to produce a judgement; and that of coaxing, ordering, or requiring would be to produce certain feelings or emotions. Some of Brentano's discussions of the purpose of language are similar to the views of Marty. See Marty's *Untersuchungen*, etc., Halle 1908.

⁵ The manuscript reads "true (*wahren*)"; the word "genuine (*echten*)" has been inserted in order to avoid ambiguity.

⁶ What Brentano here calls particles in the widest sense of the word do not quite coincide with what Marty calls synsemantic signs. See Marty's *Untersuchungen*, pt. II, ch. 1. The distinction between words that are autosemantic and those that are merely synsemantic has recently been repudiated on the ground that one always "thinks something", even in connection with so-called merely semantic words; as is well known, some ideas, especially anticipations of meaning, are regularly aroused through the "constructive inner form of language". But I should like to leave such views to self-criticism. They stand in the way of the *only* road there is which frees us from the epistemological-phenomenological fictions of ancient and modern philosophy.

⁷ According to Brentano, even names are "sentence-particles" in the widest sense of the word. These include the names which Marty called theoretical *autosemantica*—for example, "stone", "animal", "man", "table". They also include what are merely names in the grammatical

sense—words which do not name anything, but which because of the structure of the sentence serve to arouse anticipatory expectations fixing the meaning of what is said. See the references to "synkategorische Partikel" in the index to Vol. II of the *Psychologie*.

[8] "Signifying itself" (*für sich bedeuten*) and "indicating something about itself" (*für sich etwas anzeigen*) are two quite different functions. Compare note 4 above.

[9] In accordance with what is said in the previous note, we are here concerned with conveying information and not with meaning.

[10] "Considering the thing positively" should be replaced by "thinking of". At the same time that he wrote this paper, Brentano doubted whether his concept of "thinking of", in this sense, should be retained.

[11] The theory of the fictitious character of the so-called formal words (*grammatical abstracta*) is here extended to the so-called *reflexiva* and *negativa*.

[12] "That which is a thing" here signifies, as so often elsewhere, the highest general concept.

[13] Brentano does not mean to say that the expressions "thought" (*gedacht*) and "willed" (*gewollt*) are synonymous with "that which thinks" (*Denkendes*) and "that which wills" (*Wollendes*); the former words taken just by themselves are completely meaningless. He means rather that the thought of a willing or thinking being must be called up if the expressions "thought" or "willed" are to perform their synsemantic function in the sentence.

[13] Analogously, the sentence "A visible black spot is presented" says only that there is someone seeing a black spot. Bertrand Russell offers the contrary interpretation, however, on page 227 of his book, *Mensch und Welt* (Munich 1930). He does not notice that, in the sentence "An observed black spot is present," the word "observed" functions synsemantically. Instead of adding to the concept of the subject-term, it modifies it (in the way in which "deceased" may modify "man"). Because of this fact, the use of "is present" is different from its use in such a sentence as "A person is present". In the latter case, the expression "is present" or "there is" serves to complete the statement by expressing the acceptance or acknowledgement of a person. But saying "There is an observed black spot" is like saying "There is an imagined centaur"; the latter tells us only that there is someone who imagines a centaur. In *Our Knowledge of the External World*, Russell moves beyond Wittgenstein and adopts the Brentano-Marty theory of synsemantic words (beginnings of which may be found, among the moderns, in Mill's theory of the syncategorematic). Thus Russell cites "there is" among his examples of what is synsemantic. He does not notice, however, that such expressions as "the observed", "the seen", "the loved", and "the believed" are not names and hence that they too are "incapable of being the logical subject of a meaningful proposition". They signify neither things nor properties of things. The statement "There is an observed spot of colour" expresses in a misleading way the belief that someone is observing a spot of colour. For further details, see *Psychologie*,

Vol. II, p. 62, and Marty's *Untersuchungen*, etc.; note the references to "Modifizierende Bedeutung" in the index to the latter work.

[15] "Meaning" is here to be taken in its widest sense, as "use" or "function", and thus pertains, not only to what has meaning in the strict sense, but also to that which is merely synsemantic.

[16] This paragraph shows that, at the time it was written, Brentano had not completely abandoned the correspondence theory. The question raised here—"Is 'existent' a logical name?"—is answered negatively in the following paragraph.

[17] What Brentano here says about the distinction between "There is an A" and "A is existent" is not in accord with his later thought. Any distinction between "There is an A" and "A is existent" would come to this: the latter expression emphasizes one's conviction that the acceptance or affirmation of A is correct.

[18] In other words: "If there is an A then there is a B" cannot be rendered as "The being of A does not exist without the being of B". For "being" is only a synsemantic word and not a genuine name. The expression "does not exist" has one function in "The being of A does not exist", and quite a different function in "The devil does not exist"; in the latter case, it is used with a genuine name. The true function of these synsemantica is indicated in paragraphs 30 and 31 of this essay.

[19] This little essay is more advanced than the previous one of the year 1904.

[20] "The Good", "the Beautiful", and "the True", are here treated as *denominationes mere extrinsecae*. They are synsemantic expressions which appear to state something about the grammatical subject with which they are conjoined. "Knowledge is good", for example, tells us this: it is impossible at one and the same time to value knowledge correctly and not to value it positively (where "to value positively" means to love). On the predicate "true", see the Introduction and the discussion that follows.

[21] For example, the spatial falls under these determinations: the extended, the three-dimensional, the shaped, the temporal. It is impossible to conceive a spatial thing lacking such determinations.

[22] The essential determination "the spatial" overlaps with the essential determination "the temporal"; "extended" overlaps with "shaped". In other words, there are several lines or series of predications.

[23] "The thinker" is accidental with respect to "the soul", just as "the qualitative" is accidental with respect to "the spatial"; for the soul can cease to think, and the spatial can cease to be qualitative.

[24] Brentano believed that the evident, for example, inheres (*inhäriert*) in the judgement, just as the judgement, in turn, inheres in the thought or idea (*Vorstellung*), and the thought or idea in the soul. In other words: the soul underlies the thinking; the thinking underlies the judging; and the judging underlies the evident. The soul is the substratum of consciousness, the spatial the substratum of qualities.

[25] If the form or shape disappears or changes, the spatial object disappears or changes, and conversely.

26 The accident (the property, the quality) may be lost while the substance continues to exist; but the converse is impossible.
27 A collective and a continuum are wholes of which one part can continue to exist while others cease to exist.
28 Thus one who observes a continuous multiplicity of things might be called a continuously multifarious observer. For further details, see the *Psychologie*, Vol. III, pp. 81 ff. This little essay is a theory of categories *in nuce*; it is included here especially because of paragraphs 3 to 5. The theory of categories itself is taken up in a separate volume: Franz Brentano, *Kategorienlehre* (Leipzig 1933), ed. Alfred Kastil.

PART THREE (References 1 to 47)

1 This first letter is intended only to clear up a few deep-rooted errors about the theory of the "immanent object", and, in particular, certain misunderstandings propagated by some of Brentano's pupils. In thinking, I always have something as the object of my thinking, or as the content of my thinking; but whether or not there *is* such an object is something else again. Following old lectures of Brentano, some have made a threefold distinction, between the *act*, or intentional relation, the *content*, or immanent object, and *thirdly*, the object itself. But this threefold distinction cannot be made phenomenognostically—phenomenologically—with reference to the act of *thinking*. For the distinction brings up the question whether the thing that I am thinking about exists or not. And this question can be answered only by considering the acts of *judgement* which pertain to the thing I am thinking about. When our concern is only with thinking, then we should not take acts of judgement into account.
2 The report on the Fifth International Psychological Congress (Rome 1905) contained many typographical errors, and Brentano's lecture *Von der psychologischen Analyse der Tonqualitäten* had been rather badly garbled. This lecture contains Brentano's "Zweikomponentenlehre" which he had formulated long before Revesz. For further details, see Brentano's *Untersuchungen zur Sinnespsychologie* (Leipzig 1907), and *Vom sinnlichen und noetischen Bewusstsein* (Vol. III of the *Psychologie*), Part I.
3 The nature of Höfler's remarks, against which Brentano's polemic is directed, may be gathered from the wording of the letter. Evidently he had attributed the following theory to Brentano: that someone who thinks of *A* has, as his object or content, "the *A* which is thought about", where "object" and "content" are used synonymously. Compare my edition of the *Psychologie*, particularly Vol. I, where Brentano emphasizes (e.g., p. 172) that hearing has a content, or object, different from the hearing itself—namely, the sound and *not* the heard sound. But there are passages in the *Psychologie* which might be misunderstood (e.g., Vol. I, pp. 31 and 177). It is certain, however, that Brentano always held that we hear the tone and not the heard tone, we believe in God and not in the believed-in God, we deny God and not the denied God. But

he had held earlier that there is a certain correlation between the intentional relation and the object of this relation. (See the Introduction to Vol. I of the *Psychologie*.)

In Höfler's Congress lecture (*Atti*, Rome, 1906, p. 327) we also find Brentano criticized for using "content" and "intentional object" synonymously. Of course this is a matter only of terminology. But to avoid ambiguity, it is preferable not to speak of "content" in connection with judgements, where it is customary to say of two judgements, having the same *object*, that they may differ in *content*, depending upon whether they are affirmative or negative, assertoric or apodictic. Marty spoke of the contents of judgements in a wholly different sense, using the term synonymously with "state of affairs" (*Sachverhalt*) or "objective" (Meinong).

There is no terminological agreement whatever in this area. Unfortunate as this may be, no respectable psychologist or epistemologist who uses the expression "content of consciousness" would make the mistake to which the members of the Rehmke school refer (most recently Heyde, in the Journal *Grundwissenschaft*, Vol. IX). According to Rehmke and his followers, "*content* of consciousness" implies that consciousness must be spatial, like a container or vessel. I may reassure him that the "inner linguistic form" has not seduced us into taking the word in this way. Strictly speaking, one could not even use our German word for thinking—i.e., "*Vorstellen*"—without giving rise to the suspicion that we intend a kind of spatial confrontation (*Vor-sich-Hinstellen*).

Brentano does admit that the term "content" should not be used as a synonym for "object". In *Von der Klassifikation der psychischen Phänomene* (1911), now Vol. II of the *Psychologie*, Brentano states that it is advisable not to use "content" for *object* of thought: "No one could possibly say that, because the judgements 'God exists' and 'God does not exist' have the same object, they also have the same content" (p. 39). Nevertheless it is now customary to speak of the "content" of a concept (of a conceptual idea) and to distinguish it from its range or extension (*Umfange*).

Marty discusses the term "content" in considerable detail in his *Untersuchungen zur Grundlegung der allgemeinen Grammatik und Sprachphilosophie* (Halle, 1908). This term, which has been so greatly used and misused, does indeed receive still another meaning from Marty, insofar as he uses it synonymously with "state of affairs" (*Sachverhalt*) and in the way in which Meinong and Russell use "objective". On this point, there is much critical material in my edition of Brentano's *Psychologie*. In the editions of the *Psychologie*, and elsewhere, I have made it a rule never to interpret "content" as synonymous with "object", despite the fact that even now one often speaks of the content of visual sensation, meaning thereby the coloured thing which we intuit.

The Rehmke school refuses to speak of the "psychical relation to a thing" and refers instead to the "*having* of this thing". According to this manner of speaking, one who sees or perceives a house or a ducat *has* a house or a ducat. But "to have" is easily interpreted to mean possession, which comprises a spatial-physical relation. Use of this word does not improve matters in the least, for here too one must emancipate oneself from the "inner linguistic form". This is why Brentano expresses the so-called psychical relation by means of the longer expression, "to have as object", saying "I have something coloured as object (*zum Objekt oder Geganstand*)". If one understands by "relation" something requiring the existence of two terms and their connection, then admittedly we are not dealing here with a relation in the strict sense of the term. Hence Brentano late abandoned the term "relation", and referred instead to "something relative (*etwas Relativlichem*)". (Incidentally, I should take the opportunity to correct an error I made in the introduction to the new edition of Vol. I of the *Psychologie*. I said there that the psychological relation constituted the archetype of all relations. But actually the archetypes of all relations are neither the psychological or intentional relations, nor the so-called comparative relations. They are, rather, real relations, such as are involved in causation, in continuity, and in the relations between substance and accident. The error in question was not made by Brentano, as Fernkorn assumes in *Grundwissenschaft*, Vol. IX, p. 201, but by me.) It is remarkable indeed that Heyde elsewhere rejects the expression "I am related to a tree" and yet holds that the tree is related to me. How can the tree or the house have a relation to me if I am not related to it? Similarly, we should not say that, if a person sees or hears something, he thereby experiences that thing. One experiences the seeing and hearing, but one does not experience the *object* of the seeing and hearing.

One experiences states of consciousness, the state of being conscious of objects, but one does not *experience* the objects. I perceive a spot of colour, I "see" a friend or a bus, but I do not experience either one of them. The term "experience" loses its ordinary sense, and we give rise to a new source of equivocation, if we apply it not only to the perception of one's own experience (i.e., to one's conscious states), but also to the primary objects of these experiences.

4 The question whether the object exists "outside the mind" is not a question that pertains to thinking alone or to the phenomenognostic description of the act of thinking. If I think about a Pegasus, one says that "Pegasus" is the "intentional or immanent object" of the thought. In this case there would be an immanent object, but no real or existing object. But if I think about the moon, then, along with the so-called immanent object, there would also be a real object, an object which exists "outside the mind". Brentano's letter is concerned with the locution "immanent, intentional", but there is more that is left to be said. For further details, see the new edition of Brentano's *Psychologie*, and in particular my introduction to the first and third volumes. The Rehmke school also disapproves of such expressions as "inside and outside the mind", as though one here considered the mind as a kind of container or vessel. As long as there is no *characteristica universalis*, one must put up with such metaphorical expressions. After all, Rehmke and

his followers speak of "grasping a theorem" or of an "introduction to philosophy" without taking "grasping" and "introduction" in their original senses.

[5] This locution shows that the designation of consciousness as "psychic relation" is not to be taken literally, as I have indicated above in connection with Rehmke. Thus, as already noted, Brentano later described consciousness not as a relation, but as something relational (*etwas Relativliches*). Every relation, in the strict sense of the word, requires the existence of two terms. This should take care of Rehmke's "relationless having".

[6] Here Brentano expressly says "linguistic correlate". The locution "corresponding outside", once again, might give the followers of Rehmke's "Grundwissenschaft" occasion to note that this "outside" must be contrasted with an "inside" and therefore that it is spatial. I suppose it is superfluous to remark that Brentano is saying only that I can have something as object of my thinking even though that something does not exist.

[7] The meaning of this hastily written sentence, which was revised in many places in the original, is this: if we suppose that the *contemplated horse*, and not just the horse, is to be looked upon as the *object* of the thinking, then this "immanent object"—the contemplated horse— would be the correlate to the "thinking or contemplation of the horse". But correlates are such that one cannot be thought without the other; hence anyone who thinks about the "contemplated horse" must also think about the "thinking about a horse", and conversely. This "thinking about a horse" is an object of inner perception; thus the "contemplated horse" as well as the thinking about it would be objects of inner perception. But the next sentence of the letter indicates that the objects of our sense-experience—for example, the sense-qualities—and the objects of our conceptual thinking are objects only of primary consciousness; they are never objects of inner perception (i.e., of secondary consciousness).

[8] Brentano is saying that, so far as he knows, he never held the "contemplated horse" to be an object of primary consciousness. For this would have been tantamount to *denying* that there is an object of primary consciousness. The "contemplated horse", according to what was said before, is an object of secondary and not primary consciousness. Compare Franz Hillebrand, *Die neuen Theorien der kategorischen Schlüsse* (Vienna 1891)., p. 37.

In connection with all these considerations, compare the new edition of the *Psychologie vom empirischen Standpunkt*, especially Vol. I, Introduction, Vol. II (*Von der Klassifikation der psychischen Phänomene*), and, last but not least, the introduction to Vol. III (*Vom sinnlichen und noetischen Bewusstsein*) which contains several corrections pertaining to the introduction to Vol. I.

[9] Here and in other places personal communications have been left out and are indicated by " . . . ."

Finally, the following ought to be noted. Alois Höfler states in his

Logik (Vienna 1890), Section 6: "In contrast with the object (*Gegenstand oder Objekt*) which is assumed to be independent of thought, the *content* of a thought or judgement (as well as of feeling and volition) is called the 'immanent or intentional object'." What he is really concerned with here is this: if I think about something which does not exist, say a Pegasus, then the thought does have an object, which may be referred to as "immanent". But it has no "object *per se* (*Objekt schlechtweg*)", no object which is "assumed to be independent of thinking". What does this mean? Only that what I have as immanent object, i.e., what I am thinking about, does not exist, and thus cannot possibly be the object of an evident affirmative judgement.

On the other hand, if I think of a *horse* (i.e., of something existing independently of my thinking), then I have as immanent object something that cannot possibly be the object of a correct *rejection* or denial. One easily overlooks the fact—this is especially true of Husserl in the present context—that the word "object" has a twofold use. The sentence, "I have a horse as object (as object or content of my thought)", means no more than "I am thinking of a horse". The word "object" functions here *synsemantically*: it lacks autosemantic meaning. But if I say that the tree is not merely an object of my thinking, but also that it exists as an object *per se*, as a "thing in nature" (Husserl, *Ideen*, I, p. 184), then "object" means the same as "thing" (for the two words are often used interchangeably) and is thus being used autosemantically. For this reason it is misleading to distinguish between the "tree as immanent object" and the "tree *per se* (*Baum schlechthin*)". To say "The tree exists as the immanent object of my thought" is to say only "I am thinking of the tree"; so far as the mere thinking is concerned, the question whether the tree exists out there or not may remain undecided ("bracketed"). But if the tree exists and I "perceive" it, then the situation is entirely different. In this case not only do I have the tree *per se*, the *thing*, as my object (i.e. not only do I think of it), but I also accept it or believe in it and do so correctly (thus having a belief which is such that its contrary cannot possibly be evident).

When Husserl writes in the *Ideen* (p. 187) that "the real object is to be bracketed", he is saying only that the thing (the thing in nature) is not to be judged about, when one is giving an account of the nature of *thinking* as such, and that the question whether the tree can be rightly accepted or rejected is beside the point.

If Husserl also requires that the tree as a real thing be "bracketed" in the case of *perception*, then he is asking us to disregard "the suggestion of reality" (*Wirklichkeitssuggestion*), i.e. to disregard the belief in the tree and to think of perception as a mere thought or idea. He is far from having made his views clear to himself or to others. For this purpose he would have to recognize that in the sentence, "I have a tree as an intentional object", the word "object" functions only *synsemantically*, and that in the sentence "The tree is an object *per se*", it functions *autosemantically*, as I have indicated in my introduction to Vol. I of the *Psychologie*. "The tree is my intentional object" is synsemantic in more than one respect, since the word "object" and the word "is" both function only synsemantically. For the point is, not that the tree is an object, but that I am one who has the tree as an object, i.e. that I am one who is thinking of a tree. And this is also true if the tree exists. "Being an object" is not a predicate which is ascribed to the real tree; it is a *denominatio mere extrinseca*.

Husserl says that "the non-existence, or the conviction of the non-existence", of the object thought about cannot deprive the thinking of its object (*Ideen*, p. 185). But this means only that the conviction, this judgement of the "reduced perception", does not affect the thinking as such. The more one reflects on all this, the more clearly one realizes that the talk about "bracketing" yields only another unclear metaphor and not an analysis.

It requires no great phenomenological insight to realize that the tree *per se* might be consumed in flames, while the intentionally existing tree, or the tree "in phenomenological reduction" remains untouched (*Ideen*, p. 184). It has never yet occurred to anyone to take out fire insurance to protect his "idea of a tree".

[10] Marty is not entirely consistent in his treatment of the so-called "irrealia". To be sure, he follows Brentano's doctrine with respect to the analysis of form words such as "colour", "redness", etc. He believes, however, that he must acknowledge empty space and time as *entia irrealia*; see A. Marty, *Raum und Zeit* (Halle 1916), especially pp. 92 ff. On page 97 Marty says: "We should count as *abstracta*, and hence as fictions, not only colour, quality, quantity, and such like, but also similarity, difference, equality, causality, as well as existence, non-existence, possibility, necessity, impossibility, *being present, being future,* and even *being coloured, being spatially located,* and such like." In view of these concessions, Marty is hardly consistent in adding, "But I definitely do not count the contents of judgement among such fictions." He holds that, in the case of every negative judgement, there is a state of affairs constituting the basis or justification for asserting the judgement or for asserting it apodictically. But this last desperate attempt to uphold the theory of "states of affairs" and "contents of judgements" is a contradiction in terms. For "state of affairs" either signifies the *things*, concerning which we judge either that they are or that they are not, or it signifies their "existence" or "non-existence". But Marty, like Brentano, indeed even before Brentano, referred to the "existence" and "non-existence" of things as fictions. See Brentano's letter to me, dated 31 October, 1914, and my comments upon it. Recently the doctrine of "states of affairs" has come to play a role in experimental psychology; Bühler, for example, constructs his philosophy of language on the assumption of "states of affairs", as does Lindworsky.

[11] This passage is concerned with the connection between *modo recto* and *modo obliquo*; for further details see the appendix and index to Vol. II of the *Psychologie*.

[12] According to Marty, the content of judgement is most naturally conceived as that which provides the objective basis of the correctness

of the judgement, or, more exactly, as that without which our attitude could not be said to be correct or adequate. The content of the judgement "*A* is", according to this conception, would be "the being of *A*"; that of the judgement "*A* is *B*", would be "the being-*B* of *A*"; and so on. See A. Marty, *Untersuchungen zur Grundlegung der allgemeinen Grammatik und Sprachphilosophie* (Halle 1908), p. 294 and elsewhere; see index under "Inhalt".

13 See the Appendix to Vol. II of the *Psychologie* and "Neue Abhandlungen aus dem Nachlass", in the same volume, especially selection XIV and those that follow.

14 "Thing" (*Reales*), or "*res*", is a term indicating the most general concept which can be abstracted from our intuitions. The expression encompasses not only inanimate things, but everything that can be thought about at all. Ordinary language has no fixed universal term for this concept other than the pronoun "something" (*etwas*). Aristotle believed that there is no such most general concept. "Thing" is not to be confused with "actual", since one may say of many things that they are *not* actual; but everything that is actual, on the other hand, is a thing. See the Introduction to Vol. I of the *Psychologie*.

15 The example is not entirely appropriate. A more suitable one appears in paragraph 2. If I merely *think about* the impossibility of a thing, I think about an apodoctic judgement which correctly rejects the thing. The matter is different if one *affirms* the so-called "impossibility" of a thing; in this case one not only thinks about someone rejecting the thing apodictically, but one also rejects it apodictically oneself. For further details, see Vol. II of the *Psychologie* and the introduction to Vol. I.

16 Examples of temporal *entia rationis* would be the past, the present, the future, and also that which is past (*Vergangenes*), that which is present (*Gegenwartiges*), that which is future (*Zukünftiges*). On Brentano's phenomenognostic theory of time, see Vol. II of the *Psychologie*; see also note 19 below.

17 If Marty's theory were correct, I could not make the judgement "There is the impossibility of *A*" without simultaneously rejecting *A* apodictically.

18 The important question for Marty was: What is the meaning of the sentence "The judgement that '*A* is' is correct"? Marty supposed that correctness referred to the adequacy or correspondence of the judgement "*A* is" with the "being of *A*". Brentano thereupon replied, "The point is not that, if the *being* of *A* is and someone judges *A* is, he then judges correctly; the point is, rather, that if *A* is and someone judges *A* is, he then judges correctly." What does this mean? Simply that if the *A*-affirming judgement is correct and someone accepts or affirms *A*, then he judges correctly. But to say this is not to answer the question, "What are we to understand by a *correct* judgement?" Brentano immediately takes this up, however. In any case, what is said here is sufficient to show that "There is the *being* of *A*", correctly understood, says only that "*A* is".

19 If I know that a judgement is correct, then I must have judged with

insight myself. The strict concept of "correct judgement" is "judgement with insight" or "apprehension". But one does call judgements "correct" which are not in fact apprehensions or cognitions and which, furthermore, are not known by anyone actually to correspond with any cognition. We say, for example, that the judgement "2 plus 2 is equal to 4" is correct even if no one makes this judgement with insight. In saying this, we mean only to express our conviction that no one who contradicts the judgement in question could possibly be judging with evidence himself (in any of the temporal modes). Compare the letter by Brentano which is printed in my introduction to Vol. I of the *Psychologie*, and the introduction to the present book.

Brentano assumes that the reader is familiar with the theory of temporal modes on which he had been lecturing since 1894–95. He first published his theory in the *Klassifikation der psychischen Phänomene* in 1911. This note may serve to correct Husserl's lecture of 1928; the editor of the lecture makes no mention of the fact that the theory which is there represented as Brentano's had long been abandoned in favour of a theory of temporal modes. See the *Archiv für die gesamte Psychologie*, LXXV (1930), where I juxtapose Brentano's earlier and later theories and compare them with Husserl's.

[20] Suppose, for example, that *A* is in pain and that *B* judges "*A* is in pain". In this case *B*'s judgement is correct, for it agrees with the evident judgement of inner perception whereby *A* perceives his pain. A judgement contrary to this perception could not possibly be evident. Suppose now that *A*'s pain ceases, because *A* has lost consciousness, and that *B*'s judgement continues unchanged. An evident judgement referring to *A*'s pain can no longer be affirmative, since the affirmative judgement of *B* can no longer be correct.

"The being of *A* begins (or ceases)" means no more nor less than "*A* begins (or ceases)". To say that the judgement "*A* begins (or ceases)" is *correct*, in those cases where the judgement is not itself made with evidence, is to say no more nor less than this: "From now on, it would be impossible for anyone, making an evident judgement with respect to *A*, to reject (or affirm) *A*". In other words, an *evident* negative (or affirmative) judgement with respect to *A* is no longer possible.

[21] If it were necessary to grasp the *being* of *A* in order to apprehend *A*, then it would be necessary to grasp the being of the being of *A* in order to grasp the being of *A*, etc.

[22] See Vol. II of Brentano's *Psychologie*, and in particular the appendix entitled "Von der psychischen Beziehung auf etwas, als sekundäres Objekt".

[23] On Plato's theory of ideas, compare O. Kraus, "Die 'kopernikanische Wendung' in Brentanos Erkenntnis- und Wertlehre", in *Philosophische Hefte*, Vol. III (1929).

[24] Compare the letter above of 2 Sept., 1909, and that of 14 Sept., published in the introduction of Vol. I of the *Psychologie*. For further details see Vol. II of the *Psychologie*.

[25] It is this particular sentence and its application to the present question

which I found difficult; but it is clarified later in this same letter.
[26] If I think about the "non-being of a body" or, differently formulated, if I consider that a body does not exist, i.e., that there are no bodies, then either I am thinking about the correct rejection or denial of a body or I am thinking about the incorrect acceptance or affirmation of a body; I am thinking about someone apodictically rejecting the evident affirmation of a body. Either "There is the non-being of a body" tells us simply that there are no bodies, or it tells us that the judgement "There is a body" cannot possibly be evident.
[27] I had argued: Brentano contradicts himself if he holds that one cannot think about what is a non-thing, for, in the very fact of expressing this statement, he does think of a non-thing and says of it that it cannot be thought. But the error was entirely mine. To say that one cannot think of a non-thing is to say only that one cannot think unless what one is thinking about is a thing. I had asked: "What could Brentano mean by saying that there are no non-things, that there cannot be any *irrealia*?" And the answer is: "No one can judge with evidence that what it is that he accepts or affirms is not a thing."
[28] I had been puzzled by this theory of "implicit thinking". I told myself that what goes on when I think about a "sparrow" is this: at times I might think of nothing more than "that which is called sparrow" or "the creature called sparrow". Or I might think: a tiny winged creature that peeps. In short, an entirely unscientific synthesis of concepts. It would be out of the question to say that, in thinking of a sparrow, one thinks of all the physical parts, or indeed of all the logical parts, i.e., of all those characteristics which would make up a complete scientific definition of a sparrow. In this way, I contradicted Brentano's thesis.

The explication, given by this letter and the one that follows, led to the result which I may anticipate here: The "explicit thought" of a sparrow is to be understood as the thought of all of its essential characteristics (*Merkmale*), i.e., of all those conceptual properties which would be ascribed to the sparrow as a result of a complete acquaintance with it; such a thought would be a clear and distinct idea of all the sparrow's physical, logical and other "parts". But we never have such a totally explicit thought of a sparrow. If we did have such an explicit thought, then in accepting or affirming a sparrow, we would do so in accordance with the entire explicit content. But now Brentano says that when we think about a sparrow and make a judgement with respect to it, the physical and logical parts are only implicit. This "implicit thinking" and judging is not intended to be a psychological, phenomenognostic characterization. We are not concerned here with a certain kind of thinking and judging. Instead we are giving expression to the axiomatic truth that, when a sparrow is correctly accepted or affirmed, then one could not correctly deny of it any of those characteristics which a completely explicit thought would include. This is what is meant by Brentano's statement that, since the parts of the sparrow are only implicitly thought, they are only implicitly judged.

[29] If, in affirming or accepting a sparrow, I were to deny that there are birds, I would contradict myself, just as I would if I were to deny any of the parts that are essential to a sparrow. If I affirm or accept anything at all and at the same time reject or deny what is an essential part of that thing or what is one of its essential characteristics, I would contradict myself. To this extent, the positive judgement does indeed judge in accordance with the total content. We are not saying that this is something that one takes note of when one makes a judgement. The point in question is like the law of contradiction in that it is simply axiomatic.

[30] If there were such a thing as a distinct thought of a sparrow, then all the parts would have to be thought (both physical and logical parts— in short, any of the parts which cannot be correctly denied when the sparrow is correctly affirmed). By exactly the same token, the distinct, explicit thought of the *non-being* of a sparrow, if there were such a thought, would have to include all the parts of this non-being of the sparrow, hence all the parts which cannot be correctly denied when the non-being of the sparrow is correctly affirmed. If the non-being of a sparrow is correctly affirmed, then one cannot correctly deny the non-being of a healthy, sick, wild, male, young, old, or female sparrow and a dog, etc. The non-being of all these things and much more would have to be thought simultaneously with the distinct thought of the non-being of a sparrow. But all this is manifestly absurd. Moreover, one cannot deny that if the supposed thought of the non-being of a sparrow is to be completely distinct, it requires nothing more than the thought of a sparrow and the thought of its evident rejection or denial. The next letter makes this entirely clear. See note 28 above.

[31] In order to arrive at the concept of that which is not a thing (*der Begriffe vom Irrealem*), Marty was forced to imagine or invent special sources of abstraction.

[32] For example, I cannot intuit my *seeing* without also intuiting *what* it is that I see; what I see is the primary object of the intuition, and my seeing of it is the secondary object.

[33] Brentano here refers to the view that, wherever the concept of "the correct" is applicable, there must be an agreement or correspondence, and that this agreement or correspondence is a relation, not to a *thing*, but to a "state of affairs", "proposition" (Russell), "objective" (Meinong), "content" (Marty), or, in the case of valuing, a relation to a "value" or to a "state of value". But all these supposed entities are fictitious.

[34] In a letter to O. Kraus dated 14 November, 1909, which is published in the Introduction to Vol. I of the *Psychologie*, Brentano writes:

"It is paradoxical in the highest degree to say that what a man promises to marry is an *ens rationis* and that he keeps his word by marrying a real person. It would be just as paradoxical to say that, if everything real were to be destroyed, a process would continue on throughout infinity in which that which was yesterday would become that which was the day before yesterday, and then become that which was the day before the day before yesterday, and so on."

35 In fact, Brentano's epoch-making discoveries have opened up vast perspectives and we cannot even begin to envisage their significance for philosophy. To be sure, Brentano has already provided many important applications in a long series of essays, of which only a few have been published up to now (as appendices to Vols. II and III of the *Psychologie*). In carrying out these analyses one constantly encounters new problems; we have been working on these without interruption, since 1916 when we first began to understand the new theory. The later views are so revolutionary that they require an almost continuous translation of traditional modes of expression; for these modes of expression, like the ordinary language in which they originate, are almost completely permeated with fictions of the inner form of language. While the so-called *phenomenology* of Husserl sets the Ossa towering upon the Pelion of fictions, Brentano's *Phänomenognosie* strips this ontological spook-world of its very foundations.

36 The "non-being of a cow" contains the non-being of a two-year-old cow, of a white cow, of a cow with a herdsman, etc. Whatever is thought of as an essential physical or logical part of an object in a completely explicit idea of that object belongs to the "content" of that idea and could not be correctly denied if the object were correctly affirmed. And conversely: all those things which cannot correctly be denied of the object if the object is to be correctly affirmed would be included in any explicit idea of the object. If one correctly affirms the non-being of a cow, one cannot correctly deny the non-being of a white cow, of a two-year-old cow, etc. It is as if these non-beings were contained in the non-being of a cow as parts and were thus such that they would have to be thought of if that non-being were to be thought in complete distinctness. But this is only "as if", for the idea of the "non-being of a cow" is a mere fiction. Actually a clear analysis of this pseudo-concept will show that it contains none of the things it would have to contain if we really *could* think of "ideal objects" such as non-being, impossibility, and the like.

37 This extremely important theory of the universality of all our intuitions, outer as well as inner, is set forth in detail in Vol. II of the *Psychologie*; see also Vol. III. Up to this time, it has been almost universally held that our sensations can present us with that which is individual; and similarly for inner perception. But Brentano returns to the Aristotelian doctrine here, however much he may deviate from Aristotle with respect to other fundamental points.

38 See note 19 above concerning the third letter to Marty (2 September, 1906). As indicated there, Brentano first set forth his theory of temporal modes in 1894–95. In its initial version it was a theory of the modes of *judgement*; later, around 1905, it also became a theory of the modes of *thinking*.

39 Brentano's expression, "the concept horse and its *falsehood*" is inexact. The proper formulation would be "the concept *horse* and its evident rejection" or "the concept horse and the apodictic rejection of the evidence of its affirmation".

[40] The points that are set forth in this selection might be summarized as follows:

Positive judgements which have a general matter—i.e., which are concerned with the objects of general concepts—are *particular*; that is to say, they do *not* affirm the concept in its *total extension*. For example, even though the positive judgement, "There is a dog", is correct, the negative judgement, "There is no red dog, no dog that sings, no dog with a diamond necklace, no dog with a bitch, no dog with a marble palace (etc., etc.)", may also be correct. In other words: negative judgements about objects, having "dog" as physical or logical part, may be correct in spite of the fact that the judgement *affirming* a dog is also correct. Although positive judgements, therefore, do not affirm the concept in its entire *extension*, they do affirm the concept in its entire content. If a dog is correctly affirmed, then there cannot be a correct judgement which rejects any of the parts (or marks) of the content of the concept of a dog; neither the "physical parts" (e.g., the mouth and the tail) nor the "logical parts" (falling under such general concepts as mammal, creature, and thing) could be correctly denied.

We may think about what is designated by the word "dog" without thinking about everything which thus belongs to the content of the concept dog; we need only think of some part of the content. But if we were to think of the content in its totality and full distinctness, then we would have to think of the entire content; we would have to think of the concepts of mammal, creature, thing, and in their characteristic arrangement and totality.

Negative judgements which have a general matter—i.e., which are concerned with the objects of general concepts—are universal; they deny the concept in its entire extension. If the judgement "There is no dog" is correct, then no judgement affirming any dog may be correct—whether the dog be a red dog, a singing dog, a pug, a St Bernard, a dog with a diamond collar. If the judgement denying a dog is correct, then no judgement affirming a dog or affirming any object having all the physical or logical parts of "dog" can be correct.

Negative judgements having a general matter, however, do *not* deny the entire *content*. If I correctly deny or reject a red dog, then the judgement that there is a creature, a thing, a dog, something red, a mammal, may be correct, in spite of the fact that all these objects belong to the content of the concept "red dog". They are its physical or logical parts.

Let us assume that "the non-being of a red dog" is an object of a conceptual thought or idea, that we are capable of thinking of it and judging about it. Let us now apply the axiomatic truths which we just developed: if we affirm the "non-being of a red dog", we affirm it in its entire content, that is, we affirm it with respect to all its physical and logical parts. But what would these physical and logical parts be? The parts of the red dog? When we affirm the non-being of a red dog, we do not thereby affirm the non-being of a dog or the non-being of a red thing. For there may be red things and dogs of other colours. Nor do we thereby affirm the non-being of a mammal, or of a living creature, or of an organism, or of any other such thing. None of these things belong to the content of "the non-being of a dog" even though they would all have to be thought if this content were to be thought in its complete distinctness. Indeed, the content would include the non-being of a red trick-dog, of a red dog with a collar, with a doghouse, with a bitch, with a master, and so on. And so all of this, and any amount more, would belong to the concept "non-being of a dog". If this were so, then we would have to think of all this, if we were actually to think of the "non-being of a dog" in its complete distinctness, just as we must think of all the essential physical and logical parts of a dog, if the concept of a dog is to be thought in its complete distinctness. It is obvious that we cannot do this at all. What is required for such complete distinctness is nothing more than the distinct idea of the dog and the thought of its evident rejection. It is also conceivable that one might think of the evident, apodictic rejection of an evident judgement in which the dog is affirmed (and this is really what it is to have a thought or idea of the so-called "impossibility" of a correct affirmation).

Thus we have developed the thesis that "the non-being of a thing" is not the name of anything which can be affirmed or denied or even thought about. The same is true of "the being of a thing", of its "possibility" and "impossibility", and so on. All these expressions, which make up the greater part of Kant's Table of Categories, are merely synsemantic terms (or *synsemantica*); their function in language may be indicated by analyses similar to that just given. We see at the same time that Kant may have had a vague idea of all this, when he tried to relate his categories to the table of judgements.

41 As is well known, Hume and Mill deny the strict concept of causal efficacy.

42 Despite Brentano's penetrating criticism of Marty's later work, we must not lose sight of the fact that Brentano himself was significantly influenced by Marty. Marty had immediately drawn consequences from Brentano's rejection of the Aristotelian doctrine of "forms", but Brentano acknowledged these only after considerable resistance.

43 As early as the year 1909, I had corresponded with Brentano on these questions, without allowing myself to become convinced. After the death of Marty in 1914, there began a more intensive correspondence. Brentano set forth his reasons once again with great patience, and I stubbornly adhered to my untenable position. This apparent blindness on my part, which is now incomprehensible to me, tried Brentano's patience to the utmost, but it did not deter him from developing his argument. It was responsible for the good-natured ridicule which is manifested here and elsewhere.

44 I have been able to ascertain the following from the correspondence between Brentano and Marty. The subject-matter of the correspondence was Marty's investigation into language and the various questions to which these investigations led. It was Marty who set all the problems: thus he posed them to Brentano and described his own attempts at solving them. Brentano would then reply, sometimes agreeing, and

sometimes not agreeing; in this way a lively debate ensued. During the course of this debate, Brentano proposed the "far-reaching thesis" mentioned in the letter to Marty of March 1901 (the first selection in Part II of the present book): the thesis, namely, that grammatical abstracta, such as "redness', "colour", "virtue", "size", (i.e. the so-called Aristotelian "form words"), are "fictions of speech" which do not themselves designate anything. "To speak of a redness which is inherent in the thing and which constitutes the thing *as* something red", Brentano had written, "is to misconceive that property of general concepts which is revealed only through experience." Marty agreed at once and accepted the theory himself; see Anton Marty, *Die "logische"*, *"lokalistische" und andere Kasustheorien* (Halle 1910), pp. 94 ff. Indeed, Marty not only agreed, but immediately (1901) drew the important consequence that even the so-called "contents of judgement" are linguistic fictions (where the content of the judgement "*A* is" would be the *being of A*, or *that A* is, and the content of the judgement "*A* is not" would be the non-being of *A*, or *that A* is not). At first Brentano rejected this consequence. As late as 1903, he wrote to Marty: "The non-things are not fictions. They are concomitants; that is to say, the non-things are only logical consequences of the fact that there are (or are not) certain *things*, things which come into being, persist, and pass away, entirely on their own." "But non-things are dependent for their actuality upon things." And as late as 1904, it was Marty who wrote to Brentano: "It would be a mistake to suppose that true negative judgements have an objective correlate which is analogous to that of affirmative judgements. If it is true that *A* is, then there is an object which corresponds to the idea of *A*; but if it is true that *A* is not, then there is *no* object which corresponds to the idea of *A*. We must not adopt the fiction of supposing this 'non-being of *A*' to be an object." On 10 September of this same year (1904), Brentano replied in the following way: "I have made a new attempt at treating the *entia rationis* as fictions, thus denying that there are such things. It looks as though this can be carried out completely. We must understand the situation in terms of the stenogrammatical character of our language: a single word may express a wealth of intellectual activity. The ideas of reflection —the being of *A*, the existing *A*, and such like—appear to be non-things." "The old view required that these *entia rationis* be thought about only *along with* certain things. But the new view says that *only* the things can be thought about." "By denying that the form words are true names (names of what truly exists), the new view is prepared to forbid their use, as having no proper function in the language." The strange thing is that Marty proceeded to reject these consequences, which he had earlier drawn himself, and persisted in his opposition to them for the remainder of his life. To be sure, unlike the later Brentano, Marty never held that, in the cases at issue, only *realia* are thought about, or that only *realia can* be thought about.

The assertion that "form words" are not true names concerns such words as "size" and "redness"—in short, the so-called grammatical *abstracta.* These play an important role in the philosophy of Aristotle; he takes them to be logical names, indicating the "form" or "actuality" in virtue of which the potential becomes actual and the inherent possibilities in things are realized. See Brentano's *Aristoteles und seine Weltanschauung* (Leipzig 1911). In 1901, Brentano came to see that these "form words" are merely synsemantic expressions. And this conclusion, as we have noted, led him to see that other grammatical names (e.g. "being", "non-being", "possibility", "impossibility", etc.) are not true logical names and that these too are *synsemantica*; hence it is a mistake to suppose that they signify the meaning of any concept. See the letter to Marty dated March 1901 (at the beginning of Part Two of this book) and the letter dated 1 March, 1906 (the second letter in Part Three).

45 According to Brentano, external perception (i.e., the sensation of seeing, of hearing, and of the third sense, under which he subsumes all other sensory experiences) is not merely a matter of presentation or thought; it also involves belief in the colours, sounds, and other qualities—but the belief is blind and thus lacks evidence. (See Vol. III of the *Psychologie.*) This peculiar instinctive perceptual belief is also to be found in animals; anyone who doubts this would find it difficult to account for animal behaviour.

46 Brentano here refers to the biography of Marty which I had prepared as an introduction to Marty's *Gesammelte Schriften* (Halle, 1916–1920). The biography is also published separately: Oskar Kraus, *Anton Marty: sein Leben und seine Werke* (Halle 1916). At that time I was still siding with Marty on these questions.

47 The distinction between those judgements that are "merely true" and those that are "logically justified" is of fundamental importance. A judgement that is "merely true" and not logically justified may be called a true judgement which is *blind*. Its truth can be ascertained only by comparing it with some judgement which is in itself justified or evident. When such comparison is not possible, we may still speak of "a true judgement that is not evident". This would mean that the judgement is one such that no evident judgement about the same object could possibly contradict it; every evident judgement would be in agreement with it. See sections 46 ff. of the first essay, "On the Concept of Truth".

PART FOUR (References 1–49)

1 Brentano himself once held this view, as may be seen from the polemic against Windelband in Part One of the present book. See the notes by Professor A. Kastil which constitute the final selection in the Appendix.

2 See the letter to O. Kraus, dated 16 November, 1914. The present essay was written a few days after that letter and elaborates what was said there.

3 On the proof of the impossibility of infinite multiplicities, see F.

Brentano, *Versuch über die Erkenntnis* (F. Meiner, Leipzig 1925), and *Vom Dasein Gottes* (F. Meiner, Leipzig 1929).

[4] Brentano has made a mistake with respect to this point, since Husserl maintains that there *is* a perception of states of affairs. See Part Two of the editor's introduction to the present book.

[5] Cf. *Versuch über die Erkenntnis,* p. 44.

[6] Cf. *Psychologie,* Vol. III, Introduction, p. xxi.

[7] That these theses do not completely solve the problem is clear from the essay of 5 March, 1915, below. Compare Part III, note 30 concerning the letter to Marty, dated 2 Sept., 1906, and the editor's Introduction.

[8] To anyone familiar with Brentano's theory of judgement, it is obvious that "to deny the existence of a thing" means only to deny the thing.

[9] There are further details in Vol. II of the *Psychologie;* see Appendix XI, p. 179, "Vom Psychologismus."

[10] Brentano means that the proponent of psychologism, in the sense in which "psychologism" is a term of reproach, confuses a judgement's being evident with the fact that the members of a certain species of living things are more or less generally determined to judge in a certain way. See the discussion of Husserl's theory and its origin, in Part II of the Introduction to the present book. And compare the two essays on the evident that follow (the fifth and sixth essays of Part IV) and the Appendix.

[11] To say that there is no possibility of error in the case of a judgement that is evident and certain is to say this: it is impossible for anyone who contradicts that judgement to be judging with evidence. And to say that it is impossible for one contradicting the judgement *not* to be in error, is to say this: it is impossible for anyone who judges with evidence to contradict an evident judgement. In other words, the expressions "there is no possibility of error" and "it is impossible for one who contradicts the judgement *not* to be in error" come to the same thing.

[12] See the discussion of Sigwart, in Part I and Part I, note 53. Compare O. Kraus, "Die 'kopernikanische Wendung' in Brentanos Erkenntnis- und Wertlehre," *Philosophische Hefte* (1929), No. 3.

[13] Compare *Psychologie,* Vol. II, pp. 136 ff., and elsewhere.

[14] Compare *Psychologie,* Vol. II, Appendix IV, p. 147 and Appendix IX, p. 169.

[15] Brentano himself had held this view earlier; see paragraph 4 of the criticism of Windelband, in Part I. The grounds for the earlier view and for Brentano's subsequent criticism of it are set forth in detail in a letter to O. Kraus, dated 14 September, 1909, and published in the introduction to Vol. I of the *Psychologie* (p. xlvi); see also pp. 162 ff. of the same book.

[16] See the Appendix to the present book and the editor's comments.

[17] The word "nothing" is obviously not an autosemantic expression. See O. Kraus, review of Hermann Cohen's *Schriften, Deutsche Literatur-zeitung,* No. 30 (1929); "Über Nichts und Alles" (in Kraus's *Wege und Abwege der Philosophie,* Prague 1934).

[18] The word "activity" is here used in contrast with "faculty" or

"capability"—*actus* in contrast with *potentia*. But this "activity" is obviously something which is brought about, a *passio* in the Aristotelian sense.

[19] In the most general sense of the term *res*, encompassing what is mental as well as what is extended.

[20] Compare the discussion of time in Vol. III of the *Psychologie*.

[21] Brentano means it would be a mistake to suppose that, if one speaks of something past, one is thinking, not of a thing, but of an *ens rationis* called "a past thing".

[22] I believe that Brentano is here saying that we do not owe our possession of the truth to a comparision of our knowledge with a thing.

[23] All these attempts have been touched upon in the earlier criticisms. If one wished to apply the "adaequatio" theory to past and future things and yet avoid the fiction of "being in the past" and "being in the future", one would have to proceed from things which exist and draw upon their causal relations to earlier and later things. The text is directed against this latter consequence.

[24] See the comment on paragraph 24 of the lecture on truth and what is said, in Part I, note 2, concerning Windelband's definition and the fact that he was more or less getting at something correct. Brentano kept to the ordinary interpretation of the term "rule", but Windelband, as is apparent from the passage cited in the *Präludien*, understood it by reference to our normative consciousness.

[25] One could consistently add, at this point, that it would be advisable to discard the thesis altogether. And this is what is said in the next essay.

[26] One can list certain types of judgement which are directly evident and with respect to which any doubt would be entirely unreasonable; for example, the law of contradiction and certain axioms pertaining to space and time. If, in a given case, there is danger of erroneously taking a judgement to be one that is evident, we can properly reassure ourselves if the judgement in question agrees with one of those which are not exposed to any such danger. But in certain cases this help may not be available. There are further details in the following selections on the evident.

[27] The expression "someone who is judging correctly" is here meant to refer to one who judges with evidence. Thus the entire statement tells us that any reference to truth must involve the thought of someone who is judging with evidence. But this is not to say that to assert that a statement is true is to assert that there is someone who judges with evidence. Obviously the latter would be "psychologism".

[28] In thinking of a person who believes in the devil, I am thinking of the person in *modo recto* and of the devil in *modo obliquo*. A correct belief in someone who believes in the devil does not in any way imply a belief in the devil.

[29] The dictation contains "impossible (*unmöglich*)" in place of "possible"; obviously the one taking the dictation did not correctly hear what Brentano was saying.

[30] The word "affirmative" has been inserted; evidently it was not heard by the one taking the dictation.

[31] The final statement contains the solution to the whole problem. The statement which immediately precludes it, like some of the formulations in other essays (e.g. the preceding selection which was dictated at a later date), attempts to rescue the "adaequatio" principle by taking it to say that the judgement "*A* is" is correct if *A* is, and that the judgement "*A* is not" is incorrect if *A* is not. But this is more or less a tautology and, as indicated in note 106, hardly satisfactory. In this context I would like to call the reader's attention to Anton Marty's *Gesammelte Schriften*, Vol. II, Part I, pp. 204 ff. Marty there defends the view that the concept of existence involves a relation to the truth of a judgement, and indeed to an affirmative judgement. In criticizing this, Jerusalem requires that the concept of existence be reduced to that of the *evident* judgement. But Marty believes that the concept of existence may be explicated without reference to evidence; it is sufficient to relate it to the concept of truth. Marty held that truth, or correctness, consisted in the judgement having some kind of correspondence in relation to existence or non-existence. Jerusalem was right, however, at least to the extent of holding that one cannot speak of truth without reference to an *evident judgement*. But it is enough to *think of* someone judging with evidence and to believe that no one making a contrary judgement can judge with evidence.

[32] That is to say, every judgement of inner perception is evident in spite of the fact that, by its very nature, it can be evident only to *one* person; hence evidence cannot consist in the fact that *many* people agree.

[33] In such cases there is no clear and distinct conception. But there can be no doubt that the chord is heard. On Descartes, see Vol. III of the *Psychologie*, Part I, Chap. 3.

[34] Brentano does not apply the term "evident" to those *emotions* that are seen to be correct; he reserves the term for *judgements* that are seen to be correct.

[35] Compare Part IV, note 11.

[36] The term "insight (*Einsehen*)" is preferable when one is speaking of *a priori* evidence and where the term "understanding (*Verstehen*)" would be used. See O. Kraus, "Geisteswissenschaft und Psychologie", in *Euphorion*, Vol. 28 (1927).

[37] Compare the discussion of the concept of probability in Franz Brentano, *Versuch über die Erkenntnis* (Leipzig 1925), appendix, especially p. 177, and note 45, on p. 209.

[38] The question could also be put in this way: Is the evidence of a judgement related to the judgement in the way a property (accident) is related to the thing that has the property (as colour is related to what is extended) or in the way in which a species is related to its genus (as what is red is related to what is coloured)?

It could be asked whether these alternatives exhaust all the possibilities. Is there also a possibility that the evident judgement—the judgement constituting the knowledge—contains the judgement as a dependent and inseparable element, whereas the blind judgement which agrees with it may exist separately, on its own? Analogously, a three-dimensional body may be contained in a four-dimensional body as a dependent boundary or limit, and a three-dimensional body may also exist independently and on its own. I touch on the question here only because Brentano indicates, later on in the article, that he does not there complete his discussion of the problem.

A similar question arises in connection with the relation of judgement and emotions to the ideas or thoughts which are included in them.

³⁹ For further details, see Brentano's *Kategorienlehre* (Leipzig 1933), ed. Alfred Kastil.

⁴⁰ We may briefly summarize these considerations: Brentano here considers only the possibilities that the evidence is an accident of the judging and that it is a specific difference of the judging. The latter would be impossible, if judgement were a genus having only specific differences which exclude each other, as the specific differences of affirming and denying exclude each other. But this is not the case, since the judging relation may be specified in other ways; for example, it may be specified according to its object. Hence it might be possible to think of evidence as a specific difference of judgement. Brentano believes, however, that such a possibility must be ruled out; if a thing loses its specific difference, the difference must be replaced by another, since nothing can exist as a universal. But an evident judgement may cease to be evident without thereby becoming a universal. Hence the only remaining possibility is that evidence is to be thought of as an accident of the judgement; for if an accident falls away from a subject, it is not necessary that the subject acquire something else in its place.

But Brentano does not feel that the question has been entirely settled. Thus he calls attention to the fact that, in the case of secondary consciousness, if the evidence falls away then the judgement is changed; this could be reconciled with saying that evidence is an accident of judgement only if two secondary perceptions could fit into each other, so to speak; in which case, the perception of the entire evident judgement would include another secondary perception of the judgement apart from its evidence, and this latter would underlie the former as a substratum.

Such considerations, then, lead back to the third possible solution, mentioned at the end of the previous note.

⁴¹ The dictation reads "factual judgements" (*tatsächliche Urteile*), but what is intended is "vérités de fait", or assertoric judgements.

⁴² For further details see Part I of Vol. III of the *Psychologie*, i.e., *Vom sinnlichen und noetischen Bewusstsein*.

⁴³ To remember something means, according to this, to believe that one has experienced such-and-such states of consciousness, and to believe this directly or immediately, that is, without any motivation, but with a certain blind impulse. In other cases of believing about the past, however, one's belief is based upon certain documents, reports, or other indications; in such cases one believes indirectly and trusts in the reliability of these signs of what is past.

[44] "Lack of external evidence" here means: lack of evidence from external perception.

[45] Compare Vol. II of the *Psychologie*, Appendix, p. 142, and Vol. III, note 15, p. 131.

[46] That is to say, the question arises whether that which is empirically valid for us—namely, the restriction of direct factual knowledge to knowledge of the perceiver himself—is also valid, without exception, for all knowing beings.

[47] Compare Oskar Kraus: *Franz Brentano, mit Beiträgen von Carl Stumpf und Edmund Husserl* (Munich 1919).

[48] Compare Vol. III of the *Psychologie*, Chap. I, Sect. 8.

[49] At this point the dictation breaks off. Probably the following is what was meant: our rational knowledge, which is always a matter of *a priori* apodictic denial, implies simple assertoric denial; similarly, a universal and unconditional knowledge of necessity, though not within the reach of human beings, would imply simple assertoric affirmation. See Brentano's *Versuch über die Erkenntnis*.

APPENDICES (References 1–20)

[1] When Brentano speaks of logic as an "Art", he is referring to an applied art, a τέχνη, in the sense of the Greek philosophers, an *ars cogitandi*.

[2] To understand Brentano's defence against the accusation of "psychologism" and his own objections to Husserl's views, we need not ask whether the characterization in the letter corresponds to Husserl's later point of view.

[3] This is the principal point of Husserl's critique.

[4] Brentano's hope of leading Husserl back to the proper path was illusory. Husserl made no attempt to reply to these arguments, but concerned himself instead with more and more devices designed to rescue the universality of knowledge; one needs only to think of the "pure consciousness".

[5] Theoretical logic is what Husserl usually calls "pure logic".

[6] According to Brentano, all axiomatic knowledge is purely negative; there is no *raison d'être* for any scientific endeavour which is concerned only with the acquisition of such knowledge. To have any claim on the interests of research, a discipline must lead us to positive knowledge of the world.

[7] In this letter, as well as in certain later writings, Brentano is inclined to reduce all axiomatic knowledge to the principle of contradiction. But he vacillates on this point; compare his *Versuch über die Erkenntnis*. But the problems that are here discussed do not require that this question be settled.

[8] This should be supplemented by: "if we were capable of having strict concepts of these things".

[9] Editor's italics here and subsequently.

¹⁰ Compare the pertinent formulations in earlier essays of this book.
¹¹ Husserl did not reply to any of these considerations.
¹² This has abundantly been taken care of in the preceding.
¹³ According to Brentano, the laws of metamathematics need not be considered from the theoretical point of view, since they have no application to reality and thus convey no knowledge about it. But these laws may have practical importance, to the extent that they lead to new and useful methods of calculation.
¹⁴ Brentano is here concerned with this question: from the theoretical standpoint, which classifies disciplines by reference to their *objects*, where do these metamathematical problems belong? We need not decide whether mathematics and our knowledge of it pertain merely to the application of the law of contradiction, or whether mathematics has autonomous axioms of its own (compare the *Versuch über die Erkenntnis*); the point is that this knowledge is of theoretical interest only to the extent that it affords an insight into some reality or other. If there are no real objects with which such mathematics is concerned, then it is of theoretical and scientific interest only to the extent that there are acts of consciousness which are concerned with it. Hence from the theoretical point of view it is to be classified as belonging somewhere within psychology, in analogy with our knowledge of the analytic theory of colours. If the classification is not in fact made this way, the reason lies in the predominance of the practical and technological interest and in the considerations concerning the division of work, to which Brentano refers below. Compare G. Katkov, "Bewusstsein, Gegenstand, Sachverhalt eine Brentanostudie," *Archiv f. die ges. Psychologie*, Vol. 75, pp. 471 ff.
¹⁵ Compare A. Marty, *Gesammelte Schriften*, Vol. I: "Was ist Philosophie?"
¹⁶ The passages published here are from a dictation designated as a letter to Husserl. The beginning and end are missing.
¹⁷ Compare Brentano's *Von der mannigfachen Bedeutung des Seienden nach Aristoteles* (Freiburg 1862), pp. 21 ff.
¹⁸ In the lecture notes on ontology which Brentano used during the time he was at Würzburg, he writes: "The remarkable passage (*Summa Theologica*, Part I, Q. 3, art. 4) in which Thomas is at least very close to the truth, reads: 'Reply to Objection 2. *To be* can mean either of two things. It may mean the act of being (*actum essendi*), or it may mean the composition of a proposition effected by the mind in joining a predicate to a subject. Taking *to be* in the first sense, we cannot understand God's existence or His essence; but only in the second sense. We know that this proposition which we form about God when we say *God is*, is true; and this we know from His effects.' What the 'is' expresses in the statement 'God is' it also expresses in any other existential statement—no more and no less; it does not denote anything. Aristotle himself saw this clearly and said as much (*De Interpretatione*, I, and later *De Anima*, III, 6, and *Metaphysics*, IX, 10). In the last passage, he restricts himself to an obviously inexact characterization, which holds only in

185

the majority of cases, for he acknowledges a truth to which it does not apply."

[19] In saying "at most", Brentano means to convey this: to speak of the existence of the so-called "impossibility of a square circle", we need not even accept or affirm one who rejects such a circle with evidence. In saying that there is the impossibility of a square circle, we are not accepting or affirming anything at all; we are denying or rejecting one who has knowledge of such a circle and whose knowledge of it is not an apodictic denial.

[20] In a letter to O. Kraus, dated 9 January, 1915, Brentano makes the following comment on this passage in Aristotle: "I will add one brief remark to my reply to your four questions; it concerns the often cited principle of the *adaequatio rei et intellectus*. We can best see how this principle occurred to Aristotle, by looking at *De Anima*, III, 6. The formulation there is not entirely happy; a judgement is said to be true provided that it combines what is combined in reality or separates what is separated in reality (and false if it combines what is separated in reality, or separates what is combined in reality). Suppose I attribute to a subject some predicate which corresponds to nothing actual; it could be said, only in an entirely loose and improper sense, that the predicate exists in separation from the subject. The matter becomes worse as the chapter proceeds. Aristotle goes on to say—perhaps as a result of that unhappy formulation—that where there is no combining of subject and predicate, error is out of the question. Here he speaks as though the thing I think about and affirm is the thing simply *as* thought about and affirmed by me. And he excludes rejection or denial, as well as the possibility that affirmation might be in error. He here confounds so-called phenomenal truth with truth in the strict sense of the term, while previously, in speaking of affirmative and negative predication, he distinguished that which is combined and separated in our mind from that which is combined and separated in reality. But if we are mindful of our own limitations, we will hardly wish to cast a stone at this great thinker."

INDEX

187